NEW ENGLAND AVIATORS

IN TWO VOLUMES

Volume II

DAVID ENDICOTT PUTNAM

NEW ENGLAND AVIATORS

1914-1918

THEIR PORTRAITS AND THEIR RECORDS

WITH AN INTRODUCTION BY

A. LAWRENCE LOWELL

Volume II

Schiffer Military History
Atglen, PA

Cover artwork, *Red, White & Blue*, by James Dietz.
Image courtesy of the artist.

Library of Congress Catalog Number: 97-66730.

Printed in the United States of America.
ISBN: 0-7643-0346-5

We are interested in hearing from authors with book ideas on related topics.

Published by Schiffer Publishing Ltd.
4880 Lower Valley Road
Atglen, PA 19310
Phone: (610) 593-1777
FAX: (610) 593-2002
E-mail: Schifferbk@aol.com.
Please write for a free catalog.
This book may be purchased from the publisher.
Please include $3.95 postage.
Try your bookstore first.

CONTENTS

Aviators

CONTENTS

CONTENTS

CONTENTS

CONTENTS

NEW ENGLAND AVIATORS

SOLDIERS OF THE WOODEN CROSS

By Rt. Rev. Charles Henry Brent, D.D.

Medals that adorn the uniform tell of courage and endurance and heroism that braved the worst for the cause. Their wearers live to hear the acclaim of their comrades. But there is another decoration, the commonest even though the most distinguished of all, the Wooden Cross that is awarded only to the men who have done the greatest thing that man — yes, even God — can do.

Yonder they lie, along that front where with face to the foe they counted not their lives dear unto themselves but bore the standard of liberty onward. Above their graves rise the sheltering arms of the rough-hewn cross, than which no fitter monument ever reared its form over mortal remains.

Our comrades they were. Our comrades they are. Death was powerless in the face of their bold daring to rob us of them or them of us. They are separated now from us, not by the gaping gulf of time but by a veil so thin that at times we almost see their figures through its waving folds. They live — live gloriously in the land of far distances. Death stripped them of nothing essential. In the permanent society of the world beyond this they think and speak and see and love. They are what they were, except so far as the river of death has washed away the dust of earth and left them cleaner and better by reason of this their last great adventure.

The same dauntless spirit moved them, one and all. There was something dearer than life. To it they gave themselves and their all, and won the decoration of the Wooden Cross.

These men and a myriad more are calling to us, calling to us and bidding us to carry on. If we would still hold to their comradeship we must display in life the spirit they displayed in death. We must live for the things for which they died. That which we have achieved by victory we must weave into the fabric of the new world and the new age. The Wooden Cross of our dead comrades is for them a glorious decoration. For us it is the banner of our life that is to be. It challenges us to hold more precious than mortal life ideals of honor, justice, and righteousness. After all, the Cross that redeemed the world was a wooden cross, too, was it not? It was no toy or pretty bauble, but a thing of nails and pain and death — and yet a thing of glory.

THE SECOND PURSUIT GROUP

BY LIEUTENANT EARLE F. RICHARDS, THIRTEENTH AERO SQUADRON

THE Second Pursuit Group, originally the 13th and 139th Squadrons, began to operate late in June, 1918. Then came the 103d (formerly the Lafayette), which was replaced by the 22d and 49th Squadrons late in Aug., or early in Sept. This was a live Group which came to its own in the St.-Mihiel and Argonne offensives. It has some one hundred and thirty-five official victories, against thirty-eight losses.

Early in the spring there were reports from the lone Lafayette, at Dunkirk. Things were causing concern on the front from Reims to Soissons, and in June the First Pursuit Group pulled out to stave off the advancing Hun at Château-Thierry; and the neophyte 139th and 13th Squadrons moved into the vacant hangars at the "cross-roads." Raoul Lufbery had gone on to a reward, as had Dick Blodgett and others, and the new tenants were confronted with a sterner task, to meet and avenge their deaths. Then the business began and the skeleton Squadron was right busy until the eleventh day of the eleventh month.

Major Angstrom, who had been with the English, was in command of one Squadron, while Capt. Charles Biddle, of the Lafayette, had the other Squadron, as Flight Commander. In the 139th were Capt. Bridgman, who later commanded the 22d, and Dave Putnam, both of whom had been with the French. From the 103d Squadron came Hobey Baker, and Maury Jones as Flight Commander for the 13th, while George Fisher, from the First Pursuit Group, was the third on that list.

Soon the 103d came, and proved to us that there was n't any use wasting time. The summer went on in a quiet sort of way as later experiences taught, and when the 103d left our Group, the 22d and the 49th Squadrons came in.

Then in Sept. came the St.-Mihiel affair, which paved the way for large things in the Argonne. In the week beginning Sept. 12 the Group had downed twenty-five planes, against nine lost, and four of these came back. A little later, it grew noisy over west of the Meuse, and the Second Pursuit Group was very much in the activity, and over a hundred official victories resulted.

*DAVID ENDICOTT PUTNAM

First Lieutenant, A.S.A., U.S.A., One Hundred and Thirty-Ninth Aero Squadron, Second Pursuit Group

Killed in action, Sept. 12, 1918

Son of Frederick Huntington and Janet (Hallowell) Putnam; was born at Jamaica Plain, Mass., Dec. 10, 1898. He was a descendant of Gen. Israel Putnam, of Revolutionary fame. He attended the Newton High School, and entered Harvard College, class of 1920. At school he was president of his class and excelled in athletics; he was an expert swimmer, played on the football team, the baseball team, and the hockey team; he was class orator.

During his freshman year at college he successfully passed his examination for the Aviation Service, but being under age was barred from entering the U.S. Service. He left Harvard after passing his mid-year examinations and sailed for France on a cattle-ship, being determined to enter the Air Service abroad. In April, 1917, he began his training at Avord, France, where he was brevetted on Oct. 17, 1917, and sent to Pau for training in acrobatics. There he remained until Dec. 21, when he was sent to the front assigned to the Lafayette Escadrille, N 156, stationed a couple of miles outside of Châlons, near the Marne River. On Dec. 22, 1917, he flew for the first time over the enemy lines, and on Jan. 19, 1918, brought down his first enemy machine; he was given a Morane plane, and was proud of the fact that he was the only man known to have brought down a Boche while flying one of these machines.

One of Putnam's longest and hardest fights was on April 11, 1918, when he engaged four two-seaters for thirty-five minutes, and brought down one of them. The following day he fought alone a German "circus" of eight machines and got two of them.

On April 23, Putnam was credited with three official victories. His most famous combat took place on June 5, 1918, when he was alone in battle with ten German Albatross planes; bringing down five, the greatest score of victories ever credited to a flyer in one flight.

On June 16, 1918, he wrote:

> Combat after combat comes my way, and without boasting I'll say that I generally meet them head on. Friday, with another fellow, I dove into a bunch of six Germans and three fell. These are not official yet.

Yesterday I was with three other fellows when I saw two Boche biplanes. They saw us at about the same time and started to drive for home. Putting on all the speed I could, I gave chase. As my machine happened to be slightly faster than the others of my patrol, I arrived first. With both guns shooting murder, I slowly closed with one of the Boches. Nearer and nearer I drew. One gun stuck, but the other rattled on. When I was about ten yards from the German, up came his nose. A perfect target, and just at that moment my remaining gun stopped. The German gunner (I could see him clearly) took one look at me and commenced to fire. A quick turn and I was out of range. I looked back and there was the unlucky Boche falling. Suddenly his left wing broke off and he dashed into the ground. I looked for the rest of my patrol, and there they were, some five hundred yards above me watching the fight. We got together again and started to patrol some more. I kept on, for I was able to fix my guns, which were n't very badly jammed. Suddenly I saw five more Germans and gave chase immediately. As the biplanes had done before them, they, too, turned toward home, and in following them I passed through a cloud and lost the rest of my patrol. The Germans, however, went so far that I turned back. I had flown perhaps three minutes towards our lines when a German balloon loomed up directly ahead of me. "Well," I said, "I've got no incendiary bullets, but there's no harm in shooting at it." No sooner said than done. I pulled both triggers. Pfoof!!! The balloon burst into flames, and it did look queer. I supposed that there would be just one burst of flame and that would be the end. No; the thing remained in the air, a flaming mass, for perhaps twenty seconds, and then dropped slowly to the ground where it continued to burn. But how the anti-aircraft guns did shoot at me. Bang! Bang! Bang! Just a continuous roar. "Flaming onions" also were coming up from the ground. Into a cloud I went. The shooting was even more terrible there, so out I dove. Twisting, turning, circling, I finally reached our lines and made tracks for home. The others arrived about the same time, having witnessed the entire performance. That makes nine official planes and thirteen unofficial for a total of twenty-two in six months.

On June 10, 1918, Putnam was commissioned 1st Lieut., A.S., U.S.A., and four weeks later he was sent to an American escadrille, and finally assigned as Flight Commander of the 139th Squadron. During the terrific air fighting along the French front early in June, he distinguished himself by his repeated attacks on the German infantry, flying at low altitudes above the massed formations, and spraying them with machine-gun bullets with perfect indifference to the shots from the ground that riddled his wings with holes.

Lieut. Putnam's last flight was made over the lines on Sept. 12,

1918, in company with Lieut. Robertson. Fifteen German planes came down upon them from the clouds in a surprise attack. Robertson escaped; Putnam brought down one German plane in flames, and on his way back he saw an Allied biplace being attacked by eight Boches; he saved the biplane, but was himself brought down with two shots through his heart. It was for this last deed that his country awarded him the Distinguished Service Cross. He fell at Limey, and was buried with full military honors near Toul, in the forest of Sebastopol, Sept. 14, 1918, and lies by the side of Lufbery, whom he had succeeded as the "American Ace of Aces." He was credited with thirty-four planes, fourteen of which are official.

In a discourse on "Immortality," delivered after his return from France, by the Reverend William B. Geoghegan, at New Bedford, Mass., the speaker said:

> From contact with our aviators, I have felt the impulse of the soaring spirit that would carry them higher than their planes ever went, and have felt that the clouds would open to take them into a larger universe. It was my great pleasure to meet, just before he was killed, our Ace of Aces, Putnam. His was one of the most beautiful souls I have known. He was in appearance almost like a Greek statue, showing, however, the effect of his experiences. When I heard that he had gone down, I knew that that beautiful form had been broken to emancipate a noble soul, and that he had gone to flights beyond the bounds of our human imagination.

In a beautiful letter to his mother, found among Putnam's effects, to be delivered in the event of his death, he wrote:

> Mother, there is no question about the hereafter of men who give themselves in such a cause. If I am called upon to make it, I shall go with a grin of satisfaction and a smile.

Lieut. Putnam was awarded the Croix de Guerre; the Médaille Militaire, May 30, 1918; the Cross of the Legion of Honor, Nov. 11, 1918; and the Distinguished Service Cross, April 8, 1919. In addition to citations, received Feb. 21, 1918, and March 21, 1918, he was awarded the medal of the Aero Club of America July 4, 1918.

The following report of the Chief of the U.S. Air Service, Liaison Section, was sent on Nov. 15, 1918, by Major Edmund Gros, in answer to a request by the French Government for names of famous American aviators to be used in naming vessels for the French fleet.

DAVID ENDICOTT PUTNAM

First Lieutenant David Putnam. One of the American best pilots and, for some time preceding his death, the American Ace of Aces. During the time Lieut. Putnam served as a Sergeant-Pilot in the French Army, he succeeded in bringing down on the Champagne front nine enemy planes, three of which were biplace machines, and in addition he is credited with thirteen unofficially, which were too far over the enemy lines to be confirmed officially. On the date of June 5, he brought down one official enemy plane, and four others unofficially. Lieut. Putnam joined the 139th Aero Squadron, June 24, 1918, and from that time up to the time of his death, he brought down five official enemy planes as well as seven others which were so far within the enemy lines that no confirmations could be obtained. These latter aircraft were all brought down in the Toul sector during the time when that front was quiet, and it was only by means of persistent and long flights into enemy territory that he was able to gain the above number of victories.

Always seeking combat, he flew a brightly painted red machine which was known as "Putnam's Red Devil," and was never known to turn tail when attacked by superior numbers.

On July 12, Lieut. Putnam was recommended for the award of the Distinguished Service Cross for having brought down in conspicuous gallant and skillful manner an enemy biplace machine; notwithstanding the superior manœuvring ability of his opponent he dived straight into the machine gun of the observer and brought the enemy plane down by the firing of only six shots.

On August 1, Lieut. Putnam was recommended for the award of the Medal of Honor on account of his extremely brave, courageous, efficient service to the Allied cause.

As a Flight Commander Lieut. Putnam showed remarkable cool-headedness and skill as a leader and always allowed the less experienced pilots to derive benefit of his knowledge. As Acting Squadron Commander of the 139th Aero Squadron from May 16 to the time of his death, he again showed his ability by managing his squadron in most exemplary manner, yet never diminishing the number of his flights or combats.

On September 12, Lieut. Putnam and another pilot were attacked by seven or eight enemy aircraft. He succeeded in downing one enemy plane, but was overpowered by superior numbers and was brought to earth, having received several bullet wounds.

At the time of his death, Lieut. Putnam had been credited with fourteen official victories, while his unofficial victories numbered twenty.

Always a clean fighter and one who always fought out of a sense of duty and never for renown or publicity, Lieut. Putnam was loved and respected by all with whom he came into contact, and will be remembered by his friends and foes alike as a true sportsman, as well as one of the best fighters.

Edmund Gros, *Major, Air Service.*

*HOWARD R. CLAPP

First Lieutenant, A.S., U.S.A., Twenty-Second Aero Squadron, Second Pursuit Group

Killed in action, Nov. 3, 1918

Son of Clift Rogers and Gertrude (Blanchard) Clapp; was born at Dorchester, Mass., July 24, 1893. He prepared for college at the Newton High School and the Noble and Greenough School; graduated from Harvard College, in 1916; entered the Law School, and during his first year there joined the Harvard Regiment.

He attended the Officers' Training Camp at Plattsburg, from May until Aug., 1917, then entered the School of Military Aeronautics, M.I.T., graduating (with honor) Sept. 22, 1917; he continued his training at Mineola, N.Y., about Oct. 1, 1917; was commissioned 1st Lieut. Dec. 17, 1917, and sailed overseas Jan. 29, 1918. After training at Issoudun, France, Furbara, Italy, and Orly, he joined the 22d Aero Squadron, in Aug., 1918, at Toul.

This Squadron in two months lost eleven of its original eighteen pilots, and had forty-two German planes to its credit; it was actively engaged throughout the fighting along the left bank of the Meuse toward Sedan, during the last month of the war.

On the afternoon of Nov. 3, 1918, a patrol of six pilots, among whom was Lieut. Clapp, went over the lines in single-seated Spads to bomb a road leading out of Beaumont to the north. They flew about twenty kilometres inside the German lines and on their return were attacked by eighteen German Fokkers. Three German planes are known to have been brought down and only three of the American planes returned to their own lines; two of them were so riddled with bullets as to be useless. Of the three Americans who failed to return, Lieut. Tiffany was taken prisoner, uninjured; Lieut. Gibson's plane, and grave, were later identified near Létanne, but no trace of Lieut. Clapp has been found. He was last seen engaged at close quarters with several of the German planes, and the officers of the Squadron reported that his plane was probably exploded by an incendiary bullet within the German lines, near Beaumont, ten miles south of Sedan; his place of burial is unknown. Lieut. Herman C. Rorison was decorated for his conduct in this fight. The other survivors are Lieuts. Frank B. Tyndall and John Crissey.

HOWARD R. CLAPP

Extract from letter written by Lieut. Clapp, June 6, 1918, describing combat practice:

For the last few days I have been at the last field of this Group, doing combat practice, with camera-guns. It is the most thrilling and exciting work we have done so far, and wonderful practice. It accustoms you to handle the machine without paying any attention to it, or the horizon, or the ground, all old and tried friends of earlier days of instruction. But in combat your only thought is for the other machine, and how to get on his tail, or keep him from getting on yours. I have n't done very much of it yet; twice with John Agar and once with Harry Harkins. We go out together or meet over some prearranged town, and then the fun begins. We start to circle, each one climbing for all he is worth, and at the same time drawing nearer each other. Round and round, and up and up! Finally the circle gets so tight that we are both doing practically vertical banks and stretching our necks to the limit to keep an eye on the other man. Suddenly one or the other breaks — he has not handled his control properly in his anxiety to keep his place — and goes down in a side-slip or vrille (tail-spin). This is the chance that the other man has been waiting for, and he kicks the lower rudder of his machine, causing it to fall over on that side and down on the other man's tail. The latter by this time has come out of the vrille by going into a nose-dive, and with the tremendous speed thus acquired points his machine straight upwards in a terrific zoom. Then the real fun begins. It is like a juggler playing with a couple of balls.

This morning I smashed my first bird all to bits — worse luck. I was coming down to land and it was very windy and our field is terribly rough. I had her on the ground on all three points when the wheels struck a bump and over she went on the left wing. Then things happened with much speed and raising of dust. She whirled round like a top, smashing the other wing to kindling wood and wiping off the landing-gear completely. The last thing that happened was one of the wheels flying up past my left ear and embedding itself in the wing! I had a tiny scratch on my left elbow and some badly hurt feelings, for it was the first time I had done any real damage to any of Uncle Sam's expensive planes. Very much disgusted!

ARTHUR RAYMOND BROOKS

CAPTAIN, A.S., U.S.A., TWENTY-SECOND AERO SQUADRON
SECOND PURSUIT GROUP

SON of Frank E. and Josephine (Levasseur) Brooks, was born at Framingham, Mass., Nov. 1, 1895. He attended the public schools of Framingham and graduated from the M.I.T. in 1917, where he was editor-in-chief of the "Tech" Magazine.

He enlisted in the U.S. Service Sept. 1, 1917, at M.I.T.; and was ordered to Fort Wood, N.Y. He trained with the R.F.C. at Toronto, Can., from Sept. 10 to Nov. 10, 1917. From Nov. 10 to Feb. 25, 1918, he trained at Hicks Field, Fort Worth, Texas, with the 28th and 139th Squadrons. He was commissioned 2d Lieut. on Feb. 25, 1918, and sailed overseas March 12 to France, where he completed his training at the 3d A.I.C., Issoudun. On Aug. 16, 1918, he was transferred to the 22d Squadron as Flight Commander and was prominent in the brilliant exploits of that Squadron. On Sept. 14, 1918, he won the Distinguished Service Cross, and recommendation for the Medal of Honor, in combat with eight Fokkers, bringing down two and making an official credit of six.

Lieut. Howard Clapp, afterwards killed in action, wrote of this combat:

> Twelve Fokkers attacked our formation of six from above and in the sun. . . .
>
> Brooks had about five after him, and they stuck very tenaciously. But he is a fine flier and a good shot, and, though he only fired 75 rounds during the whole affair, succeeded in bringing down two of them — one in flames. They have both been confirmed, so he is now officially an ace.
>
> His machine was very badly shot up. The rudder wires were cut through on one side, so that the rudder was useless; one of the main spars in his top wing was smashed and a tire punctured. Yet, in spite of all this he brought the machine safely down in a rough field north of camp.

A quotation from Capt. Brooks's own description of the affair follows:

> We were still at 5000 metres or about three miles up. The "we" in this case referring to myself and eight red-nosed Richthofen Circus planes bent on an eight-to-one shot.
>
> We were ten miles behind the lines of the infantry and my chances of escape were so slight that I figured I had come to the end. I was frankly scared, but in spite of much high tension and futile yelling at the top of

my voice, I calculated, by nature of my training, I suppose, to get as many of the Fokkers as possible before the inevitable.

The only thing that saved me was that being entirely surrounded, the Germans could not shoot at me without being in their own way. A stream of white ribbons from the incendiary bullets and the tracers would cut through the gap in my wings so that if I reached out my hand they were close enough to cut it off. . . .

Twice I tried to ram the Fokkers that had me in a direct line with their guns. One red-nosed "Night Mare" came in from my right and endeavored to draw me under by playing as a foil in a swoop to my level and then perceptibly below.

I had just time to dip enough to see his features before I let him have a few incendiary bullets. I was n't even sorry for him after that.

Another I turned upon and after a short, close burst was satisfied that a second had quit, although he did not, like the first, apparently catch fire. . . .

Two more of the Boches, in their tactical work, happened to get in the way of my line of fire and I finally had the better feeling of finding myself with a good 2000 metres, directly over the huge, boomerang lake (Lachausée) with only four of the enemy still paying me too much attention to suit me.

This was rather more dangerous than with a swarm, because the individuals could far better get a good shot at me where they had less chance of being in their own way.

A 220 horse-power Spad can out-dive a Fokker D-7 and for 1500 metres, with almost full motor, I spun, nose-dived, and slithered, flattening out just over the rolling country, with a fair chance over those four.

Two of these, and finally one, kept up the chase for a feeble distance, but retreated to my glad astonishment, before crossing the lines.

Brooks was commissioned 1st Lieut. Oct. 7, 1918. After the signing of the Armistice he was stationed at Grand, as Commanding Officer of the 22d Squadron. He was commissioned Capt. on March 12, 1919. Stationed at Selfridge Field, and later at Kelly Field.

Citation

D.S.C.

For the extraordinary heroism in action over Mars-la-Tour, France, Sept. 14, 1918. Lieut. Brooks, when his patrol was attacked by twelve enemy Fokkers over Mars-la-Tour, eight miles within the enemy lines, alone fought bravely and relentlessly with eight of them, pursuing the fight from 5000 metres to within a few metres of the ground, and though his right rudder control was out and his plane riddled with bullets, he destroyed two Fokkers, one falling out of control and the other bursting into flames.

(*Signed*) Pershing

*JAMES DUDLEY BEANE

FIRST LIEUTENANT, A.S., U.S.A., TWENTY-SECOND AERO SQUADRON, SECOND PURSUIT GROUP

Killed in action, Oct. 30, 1918

SON of Edmund Murry and Kate (Miles) Beane; was born in New York City, Jan. 20, 1896. He took up residence in Concord, Mass., in 1909, and attended the Concord High School where he made a record on the track team. On graduation he entered the employ of the Department of Education at the State House, in Boston.

He sailed for France in June, 1916, and from July 8, 1916, to July 20, 1917, served as ambulance driver in the American Ambulance Field Service on the Verdun front. He joined the French Army in Aug., 1917, and was assigned to the Lafayette Escadrille for training. After acting as Avion de Chasse to the French, from Aug., 1917, to Feb., 1918, he was transferred to the U.S. Air Service in Feb., 1918, and shortly after commissioned 1st Lieut.

He had several German planes to his credit, when on June 27, 1918, he was shot down, badly wounded after a hard battle against overwhelming odds. He left the Hospital six weeks later with two fingers gone, but insisted on rejoining his Squadron. In Aug., 1918, he was transferred to the 22d Aero Squadron, with which he was flying at the time of his death. On Oct. 31, 1918, he was officially reported "Missing in action" near Banthéville, after one of the most important air battles of the year. For his heroic action in this engagement he was posthumously awarded the D.S.C. Not until April 29, 1919, was the fact of his death fully established. A letter from the American Military Mission in Berlin bearing that date states definitely that Lieut. Beane was killed in action on Oct. 30, 1918, and that he was buried near the place where he fell. Capt. F. W. Zinn, of the Air Service, reported that he was buried "two kilometres east of Brieulles-sur-Bar.

D.S.C.

For extraordinary heroism in action near Banthéville, France, Oct. 29, 1918. When Lieut. BEANE's patrol was attacked by eight enemy planes (Fokker type) he dived into their midst in order to divert their attention from the other machines of his group and shot down one of the Fokkers in flames. Four other Fokkers then joined in the battle, one of which was also destroyed by this officer.

(*Signed*) PERSHING

*ROBERT HEWINS STILES

First Lieutenant, A.S., U.S.A., Thirteenth Aero Squadron
Second Pursuit Group

Killed in action, Sept. 16, 1918

Son of Walter F. and Annette L. (Hewins) Stiles; was born at Fitchburg, Mass., Nov. 15, 1894. He attended the public schools of Fitchburg and graduated in 1916 from Harvard College, where he was prominent in many associations. He was on the editorial board of the *Crimson;* its managing editor in 1915, and president of the board of editors in 1916. He was a member of the freshman baseball squad, and manager of the 'Varsity baseball team in 1916; also president of the freshman Mandolin and Banjo Club. After graduation he became commission sales agent for a well-known textile firm, and was doing a very successful business at the time of his enlistment.

In the summer of 1916 he attended the Harvard Aviation School at Buffalo, N.Y., where he obtained an aviator's license. In June, 1917, he enlisted at Boston, Mass., for the Aviation Service; trained at the M.I.T. from Aug. 20, 1917, until Oct., when he was sent overseas, continuing his training at Issoudun, France. He was commissioned 1st Lieut. May 13, 1918. On Aug. 7, 1918, he was sent to the front attached to the 13th Squadron, 2d Pursuit Group. On Aug. 15 he was given credit for bringing down a German plane during his first engagement. Lieut. Stiles took part in the St.-Mihiel drive, and on Sept. 16, 1918, was reported "Missing in action." It was later ascertained that he had been killed in action on that date, having been brought down by four or five German planes. He was shot through the chest and death was instantaneous on landing. He was buried near where he fell in a little cemetery beside some Germans, who had been killed in 1871. Later, he was reburied in the officers' section of the cemetery at Thiaucourt. On the day of his death Lieut. Stiles was the leader of a patrol of three, and when seven miles southwest of Metz these men were attacked by a number of German planes. Two of the men were able to reach their own lines, but Lieut. Stiles was last seen flying straight into Germany. Although only officially credited with one plane, it has been reported by other aviators that Stiles brought down several planes after his first one. He was cited

by Gen. Pershing, "For exceptionally meritorious and conspicuous services with the 13th Squadron."

Capt. Biddle, Commander of the 13th Squadron, wrote of him:

> Lieut. Stiles was one of my Flight Commanders, and I considered him one of the most valuable men in the Squadron, and the loss to all of his friends here who admired him so much for his courage and fine character cannot be measured.

Capt. Biddle elsewhere wrote of this engagement:

> In three days, Sept. 13 to 15, the 13th Squadron shot down officially eight German machines, all single-seater fighting planes. In the meantime, however, we ourselves lost six men, two of them being among my best pilots.

Brother in Service —

Walter F. Stiles, Jr., 1st Lieut., Q.M.C., A.E.F.

LOUIS EVANS BOUTWELL

SECOND LIEUTENANT, A.S., U.S.A., TWENTY-SECOND AERO SQUADRON, SECOND PURSUIT GROUP

SON of Harvey L. and Nellie C. Boutwell; was born in Malden, Mass., Feb. 15, 1892. He was educated at the Stone School, Boston; Bowdoin College; and Boston University, Law School, LL.B. 1917. He was admitted to the Suffolk County Bar, in Sept., 1917.

On Oct. 30, 1917, he enlisted at Boston, Mass., and had eight weeks' ground training at the M.I.T. He then attended the flying school at Gerstner Field, Lake Charles, La., until Sept. 1, 1918. He was commissioned 2d Lieut. on May 13, 1918. At Gerstner Field during the summer of 1918, in addition to flying, he was detailed as Trial Judge Advocate before special courts-martial, and as such tried forty or more cases.

Lieut. Boutwell sailed overseas on Sept. 6, 1918. He spent some time in the hospital at Issoudun with influenza. Upon recovery he was assigned to 22d Aero Squadron, 2d Pursuit Group; and at last account was still overseas with the Third Army of Occupation. At Charmont he was ordered to do important work as Judge Advocate, although not relieved from his full duty as a member of the 22d Squadron.

HARRY BOIT FREEMAN

First Lieutenant, A.S., U.S.A., Ninetieth Aero Squadron
Thirteenth Aero Squadron, Second Pursuit Group

Son of Franklin W. and Helen (Boit) Freeman, of Wakefield, Mass.; was born in Newton Lower Falls, Oct. 17, 1896. He was educated at Wakefield High School; Cheshire Academy, Cheshire, Conn.; and the University of Washington (one year); also, he had two years at Yale College, class of 1919. He played on the baseball and football teams at Cheshire, and on the football team at Yale.

He enlisted on June 12, 1917, at Boston, and began preliminary training at M.I.T. Ground School, where he finished on Aug. 4, 1917. He was one of ten men chosen to go at once to France for training, and he sailed overseas on Aug. 22. He went directly to Liverpool, and from there to Southampton and Le Havre. He was one of a detachment of fifty men chosen from all the ground schools in the United States. After a few weeks at Étampes, he was transferred to Issoudun, where for two weeks he was engaged in general construction work. Following this he spent four months at the Aviation School at Tours, and was brevetted Jan. 29, 1918. He finished tests at Tours on Dec. 19, 1917, but was delayed by quarantine and change of management.

On Feb. 2, 1918, he was commissioned 1st Lieut. and went to Issoudun for Nieuport training, and then to the French Aerial Gunnery School at Cazaux, with a class of twenty men, for the month of April. He returned to Issoudun for combat training, but owing to shortage of pilots was sent out to the 90th Observation Squadron.

During May and June Lieut. Freeman was stationed with the 90th Squadron at Amanty and Ourches, flying biplace Sopwiths. On July 1 he was transferred to the 13th Squadron, 2d Pursuit Group, stationed at Toul. He served as Deputy Flight Commander to "Hobey" Baker, during July and the first half of Aug. He was then made Flight Commander. He engaged in several combats during July, Aug., and Sept., and led a formation of four against six Boches, at an altitude of 21,500 feet, the highest combat on the U.S. record. He is credited with three enemy planes.

On Sept. 14 he was one of a patrol of fourteen planes which engaged a number of Boches.

On Sept. 11, 1918, he was sent over ten miles within the lines in a heavy rainstorm to learn if the Huns were evacuating the St.-Mihiel salient. On Sept. 14 he was one of a patrol of fourteen planes which engaged a number of Boches near Pont-à-Mousson, where four men were lost. Due to a failure of his motor during combat, he was forced to land directly back of the German front lines, and was made prisoner. He was confined in the prisons of Metz, St.-Avold, Strasbourg, Karlsruhe, Landshut, Villingen, and Constance. Being released after the Armistice, he returned through Switzerland to France on Dec. 1, 1918; and sailed for America on Feb. 1, 1919. He was honorably discharged on Feb. 7, 1919, at Garden City, N.Y.

Since his discharge Lieut. Freeman has been cited by Gen. Pershing "for conspicuous bravery in Service."

Brother in Service —

Willard J. Freeman, 1st Lieut., 23d Infantry, U.S.A.; died in Service.

*JOSEPH EMMETT BEAUTON

FIRST LIEUTENANT, A.S., U.S.A., THIRTEENTH AERO SQUADRON
SECOND PURSUIT GROUP

Killed in airplane accident, June 3, 1918

SON of William F. N. and Ella Teresa (Ahern) Beauton; was born at New Haven, Conn., March 13, 1895. He was educated at the Lovell Grammar School, New Haven High School, and Sheffield Scientific School, Yale. At high school he played on the football team in 1911, '12, and '13. At Yale he played on the freshman football team in 1914.

He enlisted in July, 1917, and trained first at the Ground School of Urbana University, Ill., until about Sept. 15. From then until Dec. 1, 1917, he trained at the Flying School in Belleville, Ill.; and was commissioned 1st Lieut. Dec. 23, 1917. He sailed overseas in Feb., 1918, and received training first on Caudrons. Later he went through the courses for advanced training at Issoudun. He joined the first flight of the 13th Squadron, which was sent to the front south of Châlons-sur-Marne; the Group consisting of the 99th Observation Squadron and one French Escadrille. This Group was stationed at Haussimont-sur-Marne, and worked with an artillery camp from March until June, 1918. On June 1 the 99th Squadron was ordered to Amanty, leaving the flight of the 13th to work from this field with the French until the Squadron should be completed. On the morning of June 3, Lieut. Beauton took his mechanic, Hugh A. Tate, up for a trial flight. They left at about seven-thirty, and returned about fifteen minutes later, because of motor trouble. At that time Sopwiths were being used, and were not of the most dependable type. As the machine neared the edge of the field it was seen to side-slip and then nose over and dive. Lieut. Beauton fell and was killed. He was buried in the town of Mailly, seven miles from Haussimont, France.

EARLE F. RICHARDS

FIRST LIEUTENANT, A.S., U.S.A., THIRTEENTH AERO SQUADRON
SECOND PURSUIT GROUP

SON of Mr. and Mrs. Benjamin F. Richards; was born at West Haven, Conn., April 17, 1896. He was educated at the Suffield School, Suffield, Conn., and at Wesleyan University, Middletown, Conn. At college he was a member of the freshman and 'Varsity, football teams, the class basketball team, and the 'Varsity track team. He trained with the Wesleyan R.O.T.C.

He went overseas in the spring of 1917, and served for four months with the American Ambulance Field Service, behind Soissons, and in the Champagne, taking part in the evacuation under fire at Gueux, which won the unit a citation, and Croix de Guerre from the French, July 14, 1917.

In Oct., 1917, he enlisted at Paris in the U.S. Aviation Service, and was sent to Tours for training, where he received the French Brevet, in Feb., 1918. He trained at the 3d A.I.C. at Issoudun from Feb. to April, 1918, and he was commissioned 1st Lieut., March 8, 1918. He attended the Aerial Gunnery School at Cazaux until May, 1918, when he was assigned as Ferry Pilot to the 1st A.A.P., Orly (Seine), remaining until June 14, 1918. He was transferred to the 1st Air Dépôt, at Colombey-les-Belles, June 14 to July 14, and on July 5 was attached to the 13th Aero Squadron, 2d Pursuit Group, with which he went to the front in the Toul sector.

On Sept. 29, 1918, during the Argonne offensive, Lieut. Richards was brought down, wounded in action, and was sent to the hospital. He reported for duty on Nov. 26, and served as Flight Commander, 13th Squadron, from Dec. 18, 1918, to Jan. 4, 1919. He was honorably discharged on April 7, 1919, at St.-Aignan, France, and returned to the U.S. Inactive Status: Capt. in Reserve; per letter War Dept., June, 1919, Lieut. Richards designed the insignia of his Squadron.

Married, May 16, 1919, at Paris, France, Edith L. Armstrong.

From the Commander in Chief, A.E.F., for conspicuous and especially meritorious service.

First Lieutenant EARLE F. RICHARDS, A.S., U.S.A., Pilot, 13th Aero Squadron, 2d Pursuit Group, is hereby credited with the destruction, in combat, of two enemy Pfalz, in the region of Cormsy, at 4000 metres altitude, on Sept. 14, 1919, at 8.05 o'clock.

DAVID W. HOWE

FIRST LIEUTENANT, A.S., U.S.A., THIRTEENTH AERO SQUADRON
SECOND PURSUIT GROUP

SON of Willard B. and Annie B. Howe; was born in Burlington, Vt., June 22, 1892. He was educated at the Burlington High School, graduating in 1910; and at the University of Vermont, A.B. 1914, where he was a member of Sigma Phi and Phi Beta Kappa Fraternities. He trained for two years in the student battalion of the University of Vermont.

He enlisted at New York on May 12, 1917, and attended the First Plattsburg Officers' Camp, from May 12 to June 25, 1917. He then trained at the M.I.T. Ground School, June to Aug., 1917; and at Hazelhurst Field, Mineola, N.Y., Aug. to Oct., 1917. On Nov. 2, with a 1st Lieut.'s commission, dating from Nov. 3, 1917, he sailed overseas, and was in training at the 3d A.I.C., Issoudun, France, from Dec. to March, 1918. In March and April he was stationed at the École de Tir Aérienne, Cazaux; and acted as ferry pilot at Orly on the Seine, in May and June, 1918.

In July, 1918, Lieut. Howe joined the 13th Aero Squadron, 2d Pursuit Group, organizing on the Toul sector, and remained with this Squadron at Toul, Bebain and Souilly aerodromes until Dec. 5, 1918. He returned to America and was honorably discharged on Feb. 25, 1919.

Copy of a General Order: "Headquarters Air Service First Army, A.E.F. France, Sept. 22, 1918. General Orders, Number 8. Par. 6, 1st Lieutenants J. D. Este, J. J. Seerly, R. R. S. Converse, D. W. Howe, and 2d Lieut. F. E. Hays, 13th Aero Squadron, Second Pursuit Group, are hereby credited with the destruction, in combat, of three enemy biplane Fokkers, in the region of Chambley, at 2400 metres altitude on Sept. 13, 1918, and 18:35 to 19:55 o'clock. *By Order of Colonel* MITCHELL. (*Signed*) T. DEW. MILLING, *Colonel, A.S., U.S.A., Chief of Staff.* Official: W. P. KELLEHER, *Major, A.S., U.S.A., Adjutant.*"

HENRY I. RILEY

First Lieutenant, A.S.A., U.S.A., Thirteenth Aero Squadron
Second Pursuit Group

Son of Charles E. and Stella (Bosworth) Riley; was born Sept. 24, 1894, at North Attleboro, Mass. He was educated in the public schools of North Attleboro, and studied Electrical Engineering for three years at the Rhode Island State College. He played on the baseball team at the high school, and belonged to the Cadet Corps of Rhode Island State College.

He enlisted in the Service of the U.S. at the Officers' Training Camp at Plattsburg, on May 14, 1917. He was trained at Plattsburg, N.Y., and at the Ground School, M.I.T. He was later transferred to Mineola, Long Island, N.Y., for a course in Primary Flying.

He sailed overseas, and he attended the aviation schools in France, at Issoudun, Cazaux, Orly, Seine; at Colombey-les-Belles; at Toul; and at Belrain. Subsequently he was attached to the 13th Squadron, 2d Pursuit Group. He was commissioned 1st Lieut. on Dec. 13, 1917, and received active orders as 1st Lieut. on Feb. 11, 1918. Returning to the U.S., he was stationed at Carlstrom Field, Arcadia, Florida.

Married, Nov. 7, 1918, Catharina Slaign.

JAMES DWIGHT FRANCIS

First Lieutenant, A.S.A., U.S.A., Forty-First Aero Squadron

Son of Henry A. and Agnes (Bartlett) Francis; was born at Pittsfield, Mass., Jan. 13, 1897. He was educated at the Pittsfield High School, at Phillips Andover Academy, and at Harvard College, class of 1919. In 1916 he belonged to the Harvard Regiment and attended the Officers' Training Camp at Plattsburg, N.Y. He was a member of the Harvard R.O.T.C., 1916–17.

He enlisted in the Aviation Service at Pittsfield, Mass., on July 6, 1917. After completing the course at the M.I.T. Ground School he was sent overseas, and received the remainder of his training in French schools. He attended the 3d A.I.C. at Issoudun, from Oct., 1917, to May, 1918, as a Cadet. On May 13, 1918, he was commissioned 1st Lieut., A.S.A. He was ordered to the Cazaux Instruction Centre in June, 1918. From July to Oct., 1918, he served as Instructor at the 3d A.I.C., Issoudun. During Nov. and Dec., 1918, he was assigned to the 41st Aero Squadron, 5th Pursuit Group.

Lieut. Francis was honorably discharged at Garden City, N.Y., on Feb. 8, 1919.

Members of family in Service —

Grandfather: William Francis Bartlett, Major-General in Civil War.

Ancestors in Revolutionary War:

William Francis, Captain.

Daniel Hubbard, Captain.

Jabez Hall, Captain; died in service, 1776.

Seth Pomeroy, General; died in service, 1777.

STUART ELLIS ELLIOTT

First Lieutenant, A.S., U.S.A., Thirteenth Aero Squadron Second Pursuit Group

Son of John Stuart and Helena Forsyth (Ellis) Elliott, of Washington, D.C.; was born at Osterville, Mass., Aug. 24, 1892. He was educated at the Fay School, St. Paul's School, Concord, N.H., Harvard, A.B. 1914, and M.I.T. (graduate work). While at school and college he engaged in general athletic sports.

Previous to the war he served four years in Troop B, M.V.M. He enlisted on May 21, 1917, at Boston, and trained first at the Ground School, M.I.T. He continued his training at Mineola; and sailed for France on Oct. 27, 1917, where he had further training at Issoudun and Cazaux, France. He was commissioned 1st Lieut. on Sept. 17, 1917. During April and May, 1918, he was ferry pilot at Orly. He saw active service from July 1 to Oct. 11, 1918, being attached to the 13th Aero Squadron, 2d Pursuit Group, of which Major (then Capt.) Charles Biddle was Commander. He was stationed near Toul from July 1 to Sept. 14, and took part in the St.-Mihiel offensive. On Sept. 20 he moved to Belrain, where he remained until Nov. 4, taking part in the Argonne-Meuse drive. On Nov. 5 he was moved to Souilly. He has a record for 100 hours over the lines in a 220 Spad. He flew patrols, protections, and took part in "strafing" sorties. He returned from France on March 4, 1919, and was honorably discharged at Camp Mills, on April 11, 1919.

HUGH BRIDGMAN

First Lieutenant, A.S., U.S.A., Forty-Ninth Aero Squadron
Second Pursuit Group

Son of Lewis J. and Annie Page (Campbell) Bridgman; was born at Salem, Mass., Oct. 26, 1897. He was educated in the Salem public schools, and at Harvard College, class of 1919. He was on the staff of the *Crimson*, and was a member of the winning crew in an interdormitory boat-race in 1916.

He sailed for France on Feb. 19, 1917. with the Harvard Unit of the American Ambulance Field Service. On Sept. 15, 1917, he enlisted in the Air Service, U.S.A., and was trained at Tours, and at Issoudun. He was commissioned 1st Lieut. Jan. 1, 1918, and in June was one of the first group of ten American aviators chosen to pilot French fighting-planes at the front. He was later transferred to the 49th Squadron 2d Pursuit Group, and took part in the first "All-American" offensive in Sept., 1918. He did excellent work and was credited with one Boche.

He wrote of this exploit:

I don't think I wrote what a nice birthday I had. I got a beautiful present. The telephone rang and they told me I had official confirmation on a Fokker I got in flames, with another boy, two days before I attained my majority.

It was queer the way we got him. We have the old Richthofen Circus opposite us now, and they are marvellous pilots and full of all kinds of tricks. Seven of them laid a trap for our patrol — four staying high, and three coming down to invite us to attack them. We did just what they wanted us to do, — but left the rear man up top to protect us.

We dove 2000 metres after the Fokkers, who dove also, into Germany. They had a head start, so all we could get was a long shot with incendiaries. One of them caught fire, and as we were low, and in Germany, with the other Fokkers trying to get a chance to pick on us, we pulled up.

As I did so, my motor stopped, and I went down some more. I fiddled with it and it picked up, and I staggered back home on a level with the observation balloons.

Our Squadron now has a record of 22 Boches, with only five losses. . . . More than four to one.

In a letter dated Sept. 17, 1918, he wrote of the offensive:

Our quiet sector has been turned into an important one. I am so glad to have been in the operation as it was the first all-American offensive since we entered the war.

It was, of course, very successfully carried out. . . . We were handi-

capped in our particular line of trade by nasty weather, clouds so low we had to hop the hedges (almost) to fly at all, and squalls of rain every ten minutes. There was a strong wind, too.

Dawn of the offensive, I went out alone, more to satisfy my curiosity than to fight, as there were no enemy planes up at all. The front looked queer because my perspective was changed. We always fly high up, 15,000 to 20,000 feet, and here I was only a few hundred. It was just beginning to grow light, and in the semi-darkness the flashes of the guns we had massed on the lines looked like thousands of fireflies. I could see them twinkling constantly, fifteen or twenty miles up and down the front.

The guns near me rather worried me for a while. The shells were coming so fast that they tossed me around quite a bit, disturbing the air as they did. The detonations were very clear.

I looked around for enemy planes, but all I saw that morning were our liaison planes following infantry, and then chasing back to tell headquarters and batteries all about it by wireless. They were working at my own height, and once in a while an unusually low cloud would come by, and get two of us hidden together, whereupon I would dive out for all I was worth to avoid a collision.

During my flight I superintended the affair up and down the entire front of operations. In one place I went down and watched a local attack by the infantry supported by small tanks. Viewed from above, an attack is ridiculously slow. The tanks seem to crawl, and the men crawl with them. In reality I've seen the tanks, and they are fast for anything so clumsy.

It was tiresome to circle around and watch that particular attack, so after a time I crossed into Germany and looked over the Boches in their reserve trenches. Quantities of shells were bursting on this side and a few on our own territory. I was only machine-gunned once from the ground.

Altogether that first morning was the most impressive I shall probably ever see, and to witness it in such a complete way was worth anything I've got.

Lieut. Bridgman was honorably discharged at Camp Devens, March 18, 1919.

Citation

First Lieutenant Hugh Bridgman, A.S., 49th Aero Squadron: For distinguished and exceptional gallantry at Aincreville, France on, 23d Oct., 1918, in the operation of the American Expeditionary Forces. In testimony thereof, and as an expression of appreciation of his valor, I award this citation.

(*Signed*) John J. Pershing,
Commander-in-Chief

THE THIRD PURSUIT GROUP

By Lieutenant Chester E. Wright, Ninety-Third Aero Squadron

The Third Pursuit Group was formed at Vaucouleurs under the command of Major William Thaw, in the first days of Aug., 1918. It included the 103d, the 93d, the 213th and the 28th Squadrons. Of these the 103d, or the former Lafayette Escadrille, was the only one which had operated before. It was several weeks before the other three were equipped and ready for work. There were many difficulties, such as the lack of planes, parts, and efficient mechanics, to be met with and overcome. Yet in this short period each organization became complete and began its patrols according to schedule.

At this time there was but little enemy activity on the Toul sector, so that it was possible for the new men to gain much experience over the lines before the real contest began. On Sept. 12, 1918, the drive of the First American Army on the Boche positions between St.-Mihiel and Pont-à-Mousson commenced. With this, the group took up its duties in earnest. Patrols were constantly sent over the lines to bomb, "strafe," destroy balloons, protect observation and bombing planes, and drive back the enemy formations. With but small losses, very satisfactory results were achieved. The German formations encountered were not as strong or as skilful as they later proved to be on the Argonne and Verdun sector. Beside, their "chasse" planes, most commonly the Fokker type, were not quite as good for fighting purposes as the French 220 H.P. Spads used by the Americans. The Spads had the advantage of speed, strength, and diving ability. However, the Fokkers made up for this to a certain extent by their adeptness in climbing and manœuvring. Taken as a whole, the forces were faily well matched.

On the 24th of Sept. the First Army having reached its objectives, transferred its forces to the Argonne. The Third Pursuit Squadron accordingly moved with them, and became settled at L'Isle-en-Barrois, about 20 kilometres southeast of Verdun. In carrying out their missions here our patrols met with much fiercer opposition than before. The Germans sent out patrols in greater numbers and played a most cautious game. It was not unusual for our fairly scattered formations of three to eight planes to encounter twice as many. Yet the work went on with the same degree of success as before. A German captain who was taken prisoner after his machine had been shot down in flames, and he had been forced to escape in a parachute, made a fair statement of facts when he said: "Your organization is poor. You patrol in small numbers far into German territory, yet you get amazing results. It is due to a certain amount of daring and luck, mostly the latter."

With the retreat of the Huns, it was again necessary for the group to change position. On Nov. 6 it moved toward the lines ten kilometres to Foucacourt. Adverse weather from this day to the Armistice permitted only a few patrols and bombing expeditions. On Nov. 11 the Group Commander, now Lieut.-Col. Thaw, gave out the order "All hostilities will cease at 11 A.M." In the short three months of activity up to this time the following official confirmations on the destruction of enemy planes had been received: the 93d, thirty-two; the 103d, twenty-eight; the 28th, fourteen; and the 213th, twelve. Sharing in these victories were the following New England men: William Loomis, Richard Loomis, Bryant Woods, Clarence H. Faith, William C. Appleton, Hugo A. Kenyon, and Chester E. Wright.

WILLIAM CHANNING APPLETON, Jr.

Second Lieutenant, A.S., U.S.A., One Hundred Third Aero Squadron, Third Pursuit Group

Son of William Channing and Edna (Turner) Appleton; was born in Jamaica Plain, Mass., on March 15, 1897. He attended the Noble and Greenough School, Boston, and was graduated from Harvard in 1917. At school and college he took part in athletics; at school he played on the baseball team; and at Harvard was captain of the second 'Varsity hockey team, 1915–16, and a member of the 'Varsity hockey team, 1916–17.

He trained with the Harvard Regiment in 1915–16, attended the Plattsburg Camp in 1916, and took a Military Science course at Harvard, 1916–17. In May, 1917, he enlisted in the American Ambulance Field Service, sailed that month for France, and was attached to the Camion Service (T.M.U. 133), which operated along the Aisne and Chemin des Dames front from June to Nov., 1917.

He enlisted in the Air Service, U.S.A., in Paris on Dec. 3, 1917. He was stationed at Paris, at Tours, and at St.-Maixent from Dec., 1917, to April, 1918; and trained at Gondrecourt, Tours, Issoudun, and Cazaux, from May to Oct., 1918. On May 18, 1918, he was commissioned 2d Lieut., A.S., U.S.A. On Oct. 13, 1918, he was attached as pilot to the 103d Aero Squadron, 3d Pursuit Group (1st Pursuit Wing of the 1st Army), then stationed at L'Isle-en-Barrois, and later moved to Foucacourt Field, near the Argonne Forest. In the weeks before the Armistice the 103d Squadron patrolled the Argonne-Meuse front between Grandpré and Verdun, and later from Verdun northward beyond Stenay, during the battles which resulted in the taking of Grandpré, Dun, Stenay, etc. The following extracts are from letters written by Lieut. Appleton:

October 20, 1918

. . . Yesterday we went out to get a plane which had a forced landing near the lines. It was on a hill where eight days before the Americans had rushed up over. Old tanks, etc., lying around and lots of dead Germans, all hit in the chest by bayonet or machine gun. . . .

This country seems much more like one's idea of war than the last summer's country [the Aisne and Chemin des Dames front]. Especially yesterday with low dark clouds and misty rain and artillery rumbles. It was as dark at three as usually at five or five-thirty this time of year, and the flashes of guns twinkling all over the valleys and machine guns winnowing away in the distance, made everything very lonely. No towns left at all.

November 11, 1918

. . . We seem to have ceased hostilities. . . . You ought to see the poor old French poilus. They are weeping, they are so happy.

A couple of our fellows walked out beyond our lines just after 11 A.M., when peace came, and talked with some Germans who walked over from the other side. Germans seemed satisfied and said the Kaiser was finished, and grinned broadly.

All the church bells in the little torn-up villages began ringing and the whistles of the little narrow gauge railway locomotives began tooting at eleven, when the firing ceased.

Our squadron made the last patrol, as far as we can find out, of any American force along this part of the front, and possibly of any Allied, last evening. We went out an hour before sunset and got back after dark and landed by flares. The front was wonderfully beautiful. A thick haze up to 1000 metres, and above clear as a bell, with the moon rising in the east. You could see the earth vaguely beneath. A bunch of our chasse planes were playing around over an old town [Verdun], just on the upper edge of the haze. A few fires from burning villages behind the German lines and the artillery flashes on our side.

The sun set crimson as we headed north on our patrol, and when we reached the end of the northern stretch, there was only a pink glow. We headed home, and put our noses down and pulled on our throttles, and in a few minutes saw the flares and bonfires at our field, away to the southwest.

. . . And to-day all fighting is stopped. It is hard to believe.

After the Armistice, Lieut. Appleton was detached from the Squadron on Dec. 1, 1918; spent Dec. at Issoudun, and part of Jan. at Bordeaux. He sailed from Marseilles Jan. 20, for America, and was honorably discharged at Garden City, N.Y., on Feb. 7, 1919.

20

*ERNEST A. GIROUX

First Lieutenant, A.S., U.S.A., One Hundred Third Aero Squadron, Third Pursuit Group

Killed in action, May 22, 1918

Son of Arthur E. and Jessie (Emery) Giroux (now Mrs. Arthur E. Haley); was born in Roxbury, Mass., Dec. 4, 1895. He was educated at the Somerville High School, class of 1915, and at Dartmouth College, class of 1919. He was a member of the Phi Gamma Delta fraternity.

He left college in March, 1917, to enlist in the American Ambulance Field Service, sailing overseas on April 22, 1917; he was one of the first forty-five to sign for camion service; went to the front with the Ammunition Transport, serving as Sergeant in T.M.U. 526 B. He secured his discharge and enlisted in the Franco-American Flying Corps, and trained at Avord, Tours, Issoudun, and Cazaux; later he was transferred to the U.S. Air Service and was commissioned 1st Lieut. Nov. 20, 1917. After completing his training he acted as ferry pilot between Paris and the front. He was attached to the 103d Squadron under Major Thaw, and in April, 1918, began active service at the front. He was killed May 22, 1918, in an engagement between five American machines of the 103d Squadron, and eight German monoplace machines. He fell behind the enemy lines in the vicinity of Laventie, between Lille and Armentières, and was buried at Estaires, France. He was awarded the Distinguished Service Cross by Gen. Pershing and the Croix de Guerre with Palm.

D.S.C.

First Lieutenant Ernest A. Giroux, Pilot, A.S., U.S.A. For extraordinary heroism in action near Armeyeren, France, May 22, 1918. Lieut. Giroux, while on patrol with four other scout planes attacked an enemy formation of eight monoplace machines. Two of Lieut. Giroux's companions were forced to retire when their guns became jammed. Despite numerical superiority, Lieut. Giroux continued the attack, endeavoring to protect his leader until finally forced down and killed.

Croix de Guerre with Palm

Awarded to American Pilot, 1st Lieut. Ernest A. Giroux. Young pilot filled with energy did not hesitate on May 22, 1918, to attack in their lines an enemy patrol of superior numbers, and gave them a stubborn fight, in the course of which he disappeared.

ARCHIE R. GIROUX

Second Lieutenant, Royal Flying Corps

Son of Arthur E. and Jessie (Emery) Giroux (now Mrs. Arthur E. Haley); was born in Somerville, Mass., on Oct. 19, 1897. He was educated at the Somerville High School, and at Dartmouth College, class of 1923.

He enlisted in the American Ambulance Field Service on April 28, 1917, and served at Danmiers on the French front, as sergeant, T.M.U. 526 B, from April 28 to Oct. 28, 1917. His brother Ernest was in the same service. On April 22, 1918, he enlisted in the Royal Air Force; his brother having enlisted in the Franco-American Flying Corps. He trained at Toronto, Can., Ground School, flying 204 T.D.S.; at East Church, England, No. 7 Fighting School; and at Turnberry, Scotland, "Camel" scout Pilot. He was commissioned 2d Lieut. on Nov. 21, 1918.

On Feb. 25, 1919, he was temporarily released from Shornecliffe, Eng., and returned to the United States.

GEORGE BRYANT WOODS

First Lieutenant, A.S., U.S.A. Twenty-Eighth Aero Squadron, Third Pursuit Group

Son of George Adams and Martha Neal (Howe) Woods; was born at Winchester, Mass., May 6, 1896. He was educated at the Noble and Greenough School, and at Harvard College, class of 1919. taking his degree A.B. *Honoris Causa*. He played on the freshman football and track teams in 1915–16; on Harvard 'Varsity football squad, 1916; member 'Varsity crew squad, 1919.

He enlisted at Cambridge, Mass., on May 30, 1917, and trained at the M.I.T. Ground School from May 30 to July 17, 1917. He sailed overseas on Aug. 13, 1917, and continued his training at Foggia, Italy; and at Issoudun and Cazaux, France. He received an Italian brevet in Dec., 1917, and was commissioned 1st Lieut. U.S.A.S., at Foggia on Jan. 10, 1918. He was one of thirty men sent to France on order of Gen. Pershing in March, 1918.

On May 12, 1918, Lieut. Woods fell in a tail-spin from 400 feet (due to defective machine), with his plane completely demolished. Suffering from a broken jaw, broken ankle, and other injuries, he was three months in the hospital. He joined his Squadron, the 28th, on Aug. 30, and was sent to the front on the Toul sector.

On Sept. 12, 1918, he was leading a flight on the St.-Mihiel sector on a mission to "strafe" the infantry back of the German lines, when his motor was hit by machine-gun fire over the third-line trenches. The Germans continued shooting after the engine had stopped, riddling the plane with rifle and machine-gun bullets. They concentrated fire after the machine had been abandoned, while Lieut. Woods was making way to cover on foot, until he was captured by German infantrymen. About Sept. 29 a note dropped over the aerodrome by German flyers stated that Lieut. Woods had been killed. He was given up by his Squadron, but later was reported a prisoner of war. He was confined successively in six German prison-camps, suffering hard treatment until he reached Villingen, where there was Red Cross Service. He was released on Nov. 29, 1918, and sent by train through Switzerland with other-captured officers.

Lieut. Woods was honorably discharged on Feb. 5, 1919, at Garden City, N.Y.

CHESTER ELLIS WRIGHT

First Lieutenant, A.S., U.S.A., Ninety-Third Aero Squadron
Third Pursuit Group

Son of Richard William and Gertrude (Wesley) Wright; was born at Readville, Mass., Sept. 1, 1897. He attended the schools of Hyde Park, Mass., and spent three years at Harvard College, class of 1918. At the end of his sophomore year, he succeeded in breaking the strength test record for undergraduates, and registering second highest in the University. During the fall of his junior year he was a member of the cross-country team. In Feb., 1917, he left college to train for the Air Service.

He enlisted on March 25, 1917, at Fort Monroe, was appointed sergeant and assigned to the Curtiss School, Newport News. In the latter part of May, the school was broken up, and he was transferred to the Ground School, M.I.T. He graduated July 23, and was sent to Essington, Pa., for instruction in flying hydroplanes. On Aug. 25 he was transferred to Chanute Flying Field, Rantoul, Ill., and completed his R.M.A tests on Sept. 15. He was commissioned 1st Lieut., Oct. 9, 1917. On Oct. 23 he was assigned to active duty at Garden City, N.Y., as adjutant of the 19th Aero Squadron. He sailed overseas on Nov. 23, 1917, as Supply Officer for the 15th Foreign Detachment, and was stationed at St.-Maixent until March 14, 1918. From then until April 15 he trained at the A.I.C. at Issoudun, when he was sent to Cazaux for a month's work in aerial gunnery. He was later ordered back to Issoudun, and thence to Orly, Paris, as a ferry pilot and tester. On July 29 he reported to the 93d Aero Pursuit Squadron as pilot, and from Aug. 6 to the time of the Armistice he acted as Flight Commander of that Squadron. During that period he had numerous encounters with enemy planes and received official confirmation on eight planes and one balloon. On Dec. 5, 1918, at Souilly, he was decorated by General Liggett with the Distinguished Service Cross and one oak leaf.

Lieut. Wright returned to the U.S. on March 13, 1919, and was honorably discharged April 1, 1919, at Garden City, N.Y.

D.S.C.

For extraordinary heroism in action near Beffu, France, 10 Oct., 1918. Lieut. Wright attacked an enemy observation balloon protected by four

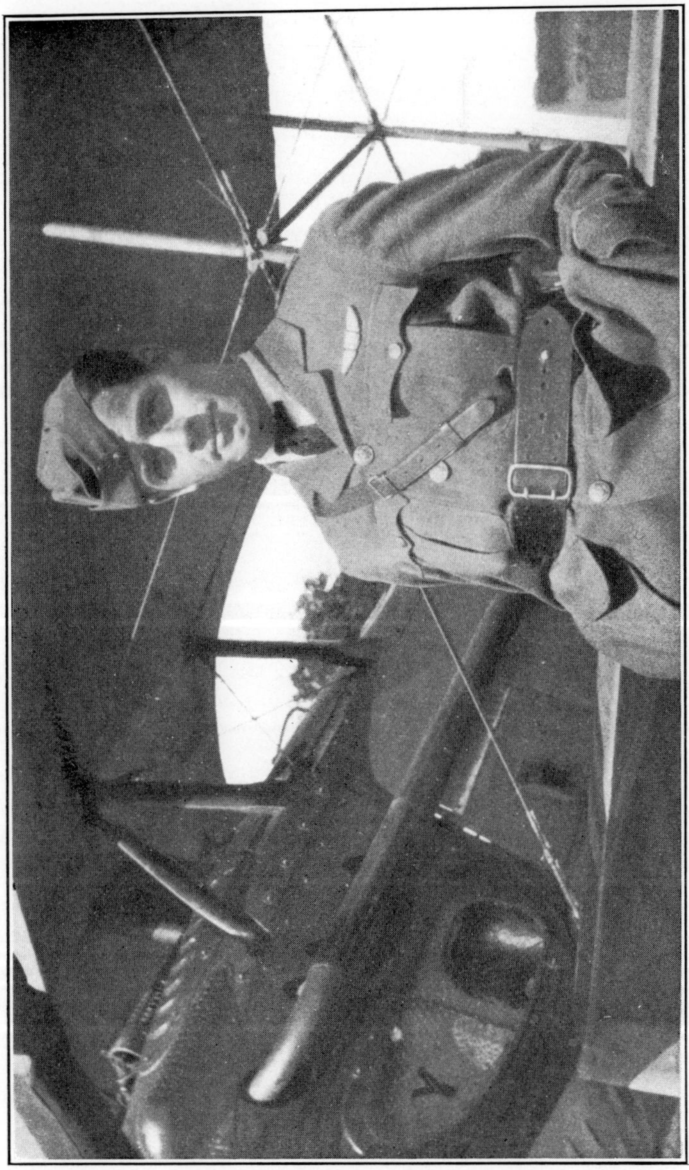

enemy planes; despite numerical superiority he forced the planes to withdraw and destroyed the enemy balloon.

A Bronze Oak Leaf

For extraordinary heroism in action near Banthéville, France, 23 Oct., 1918.

Lieut. WRIGHT, accompanied by one other machine, attacked and sent down in flames an enemy plane (Fokker type), that was attacking an Allied plane. He was in turn attacked by three enemy planes. His companion was forced to withdraw on account of motor trouble. Lieut. Wright continued the combat and succeeded in bringing down one of the enemy planes and forced the remaining two into their own territory.

(*Signed*) PERSHING

ERNEST A. GIOIOSA

CADET, A.S.A., U.S.A.

SON of Thomas and Henrietta (Baciagalupo) Gioiosa; was born at Boston, Mass., Sept. 20, 1893. He was educated at the English High School; at Boston College; and at Dartmouth College, graduating at Dartmouth with the degree B.S. He played baseball and football at Boston College, 1910–11, and football at Dartmouth College, 1911–12. He enlisted in the Air Service at Boston, Mass., Nov. 14, 1917, and was assigned to the Ground Schools at the M.I.T., and Princeton, N.J., for elementary work, completing the course at Princeton, March 9, 1918. He was subsequently transferred to Camp Dick, Dallas, Tex., where he remained from March 16 to May 6, and to Kelly Field, San Antonio, Tex., where he was stationed from May 7 to Nov. 29, 1918. He was honorably discharged at Kelly Field, San Antonio, Tex., Nov. 29, 1918.

Brothers in Service —

Alfred A. Gioiosa, Sergeant, Co. 4, Overseas Convalescent Hospital.

Albert A. Gioiosa, Coxswain, U.S.S. *Pennsylvania.*

*PERRY HENRY ALDRICH

First Lieutenant, A.S., U.S.A., One Hundred Thirty-Fifth Aero Squadron, First Observation Group

Killed in action, Oct. 29, 1918

Son of Rev. Leonard and Fannie I. (Wright) Aldrich; was born in West Kill, N.Y., Nov. 27, 1891. He prepared for college at Vermont Academy, Saxtons River, where he graduated with honors, and entered the University of Vermont; there he was also an honor student, graduating in 1915. He was a member of the Alpha Zeta fraternity, and of Phi Beta Kappa.

For two years he taught agriculture in the Waterbury High School, and was given the principalship of the junior high school of that place, resigning this position to enter the Air Service, Sept. 20, 1917. He was one of five graduates, appointed from this college to attend the aviation schools, and was trained at Fort Sill, Okla., and Garden City, N.Y., and commissioned 2d Lieut., Jan. 3, 1918.

He went overseas in Jan., 1918, received intensive training in the aerial schools in France, was commissioned 1st Lieut. Feb. 2, 1918, assigned to the 135th Aero Squadron, and was sent to the front as an observer in Aug., 1918.

On Oct. 10 he brought down an enemy plane officially. At the time of his death he was about to be made operating officer of a new squadron, which would have meant promotion to Capt., but on Oct. 29 he and his pilot, Lieut. Edward C. Landon, volunteered for an important mission for the corps commander, without the usual protection. This they declined, on the grounds that one ship, if lucky, could get away better than three, and if the enemy did overwhelm them, only one would be lost. They were forced to fly at an altitude of 1000 metres, because of poor visibility, and in the combat which ensued Lieut. Aldrich was mortally wounded.

When the plane landed he was sent with all speed to the hospital, but he passed away without regaining consciousness.

He was buried the following day, at Sebastopol, Toul, Meurthe-et-Moselle, where an impressive service was held.

The following appreciation was forwarded to Lieut. Aldrich's family with the certificate issued by the War Department stating that "Perry H. Aldrich died with honor in the Service of his country."

PERRY HENRY ALDRICH

At the time when so many officers of the Air Service are returning, I feel an earnest desire to express to you some acknowledgment on the part of the Government of the devoted sacrifice offered by your son, who died of wounds received in action in France, Oct. 29, 1918.

Lieut. Aldrich sought the front lines of danger and was one of those whose privilege it was to be selected for it. His sacrifice was made for his country, and his bravery and unflinching devotion to duty have made him one of the nation's heroes.

The Air Service of the United States Army has permanently inscribed his name upon its Roll of Honor and he will ever be remembered as one of those who contributed his best to maintain the prestige of our cause.

I join with his brother officers in expressing our deep appreciation of his loyalty and the effectiveness of the service rendered.

Very sincerely

CARR T. MENOHER
Major-General, U.S.A.

Lieut. L. W. Schlesinger, Adjutant 135th Aero Squadron, wrote:

I was with the Squadron when Perry joined it, and in my work as Adjutant the various officers of the Squadron were constantly before me. I can truthfully say that I don't believe there was a braver, truer, more Christian soldier than Perry in the A.E.F. He was a good comrade, always had a kind word and a ready smile, and was absolutely indifferent to personal danger. He showed the highest devotion to duty, and met his death while carrying out a dangerous mission.

D.S.C.

For extraordinary heroism in action near St.-Mihiel, France, 29 Oct. 1918.

Lieut. ALDRICH (Observer) with 1st Lieut. E. C. LANDON, volunteered and went on an important mission for the Corps Commander, without the usual protection. Forced to fly at an altitude of 1000 metres because of poor visibility. Soon after crossing the lines they encountered an enemy Rumpler plane, and forced it to the ground. On returning they attacked another Rumpler and drove it off. After completing their mission and seeing an enemy observation tower on Lake Lachaussée, they reëntered the enemy territory and fired upon it. Immediately attacked by seven enemy planes (Fokker type) a combat followed in which Lieut. Aldrich was mortally wounded.

By command of General PERSHING

Brother in Service –
Herbert J. Aldrich, sergeant Medical Dep't Fort Meyer, Va.

T. J. DUNCAN FULLER

First Lieutenant, A.S., U.S.A., One Hundred Thirty-Fifth Aero Squadron, First Observation Group

Son of Mr. and Mrs. Thomas J. Fuller, of Boston, Mass.; was born at Washington, D.C., Aug. 6, 1893. He was educated at the Washington public schools, and at Harvard College, class of 1915. He rowed on his freshman crew, and on the 'Varsity four-oared crew, in 1913.

He enlisted on April 23, 1917, at Mineola, N.Y., and was trained at Mineola, from April to July, 1917. He was commissioned 1st Lieut., R.M.A., July 26, 1917, U.S. Air Service, and was on duty at Chanute Field, Rantoul, Ill., from July 26, to Sept. 4, 1917; at Fort Sill, Okla., from Sept. 4 to May 9, 1918; and at Taliaferro Field, Fort Worth, Tex., from May 9 to July 1, 1918.

He sailed overseas on July 15, 1918, and trained at Issoudun, France, from Aug. 15 to Sept. 1, when he was attached to the 135th Squadron. On Sept. 12 he was forced to land on Swiss soil, his machine having been damaged by anti-aircraft fire. He refused to give his parole not to try to make his escape, and was imprisoned at Addermatt, Switzerland, until the end of the war. On Oct. 16, 1918, he made a desperate attempt to escape on a rope made from his bedclothes; but the rope broke and Lieut. Fuller fell a considerable distance and was badly injured. He was reimprisoned, and remained in captivity until Dec. 7, 1918, when he was released by the Swiss government. He returned to the U.S. on Jan. 3, and was honorably discharged on Jan. 10, 1919.

Brother in Service —

Ashmead Fuller, 1st Lieut., A.S., U.S.A.

ARTHUR L. CLARK

First Lieutenant, A.S.A., U.S.A., Twenty-Fourth Aero Squadron, First Observation Group

Son of Eugene W. and Jane (Putnam) Clark; was born at Jamaica Plain, Mass., on Dec. 18, 1892. He was educated at the Roxbury Latin School, at the West Roxbury High School, at the Mass. Agricultural College, and at the Rhode Island State College. He was a sophomore in the Agricultural Department of the Rhode Island State College when he enlisted at Plattsburg, N.Y., May 12, 1917. On Aug. 14, 1917, he was honorably discharged from the Officers' Training Camp at Plattsburg, and on the same day reënlisted in the S.E.R.C. at Mineola, N.Y., as private, 1st class.

He was assigned to the Ground School at M.I.T., and from there transferred to the Aviation School at Mineola, N.Y. He was further trained at the School for Observers at Fort Sill, Okla. On Jan. 4, 1918, he was commissioned 2d Lieut. at Garden City, N.Y., and on Jan. 5 assigned to active duty with detachment of Aerial Observers, No. 1. He sailed overseas on Jan. 9, 1918.

He was commissioned 1st Lieut. on Feb. 2, 1918, and assigned to various schools in France. On Sept. 12, he was ordered to active official observer's flying duty near the Toul sector. On Sept. 17, 1918, while flying with his pilot, Lieut. William A. Bradfield of Dallas, Tex., the motor went dead and he was forced to descend, and was captured by the Germans. For a month he was reported "missing in action," but on Oct. 15 was reported unwounded and a prisoner at Landshut, Germany.

Upon landing from their plane on Sept. 17, Lieut. Clark and his pilot were taken to Joeuf, in Lorraine, questioned closely and transferred to Karlsruhe, Baden, by train, and finally to Landshut and Villingen, about thirty kilometres north of the Swiss border. On Nov. 25, after many faithless promises, they were released, and proceeded to Konstanz, thence to the Swiss border.

Lieut. Clark was one of the first American aviators and ex-prisoners of war to be returned to the U.S., arriving on Jan. 18, 1919. He was honorably discharged in Jan., 1919, and is now attached to the Experiment Station at the Rhode Island State College.

LEO BERNARD CAUCHON

First Lieutenant, A.S., U.S.A., Twenty-Fourth Aero Squadron, First Army Observation Group

Son of Phelias, and Zelia Cote Cauchon, of Providence, R.I.; was born Sept. 29, 1895. He attended the Rhode Island School of Design. Prior to the war he was for sixteen months a member of troop N, R.I. Cavalry.

On May 11, 1917, he enlisted at Providence R.I., and was sent to the Plattsburg Training Camp, May 11 to July 16, 1917. From then until Sept. 15, 1917, he attended the Ground School at Princeton, N.J. He sailed overseas for France, arriving Oct. 28, 1917. From Dec. 25, 1917, to April, 1918, he trained at the École d'Aviation, at Châteauroux, France, and from April until July, 1918, at Issoudun, where he was commissioned 1st Lieut. in June, 1918. He concluded his training at Tours, where he was stationed from July to Aug. 23, 1918, when he was attached to the 24th Aero Squadron, and with them saw service until Dec. 8, 1918.

Between Sept. 8 and Nov. 11, Lieut. Cauchon's flying time over the lines was thirty-six hours, seventeen minutes, and he was officially credited with one enemy plane. He returned to the U.S. and was honorably discharged at Camp Pike, Ark., April 26, 1919.

Citations

First Lieutenant L. B. Cauchon, A.S., U.S.A., and Second Lieutenant B. F. Collins, C.A.C., 24th Aero Squadron, 1st Army Observation Group, are hereby credited with the destruction, in combat, of an enemy Fokker, in the region of Damvillers, at 2500 metres altitude, on Oct. 22, 1918, at 9.50 o'clock.

By order of Colonel Milling
Chief of Staff

The Air Service Commander, First Army, cites the following officers and men for exceptional devotion to duty:

First Lieutenant Leo B. Cauchon, A.S., U.S.A., Pilot, 24th Aero Squadron, has repeatedly fulfilled missions under unfavorable conditions with an utter disregard of personal risk. On Oct. 22, with Second Lieutenant Bayard F. Collins, C.A.C., U.S.A., Observer, he was flying alone over Stenay-Montmédy region and encountered five enemy formations, resulting in two combats, in which one German plane was shot down. Lieutenant Cauchon returned safely, although his plane was badly damaged. The destruction of one enemy plane has been officially confirmed on this mission.

By order of Colonel Milling

LEO BERNARD CAUCHON

First Lieutenant Leo B. Cauchon, A.S., U.S.A., Pilot, joined the 24th Aero Squadron on Aug. 30, 1918; has had thirty-six hours and seventeen minutes total flying time, of which twenty-one hours and twenty-two minutes was included in successful reconnaissance. He has displayed unusual bravery in action on several occasions, for which he was cited in General Order Number 30, Headquarters, Air Service, First Army, Nov. 26, 1918. As mess officer during his entire stay with the Squadron, he has performed his duties with good ability and untiring effort.

Maury Hill
Captain, A.S., U.S.A.

Brothers in Service —

Hervé P. Cauchon, Sergeant, Headquarters, Co. 103, F.A. 26th Div.

Henri F. Cauchon, Corporal, Headquarters, Co. 327, Infantry, 82d Div.

SIDNEY FULLER LAW

Second Lieutenant, A.S.A., U.S.A.

Son of Frederick A. and Mary E. (Fuller) Law, of Longmeadow, Mass.; was born at New London, Conn., Dec. 14, 1892. He was educated at the Springfield Technical High School, Springfield, Mass., and at the Throop Polytechnic Academy, Pasadena, Cal. He enlisted at Ludlow, Mass., Oct. 6, 1917, and was assigned to Camp Devens, Ayer, Mass., where he remained until Dec. 13, 1917. He attended the Ground School at Princeton, N.J., from Dec. 13, 1917, to March 2, 1918. He was trained at Camp Dick, Dallas, Tex., from March 2 to April 23, and at Carlstrom Field, Arcadia, Fla., from April 23 to June 29. On June 29, 1918, he was commissioned 2d Lieut., and was ordered to return to Camp Dick, where he remained until July 20. He was stationed at Brooks Field, San Antonio, Tex., from July 20 to Sept. 6, and at Call Field, Wichita Falls, Tex., from Sept. 6 to Dec. 19, 1918. At Call Field he acted as Flying Instructor, and made some cross-country flights in the interests of the United War Work Campaign. He was released from the Service at Call Field, Dec. 16, 1918.

*CHARLES HASTINGS UPTON

First Lieutenant, A.S.A., U.S.A., Fiftieth Aero Squadron
First Observation Group

Killed in airplane accident, Aug. 28, 1918

Son of Samuel and Arexzine A. (Wood) Upton; was born at Boston, Mass., Sept. 4, 1893. He was educated in the public schools of Somerville, and at Tufts College, where he spent three years in the Engineering School; he was an excellent athlete and a member of the Tufts College Glee Club.

He enlisted on June 16, 1917, at Cambridge, Mass., and entered the Ground School at M.I.T., where, after completing his course, he was selected as one of the honor men to be sent overseas to Foggia, Italy, for further training. There he won the Golden Eagle of the Royal Italian Flying Corps. He was commissioned 1st Lieut. March 2, 1918, and was given his choice of remaining to pilot Caproni planes or being transferred to France. He chose the latter course, and was ordered to Issoudun for advanced training, and then to Tours, where he was stationed for several months. He was then sent to the front attached to the 50th Aero Squadron.

On Aug. 28, 1918, Lieut. Upton, with his observer, went up for target practice; there was a very strong wind blowing, and in the process of shooting at the target an unexpected cross current of air threw the machine into a very slow "spin," which at two hundred metres altitude is often fatal. Just as Lieut. Upton was getting his machine under control again, it crashed to the ground, killing him almost instantly.

He was buried with full military honors on Aug. 29, 1918, at Gondrecourt, France. The final request in Lieut. Upton's will was that if there were services over his remains, to tell his friends to bring nothing but violets, the flowers he loved best. This request was carried out, and his grave was covered with violets. A memorial service was held for him on Oct. 6, 1918, at the Winter Hill Baptist church, at Somerville, Mass.

Lieut. Upton had a distinct literary gift; he had published some stories before he went abroad, and extracts from his inspiring letters have also been in print. A week before his death he wrote:

> I must tell you that this thing we are working for has become so much a part of our lives, that it is our life. By that I mean there is nothing I

have ever done in this world which has given me a greater degree of contentment and satisfaction. The chance to serve, oh, you know what it is, you are one of those who saw the big Ideal, who gave up things that he might serve that Ideal. . . . My chance is coming now! I am stationed temporarily twenty-five miles back of the front expecting to move up to another airdrome before long. Then our work will begin. . . . Never was much of a church man, or even a believer in prayer, yet our Big Ideal has brought something greater than many of us ever had. How else could our chance to serve come to mean what it does? It is not fear of death, or of a possible Hell; simply a full realization that there is a God whom we serve through our Big Ideal.

A few weeks earlier he wrote:

There is something more awe inspiring about an airplane crash than any other accident that may cause death. . . . I thought I had become hardened to death — I am not — my desire to fly is still with me. I do not fear my own death; there is too much beyond; but I fear to see my brothers go. And from all these accidents, sometimes fatal and sometimes not, a chap, even while seeing the injustice of it, gains a greater faith in what before may have seemed an intangible Supreme Being. It is paradoxical to have a greater faith in a Supreme Being who allows men to be killed, but it works that way.

Who can stand beside the open grave of a comrade, hear the volleys fired, and the sweet notes of "Taps," see the airplanes swoop down to drop garlands over the spot, without feeling that there is something Greater? As the last note of "Taps" sounds out over the spot, one has a vision, if you like, of a soul gone to a well-earned rest and to happiness. . . . And so through it all, we have our Grand Ideal, which tells us we have the glorious chance to grasp the opportunity of our lives, and if we come through, something to remember all our remaining days. For my part, I have never prepared to do anything comparable to what my service offers, I have never experienced anything of equal exaltation; in a word, service in a cause like ours becomes so absorbing, so impersonal, it grips one until there is *nothing too great to give, no sacrifice too great to make* for that which is now *sacred* to us. I hope I have given you something of the spirit of the boys over here, for we are all in the same situation, all in the same cause, all with the same Big Ideal. It's the greatest experience of our lives. I don't think we will lose the vision. . . . How could one lose his vision *at the front*, where if men are winged over the Biggest Top, they have gone with their Grand Ideal locked in their hearts.

*HENRY LeNOBLE STEVENS

First Lieutenant, A.S., U.S.A., Fiftieth Aero Squadron
First Observation Group

Killed in action, Sept. 12, 1918

Son of Charles and Mary Wharton (Sinkler) Stevens, was born at Pinopolis, S.C., May 23, 1892. He was educated at the Charleston and Episcopal High Schools, the University of Virginia, and the Eastman Business College. He was a member of the 'Varsity track team at the University of Virginia.

He enlisted from Providence, R.I., on May 13, 1917, at the Officers' Training Camp at Plattsburg. From Plattsburg he was sent to Toronto, Can., to train for the Aviation Service under the Royal Flying Corps. He trained at Long Branch, Camp Rathbun, and at Armour Heights, Can., and was later transferred to Taliaferro Field, Fort Worth, Tex., attached to the 22d Squadron. He sailed overseas with the 139th Squadron, on Feb. 24, 1918, and continued his training at Tours, France, where he was made Commanding Officer of a construction squadron, at 2d A.I.C., being urged to retain this position for duration of the war.

At his own request he was transferred back to active service and trained at Tours and Issoudun for reconnaissance pilot. He was commissioned 1st Lieut. on Sept. 8, 1918. On Sept. 9 he was sent to Bar-le-Duc with the 50th Squadron, and on the morning of the St.-Mihiel drive, Sept. 12, he was despatched on a dangerous reconnaissance mission, in D.H. 4 Liberty plane. Four hours later he was shot down in flames at Pont-à-Mousson, back of the German lines, and instantly killed. His mission was to see whether the Germans were withdrawing or reinforcing their lines at a very important point. As Lieut. Stevens had been up four hours before he was shot down, it was believed that he had accomplished his mission and had subsequently been lost in the heavy rain and low hanging clouds. He was buried at the military cemetery at Thiaucourt.

Married, June 27, 1917, Mary Elizabeth Carpenter.

JOHN RICHARD EDWARDS, Jr.

First Lieutenant, A.S.A., U.S.A., Ninety-Ninth Aero Squadron, First Observation Group

Son of John Richard and Harriet (DeWolfe) Edwards, of Bristol, R.I.; was born in Washington, D.C., Oct. 21, 1896. He was educated at the public schools of Portsmouth, N.H., Episcopal Academy, Philadelphia, Friends School, Washington, D.C., and Bowdoin College to the second semester of his junior year.

He completed the course of military instruction at the Plattsburg Camp of 1916. Later that year he enrolled for naval instruction and served on the U.S.S. *Virginia* during the months of Sept. and Oct.

In Jan., 1917, he volunteered for duty as an ambulance driver on the French front. Early in Feb., 1917, he enrolled in that service, took passage for France, and served for six months in the Verdun and Champagne sectors.

After completing the period for which he volunteered as an ambulance driver, he enlisted in Paris as a private in the American Aviation Service. He was a member of the first section of American aviators that was trained in France, this camp having been established at Tours. He was assigned to the French Aviation Camp at Issoudun, where he was trained to operate the various machines used by the French aviators.

In Nov., 1917, he was given the Brevet d'Aviateur Militaire by the French Minister of War. Dec. 10, 1917, he was commissioned as a 1st Lieut. in the Air Service, U.S. Signal Reserve Corps.

In Feb., 1918, Lieut. Edwards was assigned as a member of Observation Squadron U.S. No. 99. This Squadron, from March, 1918, to the signing of the Armistice, located enemy installations by observations and photographs, distributed propaganda literature beyond the battle line, located hostile munition and infantry positions, adjusted the artillery fire of the U.S. forces, performed réglage service, made repeated reconnaissances to the enemy's territory, and was likewise assigned to various special missions. This American Squadron served for a time with a French Escadrille.

While operating within the Frapelle sector, Lieut. Edwards was cited with other members of the Squadron, and Major-General

O. P. Summerall especially cited the work of the 99th and 104th Squadrons, during the closing days of the War. During the St.-Mihiel salient attack he was continually employed in connection with the work performed by this Squadron.

Aero Squadron 99 and 104 for faithful and untiring service in obtaining useful and valuable information, often under great difficulty, and in aiding the advance of the ground forces throughout the Meuse-Argonne offensive of Sept. 26 to Nov. 11, 1918.

Among other individual citations received by Lieut. Edwards, are the following:

The Air Service Commander, First Army, cites the following officers and men for exceptional devotion to duty:

1. Par. 5. First Lieutenant JOHN R. EDWARDS, A.S., U.S.A., Pilot, 99th Aero Squadron, executed exceptional mission on Sept. 14th, 1918, over Conflans, twenty kilometres behind enemy lines. His formation was attacked by twenty-five enemy pursuit planes. During combat his gas pump was shot away. Pumping gas by hand, he piloted machine free of the enemy and reached own lines. The plane landed without a crash despite the damage done to it by the enemy fire.

By order of Colonel MILLING

Brother in Service —

Allen R. Edwards, Lieut.-Col., U.S. Coast Artillery.

Father in Service —

John R. Edwards (Rear Admiral U.S. Navy) (Retired).

VINCENT E. HEYWOOD

First Lieutenant, R.M.A., Ninety-Ninth Aero Squadron First Observation Group

Son of Charles Henry and Cora M. (Eaton) Heywood; was born in Springfield, Mass., Jan. 20, 1889. He graduated from Lake Forest College, Lake Forest, Ill.

In 1915 he attended the 1st Plattsburg Camp, and that same year organized the Worcester Rifle Club, having previously qualified as an expert rifleman in the U.S. Revolver Association. In 1916 he enlisted for 30 days with the 2d U.S. Cavalry, and took examinations for a volunteer commission. On March 17, 1917, he sailed for Bordeaux, attached to the 97th Division Infantry, French Army, as Ambulancier.

The day America entered the war he took part in the French Celebration at Paris, and was one of eighty Americans to march to Lafayette's monument. At the front, near Verdun, he was assigned to S.S.U. 17, with which he had strenuous evacuation work. He was in two offensives in the Ayocourt-Esnes sector. Heywood and Stephen P. Lewis, as brancardiers went into the first-line trenches the evening preceding the German offensive near Hill 304. They remained dug in for six hours, through a terrible barrage of 77's, and went over the top with the 59th Chasseur Division, each rescuing a blessé. Heywood's Section was cited "for courage and calmness under desperate circumstances, especially during June, July, and Aug., 1917."

His enlistment in the French Army having expired on Sept. 17, he enlisted as a private in the U.S. Air Service, at Paris, and was sent to Tours for instruction, receiving his Brevet d'Aviateur Militaire on Nov. 30, 1917; he was sent to the American Chasse School at Issoudun on Dec. 3, where he remained until March 17, 1918. He was commissioned 1st Lieut. on March 6, 1918, Aviation Section, S.O.R.C., R.M.A., and assigned to the 99th Aero Squadron. On March 25, the 99th, consisting of eighteen pilots, flew their new Sopwith planes out of Le Bourge Aerodrome, Paris, under the fire of the German long-range gun.

Early in Oct., 1918, Lieut. Heywood was recalled, because of nervous breakdown, and assigned to the Technical Section of the Air Service in Paris, for a two months' rest.

He was honorably discharged at Garden City, N.Y., on Dec. 31, 1918.

Citations

The volunteer HEYWOOD came in the 17th Section on the 29th of April. During all the time he has been in the Section he did his work as well as possible. He is a very good mechanic and a very good driver; he always showed the most intelligent devotion and the highest courage, and I noted many times his calm and cool blood during the hard shelling we had in the Verdun battle (June, July, Aug., 1917). I give for Heywood my best recommendation, and I wish for him, for the good character he always shows, the best luck for anything he will undertake.

Le Sous-Lieut. Com. S.S.U. 17
(*Signed*) D'HALLEY

Croix de Guerre with Star

General Legaille, Commander of the 97th Division Infantry, cites at the Division's Order, the S.S.U. 17, attached to the Division, for the following reason. Under the Command of Sub-Lieutenant d'Halley and an American Lieutenant, Neftel, the young volunteers of the S.S.U. 17 have given proof, on dangerous, often critical occasions — notably a series of combats in June, July, and Aug., 1917 — of a calm and thoughtful courage and of most lofty sentiment of devotion. Without thought of danger, they have given themselves to go in search of, rescue, and bring back the wounded, under the enemy's fire; and have rendered to the 97th Division and to the French Cause services the value of which cannot be exaggerated.

(*Signed*) *General* LEGAILLE

The undersigned, commanding the S.S.U. 17 certifies that Mr. VINCENT E. HEYWOOD was a member of the Section at the time of the above citation.

(*Signed*) D'HALLEY

Nov. 22, 1918

To Lieut. V. Heywood:

The Administrative Officers, Technical Section, wish to express to you. their appreciation for your work in connection with the Division in which you have been associated. The results obtained have been due to the fact that each officer has performed to the best of his ability the duties entrusted to him. The organization has grown rapidly from the start, and was, at the time the Armistice was declared, in splendid shape for future functioning. Your individual part in bringing about the development of this organization is much appreciated.

(*Signed*) E. J. HALL
Lieut.-Col. Air Service
Chief Technical Section

R. NOBLE ESTEY

First Lieutenant, A.S.A., U.S.A.; Adjutant to C.O., Fifth Army Corps; Chief Photographic Officer, Ninety-Ninth Aero Squadron, Fifth Army Corps

Son of Henry P. and Mary J. (Noble) Estey; was born in Waterbury, Conn., Oct. 29, 1886. He was educated in the public schools of Waterbury, later taking up newspaper work. He became interested in aviation in 1909, and made his first flight as a member of the American Press Association at Belmont Park, in 1911. In 1913 he brought the first Curtiss Flying Boat to Providence. While he was connected with the *Providence Tribune* he formed the First Aeronautical Division of the Rhode Island State Militia, which when the U.S. declared war comprised about 100 partly trained men. On April 6, 1917, the members of the Division were taken over into the regular Navy, and soon after transferred to Marblehead. Here they remained until July 13, 1917. At this time Estey applied for and received honorable discharge from the Navy, joined the Lafayette Escadrille in New York City, and sailed for France on July 23, 1917. On Aug. 27 Lieut. Estey transferred to the Air Service of the U.S., in Paris. On Sept. 1 he was sent to Tours for training, and in Feb., 1918, to Issoudun, completing the course in March. He was then assigned to the 99th Observation Squadron, and on March 18 left Issoudun for the front. Toward the end of Aug. the Squadron was shifted to Souilly, arriving two days before the beginning of the St.-Mihiel drive. During the entire offensive the Squadron operated over the sector, photographing and carrying on artillery réglage work. There were times when it was impossible to string up telephones fast enough to keep up with the infantry, and when runners carrying messages were shot down before they could reach General Headquarters. At such times the observation planes were the only communication between the front lines and the Post Command. At the beginning of the Argonne offensive Lieut. Estey was made Adjutant by Lieut.-Col. Christie, who was then Chief of the Air Service of the Fifth Army Corps, to which the 99th Squadron was attached. After the Armistice he was ordered home, arriving at Hoboken on Feb. 17, 1919. He was honorably discharged June 5, 1919, and accepted a commission in the Reserve Corps.

HOWARD HARE POWEL

Captain, A.S.A., U.S.A., Eighty-Fifth Squadron, R.A.F.

Son of Harford W. Hare and Marion C. H. Powel, of Newport, R.I.; was born at Chestnut Hill, Philadelphia, Pa., Jan. 7, 1891. He attended St. George's School, Newport, R.I., and entered Harvard College in the class of 1914, withdrawing on account of illness in his sophomore year. He played football and took prizes in English and French in school and college.

On June 15, 1911, he enlisted as a private in Battery A, M.V.M., with which he served until honorably discharged, Dec. 13, 1913. He volunteered in the American Ambulance Field Service, Feb. 12, 1916, and during the great German drive against Verdun saw hard service with his section, "S.S.U. No. 2," which was twice cited for bravery. He was honorably discharged on Oct. 19, 1916, and in Nov. returned to the U.S.

He enlisted at Boston in May, 1917, and graduated with the first class of cadet aviators at M.I.T. He was then ordered to Mineola, N.Y., for practical flying, graduated there as a pilot, and was commissioned 1st Lieut. A.S., S.C., Officers' Reserve Corps, U.S.A., on Aug. 28, 1917. He was assigned for further advanced instruction to Kelly Field, San Antonio, Tex., where he later acted as instructor. Subsequently he was transferred to Toronto, Can.; to Taliaferro Field, Fort Worth, Tex., where he was attached to the 27th Squadron; to Toronto again; and to Kelly Field, No. 2, San Antonio, Tex.

He went overseas in command of the 183d Aero Squadron. As a member of the A.E.F. he was trained at various British flying schools, and commissioned Capt. (temp.) in the Signal Corps, U.S.A., on Feb. 19, 1918. He was attached to the 85th Squadron, R.A.F., with which he saw much active service during July, Aug., and Sept., 1918. In Sept. he was taken ill; upon recovery was given leave. He returned to the Supply Dépôt, Nov. 5, and arrived in Boston, Mass., on Jan. 22, 1919.

Captain Powel is still in the Service, stationed at Kelly Field, San Antonio, Tex. He took part in the Mid-West Flight of the Flying Circus engaged in selling Victory Loan Bonds.

Captain Powel comes of a family prominent for three centuries in the Army and Navy of Great Britain.

CHARLES HURD HOWELL

CAPTAIN, R.F.C., TWELFTH AND THIRTEENTH SQUADRONS

SON of Mr. and Mrs. George D. Howell, of Boston, Mass.; was born at Uniontown, Fayette, Co. Pa., Feb. 25, 1891. He was educated at St. Mark's School, Southboro, Mass.; at Trinity College, Hartford, Conn., and at Balliol, Oxford, and Christ's, Cambridge, Eng.

In Sept., 1915, while a student at Oxford, he enlisted in the Royal Flying Corps. He was commissioned 2d Lieut., Dec. 13, 1915; and in July, 1916, was one of a large group of flyers that accompanied Gen. Haig in his campaign on the Somme, for some nine months continuously. Lieut. Howell was then given a rest in England, and was later in service in the Coast Defence against raids, and was in charge of anti-aircraft gun crews. He gained his first promotion from successful bombing in the Somme drive.

He trained in England at Brooklands, No. 2, Res. Squadron, and at Croydon, No. 17, Res. Squadron. In France he was attached to 12th and 13th Squadrons, and to Headquarters. In England he served as instructor to the 49th and 44th Squadrons, at No. 2, Auxiliary School of Aerial Gunnery; also to the 45th, 61st, and 39th Squadrons, at Grantham.

He was commissioned 1st Lieut. July 1, 1917; Capt., Sept. 1, 1918. On Jan. 25, 1919, he was demobilized at Thetford, Eng.

His commanding officer, R.A.F., wrote in Sept., 1918, in recommending him for promotion:

> I have known Lieut. C. H. Howell for the past two and three-quarters years, first as Pilot in England, and later in France where he did splendid work in an artillery observation and long-range bombing Squadron. He can fly almost any type of machine, and is an excellent instructor. Altogether, to my knowledge, he has had that varied experience which fits him to lead formations in the Field, or command Instructional Flights at home.
>
> (*Signed*) *Lieut.-Col.* (*A.*) *R.A.F.*

Capt. Howell was mentioned in the Victory Despatches from Eng. in Nov., 1919, for his "splendid service during the war."

Married, Dec. 19, 1916, Margaret Russell.

Brother in Service —

G. Dawson Howell, Lieut., U.S. Navy.

ROBERT H. REECE

FIRST LIEUTENANT, R.A.F.

SON of John and Marietta Reece (Now Mrs. J. B. Thomas); was born in Brookline, Mass., Aug. 30, 1888. He prepared for college at the Noble and Greenough School and entered Harvard College in the class of 1911.

In Oct., 1916, he joined the Royal Flying Corps and received his aviation training in England. During the following year he was one of thirty-five chosen from his Squadron to be sent to the Ypres front, attached to the first Royal Flying Corps bombing squadron used in France. In Oct., 1917, he was attached to the Handley-Page Squadron, R.N.A.S., as navigating officer for long-distance night-bombing raids into Germany. The following Feb. he was granted six months leave and sailed for America on the S.S. *Andania*, which was torpedoed off the Irish coast. All on board were rescued by trawlers and returned to England; Lieut. Reece's leave was extended and his next voyage was uninterrupted.

In April, 1918, he returned to his Squadron in France, known as "The Bedouin Squadron." Among the places bombed by this Squadron during the following months were Metz, Mannheim, Konz, Pforzheim, Thionville, Saarbrucken, Lumez, Vahl Eberzing, Stuttgart, and Frankfort, the raid at the last place being carried out during three thunderstorms.

On July 7, 1918, Lieut. Reece was awarded the "Distinguished Flying Cross," and in Sept. 1918, he was sent to England as A.D.C. to the Inspector General of the Royal Air Force.

The D.F.C. is personally bestowed upon the recipients by King George at Buckingham Palace, and Lieut. Reece was one of five Americans to receive this honor.

Lieut. Reece was early convinced that the aeroplane would become an effective fighting machine, and during his term in the British Army he saw the development in the Air Service from the use of small machines for observation only, into a great offensive arm of warfare. This is all graphically described in the first chapter of his book, "Night Bombing with the Bedouins." This chapter he has aptly named "Per Ardua Ad Astra" which was the motto of the Royal Flying Corps. To quote his words:

ROBERT H. REECE

What would the past generation have said of a man who had prophesied great armies fighting in the air? Even in the early months of the war there were but few who realized what an important part of the war was to be carried on in the newly conquered element. When the infantry saw an occasional box-kite-looking machine drifting slowly over the lines, struggling to keep itself aloft, how many, I wonder, foresaw that in a few months these machines would be swooping down on them like swallows, raking them with machine guns by day and bombing them by night? How many artillery officers laughed at the suggestion that a day was coming when thousands of great guns would be directed from the air? Yet in a few short months two great blind fighting giants, their arms stretching from the Belgian coast to the Swiss border, learned to see each other; and their eyes were in the air.

. . . .

It was not until 1916 that the full powers of the aeroplane as an offensive weapon began to be realized. Bombing was done, but it was of a desultory nature, and although the number of machines engaged in this work steadily increased, and the work itself became more and more diversified and specialized, it was not until 1918 that the possibilities of the aeroplane as a purely offensive weapon were appreciated.

An aeroplane can operate far back of the enemy lines, both in the day and at night; enemy troops in transport can be bombed; railway stations, sidings, etc., damaged; transports of all kinds delayed; and ammunition dumps, when located, can be blown up. In fact, military targets of all sorts can be attacked from the air that cannot be reached in any other way. The very foundation of a nation's strength in war, its industry, can be attacked from the air and, if attacked on a large enough scale, can be destroyed.

. . . .

The hundreds of bombing machines which the English aeroplane factories were turning out at the time hostilities ceased, and the thousands of men being trained for bombing, make one wonder what would have happened to the German industries if the war had continued through the spring of 1919.

Besides these hundreds of aeroplanes under construction and the thousands of men in training, the Royal Air Force had in operation, Nov. 11, 1918, over twenty thousand aeroplanes, over thirty thousand aviators, and over two hundred thousand mechanics and other personnel.

. . . .

The name of Lieut. Robert Reece is next to the top on the Honor List at the Air Ministry, a record of those who did night bombing in Germany. He resigned from the Service to resume his business career in the spring of 1919.

PHILLIPS MERRILL PAYSON

FIRST LIEUTENANT, A.S.A., U.S.A.
ONE HUNDRED SIXTY-SIXTH AERO SQUADRON, A.E.F.
ATTACHED TO FIFTY-FIFTH SQUADRON, R.A.F.

SON of Mr. and Mrs. Charles H. Payson; was born in Portland, Me., Aug. 9, 1892. He was educated at St. Paul's School Concord, N.H., and at Williams College. At St. Paul's School he played football and hockey, and was a member of the crew. At college he was captain of the football team in 1914. He served with the Ohio Cavalry at the Mexican Border for ten months.

He enlisted at Boston, Mass., in June, 1917. He received his training with the Royal Air Force at various English schools; attended the Ground School at Oxford University, and the Machine-Gun School at Grantham, Eng. He was trained in night flying with the 30th Squadron, at Newcastle, and had experience in day flying at Amesbury, Eng., and Turnberry, Scotland. Ordered to France, he served at the front with the 55th Squadron, R.A.F., from June to Oct., 1918, making fourteen long-distance raids on the Rhine towns. His day raids with the R.A.F. included Cologne, Coblenz, Frankfort, Mannheim, Stuttgart, Trier, and Offenburg. He was then transferred to the U.S. Air Service, attached to the 166th Aero Squadron, A.E.F., with which he served from Oct. to Nov., 1918, and made seven raids during the Argonne offensive. From Nov., 1918, to March, 1919, he was with the 166th Aero Squadron, Army of Occupation He was honorably discharged from the Air Service at Garden City, N.Y., on March 29, 1919.

He was commissioned 1st Lieut. on April 7, 1918. He was recommended for promotion, and a letter from his superior officer Major-Gen. M. M. Patrick, dated Nov. 26, 1918, expressed regret that instructions from the War Dept. had discontinued all promotions after Nov. 11, as the recommendation for Payson's promotion had been approved by the Air Service.

Lieut. Payson was also recommended for the D.S.C. The official text, signed by Victor Parks, Jr., Capt.; Inf. att'd. A.S., and dated Nov. 12, 1918, follows:

> Lieut. Payson is English trained, having been with an R.A.F. Independent Force for several months before coming to the American Forces.
>
> He is now Flight Commander in the 166th Aero Squadron, and is a very cool-headed and efficient officer. On one raid over the lines with this

Squadron, his plane was attacked in force by the enemy, and he fought them until far back of our own lines. Lieut. Payson skilfully manœuvred his ship and evaded the German planes, time and time again. Several times he turned upon his pursuers and fired into them with his forward guns. He outmanœuvred his opponents at every stage of the battle, and with his Observer fought off five enemy planes, who seemed determined to bring him down. He landed near Révigny and his ship was salvaged, having been literally shot to pieces. The landing wires were shot away, the planes riddled, and his gas tank shot through.

A letter from the Office of the Secretary of the Air Ministry, Strand, London, Eng., dated May 23, 1919, states:

Lieutenant P. M. Payson, United States Air Service, was attached to the Royal Flying Corps and Royal Air Force from 20th Oct., 1917, until 30th Sept., 1918.

He graduated as a Pilot in April, 1918, and had completed approximately 212 hours in the air.

He served with No. 55 Squadron, R.A.F., which formed part of the Independent Air Force, from 30th June, 1918, to 30th Sept., 1918, during which period he took part in 14 successful bombing raids, and at all times displayed great ability and keenness. He was a thoroughly efficient officer and a good pilot, and on the termination of his attachment to No. 55 Squadron, the Squadron Commander reported that he should make a very satisfactory Flight Commander.

Citation

The Army Air Service Commander, First Army, cites the following officers and men for exceptional devotion to duty:

24. First Lieutenant P. M. PAYSON, A.S.,U.S.A., as Pilot of the 166th Aero Squadron, performed efficient and hazardous work in the Argonne-Meuse sector, Oct.–Nov., 1918, during operations of the First Day Bombardment Group.

By order of Colonel MILLING

*JOHN F. STAFFORD, Jr.

Second Lieutenant, Two Hundred Tenth Squadron, R.A.F.

Killed in action, Sept. 29, 1918

Son of John and Maud C. (Birtwell) Stafford; was born at Fall River, Mass., May 5, 1898. He was educated at Westminster Preparatory School, Simsbury, Conn., where he was prominent in athletics, playing three years on the football team and three years on the baseball team.

In Oct., 1917, he enlisted in the Canadian Air Service, at New York, being then nineteen years old. He was immediately sent to Canada, and trained at Camp Leaside, Camp Mohawk, and Camp Borden successively. He also attended the University of Toronto; and then went to the School of Aerial Gunnery, at Camp Hicks, Fort Worth, Tex., where he was commissioned 2d Lieut. in April, 1918. He left about the middle of May, for England, and was at the Royal Air Force Training Establishment in Cranwell, Sleaford, Lincolnshire, and later at Camp Freiston, Boston, Eng., attached to the 210th Squadron, R.A.F. At the latter gunnery school he made the best record ever held for aerial gunnery — that is, target practice from the air upon real-sized target aeroplanes, and also upon the target suspended from the pit balloon. Lieut. Stafford trained in England from June until Sept., 1918, when he was ordered to France, and stationed near Dunkirk. On Sept. 29 he left Dunkirk in a Camel Sopwith fighting scout machine, and was last seen in aerial combat with a German airplane on that date. He was reported missing by the British Air Ministry, who have been unable to obtain further information, and the presumption is that he was killed. There was a report that he had passed through Berne, Switzerland, on Dec. 9; but his family have had no further reassurance, and have given up hope of his return.

*JOSEPH BROWN BOWEN

SECOND LIEUTENANT, A.S., U.S.A.
THIRTY-SECOND SQUADRON, R.A.F., B.E.F.

Killed in action, Sept. 7, 1918

SON of Edward Steere, and Elma Sophia (Brown) Bowen; was born at Providence, R.I., April 15, 1891. He was educated in the public schools of Pawtucket, R.I., graduated from Brown University in 1915, and in June, 1917, received from Yale the degree of Master of Forestry.

On July 21, 1917, he volunteered for the Air Service and trained at Princeton, and with the Royal Air Force at Fort Worth, Tex. He was commissioned 2d Lieut., Feb. 19, 1918, and went overseas with the 148th Aero Squadron, A.E.F. On reaching England he was detached for special instruction in scout fighting, a tribute to his skill, since only the most promising aviators were chosen to fly combat planes. This training completed, the Royal Flying Corps wished to retain him as a permanent staff officer, but permission was refused and he was assigned to active duty with the 32d Aero Squadron, Royal Air Force, being one of the few American officers attached to British squadrons. During late July, and through Aug., 1918, he was in the heavy fighting in the vicinity of Cambrai, Château-Thierry, Fismes, and Douai.

His letters related violent encounters with Richthofen's "circus," from one of which he returned with twenty-two bullet holes in his plane. Of another fight he wrote: "I think I got a Hun in the scrap, but was too busy to see what happened to him."

On Sept. 7, 1918, volunteers were asked for a special patrol and Lieut. Bowen offered to go, and, as his flight-book shows, it was not the first time that he had chosen to do more than duty required. That evening he was posted as missing. Later, it was ascertained that he had been killed in the air, while engaged on the Allied side of the lines, in single combat with a Fokker scout. He was buried near the village of Pronville, west of Bourlon Wood and Cambrai. Above his grave his Squadron placed a cross made from the broken propeller of his plane, inscribed to his memory.

Lieut. Bowen was of Puritan descent; from Dr. Richard Bowen who landed in Weymouth in 1639, through six generations of

doctors, including Col. Joseph Bowen of Revolutionary fame. His mother's ancestry returns to Roger Williams.

Lieut. Bowen was passionately fond of outdoor life and of the trees, which he meant to make his profession; his enthusiasm for the freedom of the outdoor world made him more prompt to respond to the call of Liberty and his attitude toward his work in aviation is set forth in his own words written to his family:

It is true that the aviator's job is dangerous, but death has never held any dread for me. In fact, I think I have a philosopher's point of view, and I can look upon it as an interesting experience that will come sooner or later. I am not married and therefore should go at once, but even if I had a wife and children, I should consider it my duty to go if the war lasts much longer, for it is a plain case of doing the fighting abroad while the loved ones at home are in safety. It does not matter *when* a man dies, but *how*."

Brother in Service —

Harold Clovis Bowen, A.S., U.S.A., 810th Aero Squadron.

LYMAN PERLEY WHITTEN

SECOND LIEUTENANT, A.S.A., U.S.A.

SON of Francis and Susan S. Whitten; was born at Malden, Mass., March 25, 1897. He was educated at the Malden High School, and at the Mass. Institute of Technology. He was a member of the sophomore relay team at M.I.T. in 1917. He enlisted at Boston, Mass., Nov. 3, 1917, and on Dec. 8 reported at the U.S. School of Military Aeronautics at Princeton, N. J. He was transferred to Camp Dick, Dallas, Tex., on Feb. 22, 1918, and to Taliaferro Field, Hicks, Tex., on March 13, 1918. On June 3 he was ordered back to Camp Dick, and on July 5 assigned to Ellington Field, Houston, Tex. He was commissioned 2d Lieut. on May 23, 1918, and honorably discharged at Ellington Field, Houston, Tex., Jan. 6, 1919.

Brother in Service —

Louis Osborne Whitten, Private, M.E.R.C., Base Hospital No. 44, Mesves, France.

HENRY JAMES GRAY RUDOLF

FIRST LIEUTENANT, R.A.F., FORTY-FIRST SQUADRON, WITH SECOND ARMY, B.E.F.

SON of James R. and Edna (Havelock) Rudolf, of Boston, Mass.; was born in Canada, July 20, 1891. He attended the Brookline High School, and graduated from M.I.T., S.B., 1915. He was president of the rifle club, M.I.T., and capt. of the rifle team. He spent a year experimenting in the laboratories of Thomas A. Edison, and later entered the ammunition plant of the Bartlett-Haywood Co., Baltimore, Md., as inventor and head of several departments of production.

He enlisted on Aug. 7, 1917, in the Royal Flying Corps, and was ordered to Toronto, Can., where he trained at Long Branch, Ontario; at the University of Toronto; and at Camp Mohawk. In Nov., 1917, he was sent to Camp Everman, Tex., and then to Camp Hicks, where he was commissioned 2d Lieut., R.F.C., on Jan. 29, 1918. He was sent overseas in Feb., 1918, and completed his final training at Hooten Park, Cheshire, Eng., where he graduated with distinction as scout pilot and was commissioned 1st Lieut., R.A.F., April 1, 1918. After additional courses in aerial gunnery at Turnberry, and at Gulane, Scotland, he was ordered to France on Aug. 14, attached to the 41st Squadron, with the 2d Army, B.E.F. From then until the end of the war this scout squadron did patrol work around Ypres and as far south as Arras. The fighting was all well over the lines, and seldom below 12,000 feet, which made it difficult to determine the exact results. This Squadron succeeded in keeping the Germans on their own side, but paid heavily for it, as in three months the personnel changed three times.

Lieut. Rudolf is credited with three Fokker biplanes out of control (confirmed). On one occasion he and two others were attacked by fifteen Fokkers that came down on them through the clouds. After losing his two companions, one of them being shot down in flames, Lieut. Rudolf fought his way back alone, and on landing found that there were fifty-seven bullet holes in his machine. On another occasion he was alone watching a flight of Bristol Fighters manœuvring toward a flight of Fokkers. Two of the British machines collided, and one crashed. The other gained control near the ground with one wing badly damaged, but was attacked by a German two-seater. To help him, Lieut. Rudolf was obliged to go down under the Fokker; he drove the German plane off and flew home ahead of the crippled Bristol, diving on the machine guns in his path. For this exploit he was mentioned by the second Brigade at the request of the 48th Squadron.

At another time he was congratulated by the British 2d Army for his part in a duel which they observed from the front line. In the midst of the fight, Lieut. Rudolf shot off one blade of his own propeller. At the same time the German went into a spin. Rudolf was forced to stop his engine but followed him down 6000 feet, getting in bursts as he came out of his spin, and left his enemy out of control, himself landing safely just across his own lines on a narrow road among the shell craters east of Ypres.

The principal work of Squadron 41 was to furnish offensive patrols and escorts for bombers, but on all patrols they dropped twenty-five pound bombs at railroads and bridges, besides doing some ground-strafing. On Aug. 27, at dawn, they dropped down on the Linselles aerodrome, some twelve miles over the lines, and flying low, bombed and shot up the hangars, leaving all in flames.

On Sept. 28, during the great offensive in front of Ypres, they swept the roads in front of the advance, which took place in a driving rain storm. All the squadrons of the 11th Wing took part. Ten went out from the 41st Squadron, but only five of them returned. King Albert of Belgium was in personal command, and sent his congratulations to the aviators.

On July 15, 1919, Lieut. Rudolf was placed on the unemployed list, R.A.F., retaining rank.

ROBERT SIDNEY BOWEN, Jr.

SECOND LIEUTENANT, R.A.F.

SON of Robert Sidney and Catharine Sinclair (Fenton) Bowen; was born at Allston, Mass., Oct. 4, 1900. He was educated in the public schools of Newton, Mass., and was prominent in track athletics at the Newton High School. He went overseas as an ambulance driver in the American Field Service, and was serving in France when the U.S. took over this organization, and returned him to this country as under military age.

He enlisted with the Royal Flying Corps (British) in New York City, in Oct., 1917. He received his training at Toronto University; at Camp Mohawk, Deseronto, Can.; at Camp Leaside, Beamsville, Can.; and at Camp Taliaferro, Fort Worth, Tex. He was ordered overseas in July, 1918, and trained at Herts, Eng., until called into active service as scout Pilot in France, where he joined the 84th Squadron a short time before the Armistice was signed. He was commissioned 2d Lieut. in the Royal Air Force in July, 1918. Since the Armistice, Lieut. Bowen has been on special service in England; in active service in France and Belgium; also attached to the 80th Squadron serving in France and Egypt.

On Nov. 12, the day after the signing of the Armistice, Lieut. Bowen sent home a vivid account of his unofficial downing of two enemy machines a few days previous to that date; his letter closed with the words:

> I reported my flight, but it was hard lines for me because I have no idea where the German planes went down and therefore they can't be credited as official. . . . My bus has 33 bullet holes in it and three in my flying suit. which shows I was in some close action.

Grandfather in Service —

Charles F. Bowen, served in 5th Mass. Regiment in Civil War.

*ALFRED THEODORE WYMAN

SECOND LIEUTENANT, R.A.F.

Killed in airplane accident, May 27, 1918

SON of Alfred A. and Flora M. Wyman; was born at Fitchburg, Mass., Dec. 28, 1892. He was educated at the Fitchburg High School, and at M.I.T., from which he graduated with the degree B.S. in June, 1916. He was a member of the class relay team at M.I.T., class treasurer in 1913; class president in 1914, and a member of the Delta Upsilon Fraternity, Osiris, the Institute Committee, and the Architectural Society. In June, 1916, he received the Medal of the American Institute of Architects for General Excellence in Architecture, and the Rotch Prize of two hundred dollars.

He enlisted in the Royal Flying Corps, at Toronto, Can., from Fitchburg, Mass., in Sept., 1917. He received provisional appointment as 2d Lieut., Cavalry, U.S.A., as a result of the examination which he passed earlier in Sept., but did not accept because he was already a member of the R.F.C. He was trained as a cadet at various flying schools in Canada, and at Fort Worth, Tex. He received sailing orders and proceeded overseas to England, where he received further training outside London. He was commissioned 2d Lieut. in the Royal Air Force, on April 1, 1918. On May 27, 1918, just after he had completed his training, Lieut. Wyman was killed as the result of an airplane crash at Chichester, Eng. He was buried at Chichester, Sussex County, Eng.

Brothers in Service —

Philip Wyman, Capt., A.S.A., U.S.A.
Franklin Wyman, 1st Lieut., A.S.A., U.S.A.
Kendall Wyman, 2d Lieut., Infantry, U.S.A.
Donald Wyman, 2d Lieut., Royal Air Force.

HAROLD A. KULLBERG

First Lieutenant, R.A.F., No. 1 Squadron

Son of Charles A. and Hilda (Streed) Kullberg; was born at Somerville, Mass., Sept. 10, 1896. He attended the public schools of Concord and Somerville, and the Wentworth Institute, Boston.

On Aug. 7, 1917, he enlisted in the Royal Flying Corps, at Toronto, Can., having been pronounced too short to pass the requirements of the U.S. Air Service. He attended the School of Military Aeronautics in Toronto; trained at Deseronto, and Camp Borden, Can.; and also at Camp Hicks, Fort Worth, Tex. He was commissioned 2d Lieut., Dec. 12, 1917. He sailed overseas to England, in Jan., 1918, and was assigned to a scout squadron in the Surrey district, and stationed at Stockbridge and Tangmore. He was commissioned 1st Lieut., April 12, 1918. In May he was sent to France, attached to Squadron 1, of the R.A.F., and was in action on several fronts. He was officially credited with fourteen Hun planes and two balloons, and was awarded the Distinguished Flying Cross by King George. The victory for which Lieut. Kullberg was decorated, was an encounter alone with ten enemy planes, during which he brought down two and routed the others.

His last experience was to be shot down in Germany, two months before the Armistice was signed. He spent six months in the Prince of Wales Hospital recovering from his wounds. On July 12, 1919, he was demobilized in England.

Distinguished Flying Cross

This officer has destroyed six enemy aeroplanes and has taken part in seven engagements when others have been destroyed by members of this patrol. A bold and keen officer who possesses fine fighting spirit.

R.A.F. Communiqué No. 22

Lieut. H. A. Kullberg, No. 1. Squadron, dived on a Fokker biplane which was attacking a D.H. 9, and, after a long burst of fire, saw its wings break off in the air. A little later he attacked another Fokker biplane, which was seen to go down and crash.

He was also awarded the Diploma of Aerial League of America.

Brother in Service —

Frank O. Kullberg, Sergeant, U.S. Signal Corps, A.E.F.

HARRY DEPEW COPLAND

First Lieutenant, R.A.F.

Son of Mr. and Mrs. Henry B. Copland; was born in Cambridge, Mass., April 17, 1896. He was educated in the schools of Detroit, Mich., and Cambridge, Mass., graduating from the Rindge Technical School in Cambridge, in 1915. He early became interested in aviation. In 1908 he made flights at Franklin Field, Boston, and in 1911 conducted experiments with a power-driven airplane of the Curtiss type at Detroit. During 1915 and 1916 he made several trips to England and France, and was wireless operator on board British munition ships.

In the spring of 1917 he endeavored to enlist in the U.S. Naval Aviation, but was rejected because he was under weight. In Aug., 1917, he joined the Royal Flying Corps in Boston, Mass., and proceeded to Toronto, Can., where he was trained as pilot. In Nov., 1917, he was transferred to Taliaferro Field, Fort Worth, Tex., where he completed a course in aerial gunnery. On Dec. 18, 1917, he was commissioned 2d Lieut., R.F.C., and given an appointment as Flying Instructor at the School of Aerial Gunnery in Texas. From that date until April he trained British and American cadets in aerial gunnery. On April 1, 1918, he was commissioned 1st Lieut., R.A.F., and assigned to the Aerial Fighting School at Beamsville, Ontario, Can., as Instructor. In July, 1918, he was appointed Flight Commander of B Flight No. 1, Aerial Fighting Squadron, which he instructed until Oct. 1. From the time of his appointment as instructor up to Oct. 1, he made over 1500 flights and carried over 800 cadets without accident.

In Oct., 1918, Lieut. Copland was sent overseas, and attached to the Felixtowe Air Station. Here he did patrol duty in the North Sea and on the coasts of Germany, Belgium, and France, for submarines. After the Armistice was signed, he patrolled the North Sea in large flying boats in search of floating mines which menaced shipping. These patrols lasted from four to six hours. On Nov. 21, 1918, he escorted the surrendered German submarines into Harwich Harbor. In May, 1919, he was ordered to No. 4 Communication Squadron from No. 231 Squadron. The new Squadron carried passengers and mail between England and Holland across the North Sea. Lieut. Copland sailed for the U.S. on June 29, 1919.

JOHN KENT BLAIR

FIRST LIEUTENANT, R.A.F., FIFTY-SIXTH SQUADRON

SON of George H. and Marion L. Blair; was born in Boston, Mass., May 8, 1894. He attended the Mechanic Arts High School, Boston, from which he graduated in 1912.

On July 15, 1917, he enlisted in the Royal Flying Corps at Toronto, Ont., having four cousins with the Canadian Expeditionary Forces. On July 6 he was assigned to the Cadet Wing, R.F.C., and sent to the Toronto University School of Military Aeronautics for training. He attended successively the flying school at Armour Heights (Y Squadron, C.T.S.), from Aug. 20, 1917; Leaside, from Oct. 23 (90th Squadron, C.T.S.), for bombing, photography, artillery, and observation; Camp Hicks, Tex., from Nov. 25, 1917, for aerial gunnery; and Camp Everman, Tex., from Dec. 13, where he was instructor to the 80th Squadron. He was commissioned 2d Lieut. in Dec., 1917, and 1st Lieut. in April, 1918.

On April 9 he sailed overseas, and was stationed with the 3d Squadron at Shoreham-by-the-Sea, Eng., on April 29, 1918. He was later transferred to Turnberry, Scotland, for aerial fighting. He was ordered to France in June, and served there with the 56th Squadron, encamped a few miles south of Doullens, until just before the Armistice. During this time Lieut. Blair was flying a single scout machine, S.A. 5, and was engaged in patrol work. He was in numerous air fights, "ground-strafing" expeditions and balloon hunts. He was shot down three times while ground-strafing, but managed to get back to the British lines, being twice forced to land among the trenches and shell-holes. He was with the British advance on the Cambrai front from the beginning of his active service.

He was still with the Royal Air Force at Todcaster, Yorkshire, Eng., on June 12, 1919.

DAVID CLENDON HALE

OBSERVER, R.A.F., TWO HUNDRED FOURTEENTH SQUADRON

SON of Davis Campbell and Elizabeth (Sheen) Hale, of Cambridge, Mass.; was born in Longmont, Col., Aug. 18, 1894. He graduated from Phillips Andover Academy in 1913, and from Amherst College, S.B., 1917. He belonged to the track team at school and college.

He enlisted in the U.S.N. Air Service at Boston, Mass., on June 5, 1917, and was assigned to the Ground School of Naval Aviation at M.I.T. He transferred to the Royal Flying Corps at Taliaferro Field, No. 1, Fort Worth, Tex., and was sent overseas to England, on March 1, 1918.

He completed his training in night bombing at the R.A.F. Officers' Night Flying School at Stonehenge, Salisbury Plain, where he passed a thirty-two days' course on May 7, 1918. He was later ordered to London, and attached to the 214th Squadron, R.A.F., one of the R.A.F. Independent Air Squadrons, which was shortly ordered to St.-Inglevert, France. He qualified as Sub-Lieut., R.A.F., and Observer on June 26, 1918.

He saw service at the French front from July 9, 1918, flying Handley-Page bombing machines, and taking part in raids on Ostend, Bruges, Zeebrugge, and the various German aerodromes in Belgium, during the summer. On Aug. 15, 1918, while attached to an American Squadron, he was observer in the first (official) American night bombing plane to cross the lines on the western front, en route to a raid on the Ostend docks. While he was carrying out a similar raid on Zeebrugge on Aug. 22, Observer Hale's machine crashed and he was slightly wounded. During the autumn of 1918 the 214th Squadron made a number of closely concentrated raids in connection with army operations in the lines, bombing railroad junctions and ammunition dumps during the retreat from Belgium. At the time of the Armistice, Hale was stationed at Maria Aeltre, Belgium. From there he wrote that the most interesting experience of all was entering the city of Ghent on the day of its release from the Germans, and receiving the welcome of the people of all ages and conditions.

He was honorably discharged on Jan. 28, 1919, at Hampton Roads, Va.

GEORGE CLARKE WHITING

First Lieutenant, A.S., U.S.A., Forty-Third Pursuit Squadron, R.A.F.; One Hundred Forty-Eighth Pursuit Squadron, U.S.; Flight Commander

Son of Walter Rogers and Gertrude (Clarke) Whiting; was born in Boston, Mass., Jan. 28, 1894. He was educated at the Stone School, Boston, and Harvard University, class of 1917. He rowed on the crew at school and at college, and was a member of the Union Boat Club crew. In 1916 he was instrumental in forming the "Harvard Flying Corps," with the result that twenty undergraduates and two members of the graduate committee received training at flying schools and became licensed aviators.

On April 17, 1917, he enlisted in the Aviation Section, Signal Corps, at New York, and trained at Miami, Fla., and Ground School, Austin, Tex. On Aug. 17, 1917, he sailed overseas with one of the first detachments of forty-eight aviators, picked from American flying schools for training in the foreign fighting schools. He arrived in England Sept. 1, and was attached to the Royal Flying School at Oxford; then at Croyden, 43 T.S., for scout training. In Dec. he trained at Turnberry, Scotland, after which he had a course at the Aerial Fighting School, Ayr, Scotland.

On March 2, 1918, he was commissioned 1st Lieut., and on March 12 crossed to France, attached to the 43d Squadron, R.A.F., as flying officer, one of the first three to cross from English schools. He remained with the 43d until July 1, 1918, operating from the aerodromes of La Gorge, Avesnes, Le Compt, Fouquerelle, Liètre.

On July 1 Lieut. Whiting was transferred to the 148th American Air Squadron at Dunkirk, acting as Flight Commander, and operating successively from Dunkirk, Allonville, Ramasmill, and Albert. This was a Pursuit Squadron which acted in coöperation with the R.A.F. and was under British command. Lieut. Whiting was in active service with this Squadron until Oct. 4, 1918, when he was shot down, and was admitted to General Hospital No. 14, at Boulogne. From the General Hospital he went to Issoudun for the Medical Board, and inspected the school while there. He then received orders to return to the U.S. On Feb. 4, 1918, he was honorably discharged at Washington, D.C.

Married, Oct. 4, 1917, Martha Clay.

*EDMUND GRAHAM TART

First Lieutenant, R.A.F., Eighty-Fifth Bombing Squadron
Group Nine

Killed in airplane accident, May 31, 1918

Son of Edmund and Margaret (McNab) Tart, of Everett, Mass.; was born in Montreal, P.Q., Nov. 28, 1892. He was educated in the public schools of Chelsea, and graduated from the Wentworth Institute, Boston, with a fine record in mathematics. In athletics he took two running prizes, for 200 and for 400 yards. He had acted as assistant commissioner of the Everett and Chelsea Boy Scouts. He was in business as an electrical engineer at the time of his enlistment.

He enlisted at Boston, Mass., in the spring of 1917, during Col. Guthrie's recruiting mission, and left Boston on June 12, 1917, for Frederickton, N.B.; he then trained at Camps Gordon and Rathbun, at Toronto University, Camp Borden, and Leaside, Can. He was commissioned 2d Lieut., R.A.F., in Nov., 1917, and sailed overseas. In April, 1918, he was commissioned 1st Lieut., and attached to the 85th Squadron, Group 9. It was said by his Major that he was a very keen pilot, and that "he could go to crashes blindfolded." He had made a special study of map-reading.

Lieut. Tart was accidentally killed during a flight with his bombing squad, in England, on May 31, 1918, and was buried in Bebington Cemetery, England.

Brother in Service —
Harry Tart, Royal Air Force.

EDWARD MILTON WILCOX

FIRST LIEUTENANT, A.S.A., U.S.A., NINETY-NINTH SQUADRON BRITISH R.A.F.

SON of George C. and Gertrude (Smith) Wilcox; was born at Winsted, Conn., July 14, 1896. He was educated at the Winsted public schools, Gilbert High School, and Sheffield Scientific School, Yale University. He was made a member of Sigma Chi, at Yale. He trained with the Yale S.A.T.C., April–June, 1917.

On June 1, 1917, he enlisted at New Haven. In eight weeks he completed a course in Military Aeronautics at M.I.T., and was ordered overseas, sailing Aug. 18, 1917. He was a member of the 1st American Detachment attached to the Royal Flying Corps for training in England as pilot. He trained at Oxford, Stamford (flying a Curtiss machine); Lincoln (advanced flying), where he nearly lost his life when his engine failed at the height of 3000 feet, and he fell on a concealed embankment, destroying his de Haviland machine; he was slightly wounded, and was in a hospital for five weeks. During July, 1918, he was trained in aerial gunnery at Marske, Yorkshire, and was ready for the front. But he had further training in wireless telephony at Salisbury Plain, England. On May 13, 1918, he was commissioned 1st Lieut. Having trained from Sept. 4, 1917, to Aug. 5, 1918, Lieut. Wilcox served one month as ferry pilot in England, then as ferry pilot in France for the Independent Force, Royal Air Force, employed in bombing. He was sent to Courban, an aircraft dépôt, eleven miles behind the lines, which supplied machines for bombing squadrons, and it was then his duty to take machines to the front to replace casualties. The machines used for bombing trips were de Haviland 4's with the Rolls-Royce engine, de Haviland 9's and de Haviland 9 A's, equipped with the Liberty motor.

On reaching France, Lieut. Wilcox applied to go to the front, but was sent there only a week before the war ended, with the 99th Squadron, R.A.F. He had, however, 150 hours in the air to his credit before sailing for America, on Jan. 28, 1919. He was honorably discharged at Garden City, N.Y., on Feb. 14, 1919.

ARTHUR KELLAM TYLEE

Lieutenant-Colonel, R.A.F., Headquarters, Canada

Son of Arthur Mailland and Harriet F. (Kellam) Tylee, of Quincy, Mass.; was born in Lennoxville, P.Q., Can., April 24, 1887. He attended the Brookline public schools, and graduated from M.I.T., B.S., 1907.

On Aug. 4, 1915, he enlisted in the R.F.C., at Toronto, Can., and was commissioned 2d Lieut. in the Canadian Expeditionary Forces, on Nov. 18, 1915, and was stationed at Toronto until Dec., 1915. On Dec. 7, 1915, he was commissioned 1st Lieut., Royal Flying Corps, and ordered overseas. He was stationed at Thetford, Eng., until April, 1916; first attached to the 12th then to the 35th Squadron, R.F.C. Ordered to France, he was attached to the 23d Squadron until Aug., 1916. From then until Jan., 1917, he was attached to the 65th Squadron in England. On Jan. 1, 1917, he was commissioned Captain, and transferred to the 48th Squadron in England, remaining until Feb., 1917. During the next six months he was with the 81st Squadron in England and Canada, being commissioned Major on March 21, 1917. He was attached to the 42d Wing, in Canada, until Nov., 1917, and was in Texas from Nov. to Jan., 1918. From Jan. to April, 1918, he was with the Training Division in England.

On April 1, 1918, he was commissioned Lieut.-Col., and attached to Headquarters, R.A.F., Canada, as Inspector of Training, until the close of the war.

On Jan. 1, 1919, Lieut.-Col. Tylee was made Officer of the British Empire (O.B.E.). In March, 1919, he was still in the British Service.

THOMAS A. KIRWAN

CAPTAIN, A.S., U.S.A.

SON of Michael J. and Marcella L. (Aiken) Kirwan; was born at Oswego, N.Y., March 12, 1892. He attended the high school at Oswego, N.Y.; Columbia University, class of 1914 (two years); and the University of Pennsylvania (two years, special course).

In March, 1915, he enlisted in Battery A, 1st Mass. F.A., and served on the Mexican Border in 1916 as private. He was elected 2d Lieut., June 14, 1917, and sailed with Battery A, 101st F.A., for France, Sept. 9, 1917. He was commissioned 1st Lieut., Nov. 16, 1917, and on Nov. 28 transferred to the Air Service as Observer; trained for six weeks at Camp Valdahon, France, and returned to his regiment, with which he went to the front in the Chemin des Dames sector. He was then attached to French Escadrille 55, which was located at Mont de Soissons, and assigned to the 26th Division, for aerial observation and for photography. When the 26th Division left the Chemin des Dames sector he was sent to French Escadrille 51, in the Reims sector. After two months' training he was ordered to report to the 88th Squadron and, on its arrival at the Toul sector, was appointed Chief Observer of the squadron.

In July, 1918, the squadron took part in the Château-Thierry offensive, and on July 15 Capt. Kirwan was made Operations Officer of the Fourth Observation Group. This group performed the aerial observations for the divisions which came into the Toul sector. Shortly before the St.-Mihiel drive Capt. Kirwan was promoted to Operations Officer of the Air Service, Fourth Army Corps, and took an active part in assigning the squadrons and balloons to the divisions in the corps. Following this offensive the Fourth Army Corps remained in this sector as part of the Second American Army, and after the Armistice went into Germany as part of the Army of Occupation.

Capt. Kirwan spent three months in Trier and Coblenz, and served for a month as Commandant of the University of Rennes. At his request he was relieved, and sailed for the U.S., March 28, 1919. He was honorably discharged, April 19, 1919.

Capt. Kirwan was awarded a citation signed by Gen. Pershing, for "exceptionally meritorious and conspicuous services as Aerial Observer, Fourth Army Corps."

VAN ZANDT STONE

LIEUTENANT, R.F.C., EIGHTY-THIRD AERO SQUADRON
TWENTY-THIRD SECTION

SON of Charles Emerson and Ada Menzies (Dailey) Stone; was born in Andover, Mass., Sept. 14, 1893. He was educated at Phillips Andover Academy, graduating in 1912.

On Aug. 11, 1917, he enlisted in the Royal Flying Corps, and was sent for training successively to Long Branch, Ontario, Toronto University, and Camp Mohawk, Deseronto, Can. On Nov. 15, 1917, he was commissioned 2d Lieut., and attached as instructor in turn to Camps Benbrook and Hicks, Fort Worth, Tex. He was commissioned 1st Lieut. in Feb., 1918, and made Flight Commander at Camp Leaside, Toronto. He was sent overseas and stationed at the Central Flying School, Upavon, Wilts, Eng., where, owing to his efficiency as Instructor, the War Office retained him until the end of the war.

Lieut. Stone was honorably discharged from the Royal Flying Corps and has returned to the U.S.

The following "Tribute to the Phillips Andover Boys in the War," by Charles Emerson Stone, father of Lieut. Stone, seems worthy of inclusion here:

> I was thinking only the other day of the more than two thousand boys of our alumni and students who have been in this great war, and what a poignant regret it would always be that we had failed to see, in the years before it was certainly upon us, that the spirit of daring and the thirst for action was put in them in actual preparation for this awful event. How blind we are after all our research and years of study and thought, that we should not have seen it, and have had a little more charity and greater love for the rare souls that were given into our keeping! But ten years ago who could have foretold it all? Still the regret is there all the same. And we mourn the loss of eighty-three of earth's noblemen. R.I.P.

WALTER P. MUTHER

First Lieutenant, A.S., U.S.A., One Hundred Forty-Seventh Aero Squadron

Son of Lorenz and Louisa (Ebert) Muther, of Newton, Mass.; was born at Oak Park, Ill., March 1, 1890. He attended the Mass. Institute of Technology, graduating in 1913. On June 2, 1917, he enlisted at Cambridge, Mass., and trained at the M.I.T. Ground School and at the Flying School at Essington, Pa. He was commissioned 1st Lieut., Air Service, Nov. 8, 1917. He sailed overseas from New York, Nov. 2, 1917, and continued his training at the 3d A.I.C., Issoudun, France, Dec. 4, 1917, to April 15, 1918, and at the American Aviation Acceptance Park, Orly, Seine, April 15 to July 24, 1918. Lieut. Muther was then attached to the 147th Aero Squadron, 1st Pursuit Group, with which he remained until Dec. 4, 1918. With this Squadron, which did notable work at the front, he was in action at Château-Thierry, St.-Mihiel, and in the Argonne Forest. Lieut. Muther was honorably discharged, Feb. 17, 1919. (Portrait on opposite page.)

GEORGE W. TUTTLE

Second Lieutenant, A.S., U.S.A.

Son of Dr. Walter and Anna A. (Woodbury) Tuttle; was born at Exeter, N.H., April 10, 1894. He was educated at Phillips Exeter Academy and at the Mass. Institute of Technology. He won scholarships at Exeter, and at M.I.T. for the entire course. He enlisted in U.S. Army School of Military Aeronautics, and trained at U.S.A.S., Mineola, N.Y. He was commissioned 2d Lieut., July 18, 1918, and assigned to the 48th Aero Squadron, 1st Prov. Wing, at Mineola, N.Y.; then to the 3d Prov. Squadron, Armorers' School, Wilbur Wright Field, Fairfield, Ohio. He was transferred to the U.S. Army Aviation School, Payne Field, West Point, Miss., where he was stationed until the end of the war. He was honorably discharged on Dec. 5, 1918, at Hoboken, N.J.

Married, April 29, 1918, Edith Pelletier.

Father in Service —

Dr. Walter Tuttle, examining physician, Rockingham County, N.H.

*EDMUND PIKE GRAVES

First Lieutenant, Royal Air Force

Killed in airplane accident, Nov. 22, 1919

Son of Edmund Pike and Mary Warner (Caldwell) Graves; was born in Newburyport, Mass., March 13, 1891. He was educated at St. George's College, Buenos Ayres; Middlesex School; and Harvard College, A.B. 1913. He enlisted in the Royal Air Force at Toronto, Can., July 9, 1917. In Oct. he was commissioned 2d Lieut., "winning his wings." He instructed in the School of Aerial Gunnery at Fort Worth, Tex., until March, 1918, when he was appointed Instructor of Acrobatics in the new School of Special Flying at Armour Heights, Toronto; where he was commissioned 1st Lieut. He went overseas in Oct., 1918, and was stationed at London Colney, until honorably discharged in July, 1919. His failure to get to the front was such a disappointment to him that he enlisted in the Kosciuszko Squadron of the Polish Army, to fight the Bolsheviki, in Sept., 1919, and was engaged in operations against them just previous to his death. He was killed while taking part in a Polish celebration at Lemberg, on Nov. 22, 1919. After the squadron had flown over the town, he flew down the main street, performing the "double roll." During the manœuvre the right wing broke. He coolly cleared himself and jumped, but was too near the ground for his parachute to be effective.

While in England he had agreed to pilot a machine in a trans-Atlantic attempt when Alcock's success intervened. Of the Bolsheviki he wrote:

> We entertained a Bolshevik Squadron Commander who deserted to the Poles with all his squadron, officers and men. They had been forced into the Red Army by threats that otherwise their families would be shot. When the territory occupied by these families had been taken, he and his squadron deserted. The Bolsheviki have few planes and pilots, all flying under compulsion, and they never venture within forty kilometres of the lines. Also, each officer has attached to him a true blue or "red" Bolshevik who, if suspicious, has him shot, or shoots him himself. It all seems incredible.

HENRY JOSEPH LEAVITT

SECOND LIEUTENANT, R.A.F., B.E.F., SIXTY-FIFTH SQUADRON
TWENTY-SECOND WING

SON of Henry and Cora (Holmes) Leavitt, of Auburn, Me.; was born at Sanford, Me., Oct. 4, 1892. He was educated at the Sanford High School, the Tennessee Military Institute, and the Northeastern College, Boston, graduating in the class of 1915.

He enlisted in the Royal Flying Corps, in July, 1917. He received his training at Toronto University; Camp Deseronto; Camp Mohawk; and Camp Leaside, Ontario; and subsequently at Camp Taliaferro, Fort Worth, Tex. In Jan., 1918, he sailed overseas and completed his training at Montrose, Scotland. He was commissioned 2d Lieut., Dec. 19, 1917, in the British Land Force. In April, 1918, he was assigned to the 65th Squadron, R.A.F., and went to the front. Lieut. Leavitt was a skilful and daring flyer, but owing to a mishap to his machine while flying over German territory, on May 17, 1918, he was forced to land between the German trenches, and was captured by the enemy. From then until Dec. 13, 1918, he was confined in German prison camps, at Karlsruhe, Rastadt, and Stralsund. From the last camp he wrote:

> Only a fellow who is unfortunate enough to be a prisoner can know how cruel the Hun really is. Our camp is on an island some twenty yards from the shore, a barbed wire fence runs around it. On the inside of the fence are armed sentries; outside the wire is a dog patrol. These dogs are trained to jump on any man wearing khaki. We used to watch them sometimes when the keeper taught them to attack a well padded man in khaki. One day he was leading three dogs through the camp on a rope; an officer was walking along minding his own business when the Hun let them go. If a crowd of British officers had not hurried to the scene with clubs the dogs would have killed him. As it was the poor fellow will wear the teeth marks of the dogs in his face for life.

On his release Lieut. Leavitt was given a two months' furlough and was then assigned to another squadron on Feb. 26, 1919. He returned to the U.S. in July, 1919.

Brother in Service —
Harold E. Leavitt, U.S.N.

Previous war records of family show one uncle and three granduncles in Civil War; great-grandfather, David Chase, in War of 1812; great-great-grandfather in Revolutionary War.

WALTER AMORY

First Lieutenant, R.A.F., Fourth Squadron

Son of Copley and Mary (Russell) Amory; was born at Walpole, N.H., in June, 1899. He attended the Groton School, Groton, Mass., and in Aug., 1917, soon after passing his 18th birthday, enlisted in the Royal Air Force, Canada, being too young to enter the U.S. Air Service. He passed his examinations successfully and was sent to Fort Worth, Tex., where he was kept as Instructor until March, 1918. He was commissioned 2d Lieut. in Jan., 1918, and in April was commissioned 1st Lieut. and given his wings.

He sailed overseas in April, 1918, and continued his training in England, being in a serious crash in June, which disabled him for over two months. Upon his recovery in Sept., 1918, he was sent to France attached to the 4th Squadron, R.A.F., and entered active service at the front. On Oct. 30 he flew over the enemy's lines, after a skirmish in which one of his friends was shot; in a vain endeavor to aid his friend, Lieut. Amory was himself wounded in the leg, and his machine brought down in Belgium, where he was captured.

He was reported "missing" on Nov. 7, but two weeks later his family received word, through the British Red Cross, that he was alive and in a hospital. His recovery was retarded as his wounded leg was neglected and dressed in paper bandages while he was with the Germans, at Aix. After the Armistice he was taken to a British hospital, and late in Dec. carried to England, where he is waiting to recuperate before returning overseas.

Brothers in Service —

Copley Amory, Jr., Lieut., U.S.A.
John Forbes Amory, Private, U.S.A.,
(Both in active fighting, severely wounded, Sept. 28, 1918.)

FRANCIS PEABODY MAGOUN, Jr.

First Lieutenant, R.A.F., No. 1 Squadron

Son of Francis Peabody and Jeanne (Bartholow) Magoun, of Cambridge, Mass.; was born in New York City, Jan. 6, 1895. He attended the Noble and Greenough School, Boston, and graduated from Harvard College in 1916. In Feb., 1916, he joined the American Ambulance Field Service, and sailed overseas; he served as volunteer driver with S.S.U. No. 1, from March 3 to Aug. 3, 1916, during which time this section was cited in French divisional Orders, July 15, 1916.

He returned to the U.S., and in Feb., 1917, again went overseas, enlisting in London, in March, with the Royal Flying Corps. He attended the School of Military Aeronautics at Oxford, Eng., and trained in elementary flying at the R.N.A.S. School, Vendôme, France. He trained at Catterick, Yorks, in advanced flying, and at the School of Aerial Gunnery at Turnberry, Scotland. On July 4, 1917, he was commissioned 2d Lieut. R.A.F.; and on Aug. 1, 1918, 1st Lieut., R.A.F.; "wings" gazetted Sept. 3, 1917.

Lieut. Magoun was attached to No. 1 Squadron, R.A.F., B.E.F., and served in France from Nov. 15, 1917, to April 10, 1918, when he was wounded while ground-strafing. On April 9 he was awarded the British Military Cross. In the summer of 1918 he returned to the U.S. on a furlough, but on Oct. 9 rejoined his Squadron and was again at the front, remaining in active service until the first of Jan., 1919. He was demobilized at Folkestone, Eng., Jan. 10, 1919, and enrolled for graduate work at Trinity College, Cambridge, Eng. In the summer of 1919 Lieut. Magoun returned to the U.S.

PATRICK GRANT, Second

Flight Cadet, R.A.F.

Son of Judge Robert and Amy Gordon (Galt) Grant; was born at Boston, Mass., April 30, 1886. He was educated at the Roxbury Latin School, Roxbury, Mass., and at the Noble and Greenough School, Boston; he graduated from Harvard College, A.B., 1908. He was a member of the Harvard 'Varsity football team.

He attended the First Officers' Training Camp at Plattsburg in Aug., 1915.

On Nov. 1, 1917, he enlisted at Philadelphia, Pa., as Ensign, U.S.N.R.F. He resigned on April 21, 1918, to enter the Royal Air Force, Canada, April 25, 1918. He trained at Ontario, Can., and at Camp Borden, Squadron 88, Flight C.

He was honorably discharged at Camp Borden, Ontario, Can., after Nov. 11, 1918. (Portrait on opposite page.)

Married, Sept. 7, 1912, Marie S. Diston.

Brothers in Service —

Alexander Galt Grant, 2d Lieut., U.S.A. Field Artillery.
Gordon Grant, Capt., U.S.A., A.E.F., Field Artillery.

ALAN HENRY BOYNTON

First Lieutenant, Marine Aviation Force

Born at Lynn, Mass., Oct. 23, 1892. He was educated in the public schools of Lynn, and at the Stone School, Boston. He enlisted in the U.S. Marine Corps, and was commissioned 2d Lieut., Sept. 17, 1917. He trained at the Curtiss School, at Newport News, Va., and was then stationed at the Philadelphia Navy Yard, with Aeronautic Co., Advanced Base Force, U.S. Marine Corps. He was transferred to the 1st Marine Aeronautic Co., Cape May, N.J., and then sent to the Cape May Naval Coastal Air Station. He was next ordered to Naval Base 13, at the Azores, and subsequently returned to the Marine Aviation detachment at Miami, Fla. He was commissioned 1st Lieut., Marine Corps, June 10, 1918. Discharged at his own request, at Miami, Fla., Nov. 25, 1918.

Brother in Service —

Charles Raymond Boynton, Sergeant, Supply Co. 311, Q.M.C., Bordeaux, France.

WILLIAM GASTON

Lieutenant (*j.g.*), N.A.F., Royal Aviation Bombing Corps

Son of William A. and May L. (Lockwood) Gaston; was born in Boston, Nov. 12, 1896. He was educated at La Villa, Ouchy, Switzerland; at St. Mark's School, Southboro, Mass.; and graduated, Harvard College, class of 1919.

He enlisted in the U.S. Navy in April, 1917. In May he was transferred to the Naval Aviation Squad at Squantum, Mass., where he was commissioned Ensign on Jan. 2, 1918, and received a pilot's license. He was ordered to the Aviation Detachment, Naval Operating Base, Hampton Roads, Va., on Oct. 18, 1917, and served there as an instructor. On Feb. 6, 1918, he was assigned to the Royal Flying Corps, at Fort Worth, Tex., for a course in Aerial Gunnery. He sailed for Europe on March 22, 1918.

On his arrival in England he patrolled the North Sea and English Channel, and later was attached to the R.N.A.S. at Hornsea, Yorkshire, in April, 1918. He was sent in May to No. 1 School of Navigation and Bomb Dropping at Stonehenge Mills, Salisbury, and remained there as instructor for one month. He was then assigned to the U.S. Northern Bombing Squadron with headquarters at St.-Nylevert, France, in July, 1918; in Aug. he was attached to the U.S. Air Service at Milan, Italy. Subsequently, from Sept. to Dec., 1918, he was with No. 214 Squadron, R.A.F., in France, and was in command of a Handley-Page bombing plane. He was promoted to the rank of Lieut. (j.g.), Dec. 12, 1918. Ordered home to the U.S. in Dec., 1918, and relieved from active duty in Feb., 1919. He returned to Harvard, and graduated with the class of 1919.

Brother in Service —

John Gaston, Lieut., U.S. Marines, 18th Co., 5th Division, Army of Occupation, Germany.

*LLOYD ANDREWS HAMILTON

First Lieutenant, A.S.A., U.S.A., Seventeenth Aero Squadron

Killed in action, Aug. 24, 1918

Son of Dr. John A. and Jennie B. (Andrews) Hamilton, of Burlington, Vt.; was born at Troy, N.Y., June 13, 1894. He graduated from the Pittsfield High School with honors in 1911; there he was president of his class and captain of the school track team. In 1912 he graduated from the Jacob Tome Institute in Maryland. He was valedictorian of the class, was awarded the school's scholarship prize, elected to Alpha Delta Tau for "meritorious attainments," associate editor of *The Trail* publication, member of the debating team, and of the track team and football squad.

He graduated from Syracuse University, A.B., 1916. He was a member of the freshman football and track teams, the 'Varsity football and track squads, and member of the Psi Upsilon Fraternity. He was awarded Phi Beta Kappa honor, and Liberal Arts honor, in the Department of Economics, and graduated *Magna cum Laude.*

In the fall of 1916 Lieut. Hamilton entered the School of Business Administration in Harvard University. Following the declaration of war he enlisted, April 23, 1917, and on May 12 was sent to the R.O.T.C. at Plattsburg. On July 12 he signed for Aviation and was transferred to the M.I.T. for ground-school work. He left Mineola, Sept. 18, with 150 others, for England. Further ground-school work was taken at Oxford University, and Grantham Gun School. His first flying was at Tadcaster, and was continued at South Carlton aerodrome, and at Turnberry and Ayr, Scotland.

He was commissioned 1st Lieut. March 2, 1918, and at once sent to the front in France, attached to the famous British Third Aero Squadron. He had the distinction of being the first American officer to fight with the Royal Flying Corps, and was the first of the 150 of his Squad to bring down an enemy machine. While with the R.F.C. he was under the well-known Capt. Bell, of Australia, who was credited with twenty-three machines, and who, because of his dash and skill, was called "Ginger Bell." Lieut. Hamilton was with Capt. Bell in the air when the latter was shot down by

a German explosive shell, and at once avenged his Captain's death by shooting down the enemy observer and pilot in their machine. The day before the well-known Von Richthofen was killed Lieut. Hamilton was in the flight that fought the famous "flying circus" and engaged Von Richthofen himself for a few minutes, but later engaged another and sent him down.

On June 20 he was transferred to the U.S. Air Service and made Flight Commander in the 17th Aero Squadron. This he helped to form and train. He was one of three recommended for commanding officer of the Squadron, but an older man of more military experience was chosen. His operations throughout his work at the front were from Amiens north to the coast. On Aug. 24 he was returning from an attack ten miles over the lines when he saw an enemy kite balloon and dove on it, causing the observer to jump, and then shot the balloon down in flames. But before getting away he was hit by enemy machine guns from the ground and fell about three miles over the lines and near Langecourt. Ten months later his grave was found and the body removed and buried at Bomy, France.

Lieut. Hamilton was awarded the British Distinguished Flying Cross before he was killed. This is the highest decoration awarded an Aviator by that nation. This citation reads:

> Lieut. L. A. Hamilton is an excellent Patrol Leader, and his dash and skill materially helped in the success of the operations.

In company with four others he received the award for bringing down seventy-five machines in one month.

He was also awarded the U.S. Distinguished Service Cross through citation by General Pershing. The citation is as follows:

> Lieut. Lloyd Andrews Hamilton is cited for extraordinary heroism in action at Varssenaer, Belgium, on Aug. 13, 1918. Leading a low bombing attack on a German aerodrome thirty miles behind the lines he descended and destroyed the hangars on the north side of the aerodrome and then attacked a row of enemy machines, flying as low as twenty feet from the ground despite intense machine-gun fire, burning five German planes. He then turned and fired bursts through the windows of the château in which the German pilots were quartered, twenty-six of whom were afterward reported killed.

This destruction was made without the loss of a man or a machine making the attack.

LLOYD ANDREWS HAMILTON

Lieut. Hamilton was rated as a Military Aviator Aug. 3, 1918, by order of the Secretary of War at Auxi-le-Château. He is credited with at least seven German planes, some reports making the number twelve. Six other machines were brought down for which official credit was not given. He brought down six observation balloons, one upon the day of his death and one the day before. While training in England he is said to have perfected a stunt not before used at the front and that most of his victories in the air resulted from its use. Among his effects was found a snap-shot of his Sopwith Camel machine, giving a tail view, and on the back of the picture he had written, "This is a view no Hun ever had of my bus." Often he wrote that he had no fear of any machine the enemy might send up, but that in low flying upon transportation and balloons it was mere chance if one escaped machine-gun nests. It was in this work that he finally lost his life.

An officer wrote:

> Ham and his fighting partner, Tipton, were known as the first and finest American pilots on the front when they were with the British, and had the reputation of never "letting any one down," as the expression is, in a tight corner.

The only officer who, from another machine, saw him shot down, wrote:

> Ham was one of the most popular fellows out here. He was most fearless in the face of danger and as stout a pilot as ever flew in France; he was a very capable Flight Commander and we all felt safe when behind him.

His Major, Commander of the Squadron, wrote:

> "Ham," as he was endearingly known to us all, has been a great help in training our new men and in developing our organization. His lovable personality, steadfast purpose and remarkable ability as a flyer have set an example that we all are striving to emulate.

His great-great-grandfather, Ebenezer Andrews, was in the Vermont Militia, served in the Revolutionary War under Ethan Allen, and with some sixty men captured Ticonderoga. He also fought at Bennington.

*EDWARD HOOPER GARDINER

SECOND LIEUTENANT, A.S., U.S.A., ARTILLERY OBSERVER
ATTACHED TO FIFTIETH SQUADRON

Killed in action, Sept. 12, 1918

SON of Edward G. and Jane G. (Hooper) Gardiner; was born in Boston, May 14, 1896. He graduated from the Berkshire School, Sheffield, Mass., and entered Harvard College, class of 1919 (A.B. posthumously awarded him). At school he played for three years on the football team, and at college was on the freshman crew squad.

He trained with the Harvard R.O.T.C. and attended the Plattsburg Training Camps in 1916 (one month), and 1917 (three months). On Aug. 15, 1917, he was commissioned 2d Lieut., U.S. Cavalry, and on Aug. 29 reported at Camp Devens, attached to the Field Artillery. He was transferred to the 103d Machine-Gun Bat., 52d Brigade, at Camp Bartlett, on Aug. 31. On Sept. 17 he volunteered to fill a vacancy in Headquarters Det., 51st Artillery Brigade, 26th Division, at Boxford, Mass. He sailed overseas under "confidential orders," on the *Finland*, as General's Aide, attached to Battery C, and landed at St.-Nazaire on Oct. 5, 1917. During Oct. and Nov. he was attached to the 102d F.A. He was transferred on Dec. 9, 1917, to the Aviation School for Instruction in Observation, at Le Valdahon, remaining there until Jan. 15, 1918, when he was returned to the 102d F.A., and went with them to the front in the Chemin des Dames sector. He was appointed Assistant Instructor in Aerial Observation on March 3, 1918. He was ill with grippe at Base Hospital No. 6 from May 21 to Aug. 3.

On Aug. 16 he was attached to the 50th Aero Squadron, and on Sept. 12 he disappeared in action near Pont-à-Mousson, during the St.-Mihiel offensive. For several months after his death there was great uncertainty as to Lieut. Gardiner's fate, and it was not until May, 1919, that an official report from the American Military Mission in Berlin secured the German record which stated that he had been shot down at Thisnonville, a small town twenty-five kilometres northeast of Pont-à-Mousson. He was buried in the American Cemetery at Thiaucourt, France.

*STAFFORD LEIGHTON BROWN

First Lieutenant, A.S., U.S.A.

Killed in airplane accident, Sept. 28, 1918

Son of George W. and Eugénie (Stafford) Brown; was born at Newton, Mass., Oct. 25, 1895. He was a graduate of the Newton High School, and entered Dartmouth College in the class of 1920. At college he was captain of the tennis team, and played on the football and hockey teams.

He attended the Plattsburg Training Camp in 1915; and in March, 1917, went overseas to France as driver in the American Ambulance Field Service. He served for five months, chiefly in the vicinity of Verdun, and then joined the Air Service. He trained at Tours and Issoudun, and was commissioned 1st Lieut. in June, 1918.

In at least three instances, before the accident in which his life was sacrificed, Lieut. Brown escaped fatal consequences solely by his remarkable skill as pilot. On one of these occasions his companion was killed. He had almost finished formation flying in the Seventh Class, when he was killed by a fall due to a defect in his machine, on Sept. 28, 1918, while flying a Spad monoplace to the front, in the Arrondissement de Mantes. He was buried at Hargeville, Suresnes, France.

*STURGIS PISHON

FIRST LIEUTENANT, A.S., U.S.A., THREE HUNDRED FORTY-FIRST AERO SQUADRON

Killed in airplane accident, Oct. 26, 1918

SON of Mr. and Mrs. Josiah Sturgis Pishon; was born at Las Vegas, New Mexico, May 30, 1888. When a boy he removed to West Roxbury, Mass., where he attended the public schools. He graduated from the English High School, Boston, in 1906, as a Franklin Medal scholar, and entered Dartmouth College in the class of 1910, graduating there *magna cum laude.* He was prominent in athletics, playing on the 'Varsity football team, where he was famous as quarter-back; he also played baseball and hockey, and belonged to the Theta Delta Chi Fraternity and the Casque and Gauntlet Society; was member of Phi Beta Kappa; was permanent secretary of his class. On leaving college he entered the wool business and later associated himself with an advertising firm, with which he was connected at the time of his entry into the U.S. Service.

He enlisted Aug. 8, 1917, at the Army Aviation Ground School at Cornell University, Ithaca, N.Y., graduating there Sept. 29, 1917, with special recommendation to the War Department. He sailed overseas Oct. 13, 1917, and trained at Issoudun, France. After four months he was transferred to Foggia, Italy, where he was one of the first detachment of American Aviators to train with Italian officers. He was commissioned 1st Lieut. May 18, 1918, and returned to Issoudun for further training. Later he was sent to St.-Jean-des-Monts for aerial gunnery instruction, and it was there that he was killed in an airplane accident, on Oct. 26, 1918. He was buried in the French Military Cemetery at St.-Jean-des-Monts, Vendée, France.

The following extract is from a letter written by Lieut. Pishon, and found with his papers after his death:

> What little I have to give to my country I give without reservation. If there ever was a righteous cause it is ours, and I am proud to have worked and died for it. Pray God this war will be over soon and that it will be the last war. I leave you with a smile on my lips and a heart full of love for you all. God bless you and keep you.

Brother in Service —

Emmet Pishon, 1st Lieut., U.S. Infantry.

*EDWARD RALPH KENNESON

FIRST LIEUTENANT, A.S.A., U.S.A., COMMANDER, NINTH AERO SQUADRON

Died of pneumonia, Jan. 9, 1919

SON of Edward S. and Esther (Martin) Kenneson, of Arlington Heights, Mass.; was born at Somerville, Mass., Nov. 4, 1895. He attended the Somerville High School, graduating in 1913.

In Oct., 1916, he entered the School of Aeronautics, at Newport News, Va., and was given a Pilot's license, Dec. 2, 1916. On Dec. 18 he enlisted in the U.S. (Regular) Army, at Fort Monroe, Va., where he continued his studies until graduation. On April 4, 1917, he was commissioned 1st Lieut., A.S., Signal Officers' Reserve Corps, and was transferred to Princeton, N.J., as Instructor of Aeronautics. In July, 1917, he was sent to Kelly Field, San Antonio, Tex., where he received overseas orders, sailing Aug. 22, 1917, in command of the 36th Aero Squadron. He was retained as Instructor at the 3d A.I.C., Issoudun, France, for over a year.

In the spring of 1918 he applied to go to the front, and after some advanced training in bombing he was assigned to the 91st Squadron as an observer. On Sept. 2, 1918, he was transferred to the 9th Squadron, and on Sept. 30 was appointed Commander. He saw active service at the front from Oct. 1 to the signing of the Armistice, when he was assigned to the Army of Occupation. On Jan. 9, 1919, he died of broncho-pneumonia and was buried at Suresnes, France.

Lieut. C. E. Kennedy of the 9th Squadron wrote of him:

> Lieut. Kenneson joined our Squadron about the middle of Sept., when we were at Amanty, France. It was about the time of the St.-Mihiel drive, and your son accomplished several successful missions over the lines at night, bringing back very important and valuable information.
>
> He was an excellent pilot, capable and courageous. He had more hours in the air than any other man in the Escadrille; I believe his flying time totalled more than one thousand hours. All our observers had absolute confidence in his ability and never had hesitancy in starting out on a mission with him. A splendid pilot, he was equally as capable as a soldier. He was devoted to his duty, performing all his military offices with qualities of unusual judgment and fairness.

Lieut. Kenneson was recommended for promotion to a Captaincy.

Married, June 14, 1917, Mary Aileen Cubberly, of Trenton, N.J.

* WILLIAM F. HERRICK

SECOND LIEUTENANT, A.S., U.S.A.

Killed in airplane accident, Sept. 16, 1918

SON of William B. and Lucy A. (Fisk) Herrick; was born at Natick, Mass., July 31, 1890. He graduated from the Newton High School in 1906, and spent one year at M.I.T. He went abroad for one year as private tutor, and after his return was engaged in business up to the time of his enlistment, in June, 1917.

He attended the Ground School, M.I.T., and upon the completion of his course was sent overseas to France. He was transferred to Foggia, Italy, where he was commissioned 2d Lieut. in May, 1918. He was then given the option of service in the bombing-planes at the Italian front, or of returning to France to qualify as a fighting pilot. He chose the latter course, and was nearly ready to go to the front when the fatal accident occurred at Issoudun.

The following extract is from a letter received by the father of Lieut. Herrick from a Red Cross representative:

> Lieut. Herrick was engaged with a number of other aviators in mass-formation practice on Field 7. At a certain signal he and Lieut. Sylvester B. Moore were to pass each other, one flying up and the other down. Through some misunderstanding both aviators ascended. The result was a collision; the airplanes were smashed and the men fell, being instantly killed. . . . I was talking with some of the men about Lieut. Herrick, and it would be a satisfaction to you to know with how much affection and admiration they spoke of him. They said he was always full of fun and helped to keep them all in good spirits. He was considered an unusually good flyer. You may rest assured it was no fault of his own that caused his death, but an accident coming in the regular performance of duty.

Lieut. Herrick was buried with military honors at cemetery No. 32, about seven miles from Issoudun, France.

*ELWIN F. CHAPMAN

CADET, A.S., U.S.A.

Killed in airplane accident, June 3, 1918

SON of George F. and Eliza M. (Capen) Chapman, of Canton, Mass.; was born at Evanston, Wyoming, July 3, 1891. At an early age he moved with his family to Jamaica Plain, Mass., where he attended school. In 1906 he entered Bordentown Military Academy, at Bordentown, N.J., graduating in 1910. He was regarded as one of the finest athletes that this school had ever produced, and while there he was captain of the baseball team, and in his senior year captain of the football team; also a member of the basket-ball team. In the fall of 1910 he entered the University of California, graduating in 1914; there he was one of the leading athletes; he was pitcher on the 'Varsity baseball team, and member of the Theta Delta Chi fraternity, the Wolf's Head Club, and the Gun Club.

He enlisted at Brookline, Mass., in Nov., 1917, and in Feb., 1918, entered the School of Military Aeronautics, at Princeton, N.J., where, in a class of ninety, he was one of nineteen to successfully complete the course. He was then ordered to Camp Dick, Dallas, Tex., in April, 1918. During the drive for the Third Liberty Loan he was chosen as the speaker to represent his Squadron in that part of Texas. About the middle of May, 1918, he was sent to Rockwell Field, San Diego, Cal., where he was killed in an aeroplane collision on June 3, 1918. He was buried at Canton Junction, Mass.

Brother in Service —

George H. Chapman, 1st Lieut., U.S.A., 15th Aero Construction Co.

*ROGER S. DIX, Jr.

Second Lieutenant, A.S.A., U.S.A.

Killed in airplane accident, May 15, 1918

Son of Roger S. and Louise (Parrish) Dix; was born at Boston, Mass., Dec. 9, 1896. He was educated at the Country Day School, and at Harvard College, entering with the class of 1918. He left Harvard at the end of his junior year, and attended the Plattsburg Training Camp, in 1915, and again in 1916. He served with the American Ambulance Field Service, Section 1, at Verdun, in 1917, at which time his section received a Citation Militaire. In Nov., 1917, he enlisted in France, in the U.S. Air Service, but was forced to remain inactive during the winter, owing to lack of planes. In the spring of 1918 he was one of twenty-five to volunteer for instruction as bombing observers in the French Bombing School at Le Crotoy, Somme, France, with the understanding that they should be sent at once to the front for the spring offensive. He was commissioned 2d Lieut., May 12, 1918.

Lieut. Dix had completed his course, and was to leave that week for the front, when he was killed in an airplane accident at Le Crotoy on May 15, 1918. He fell from a height of 200 metres, and his French pilot was also killed. He was buried with military honors at Le Crotoy.

A letter signed by the twenty-four comrades of his flying detachment which was sent his parents, states:

> Cadet Dix was easily the most popular member of this detachment. He was a loyal, gallant soldier, an assiduous student, an excellent airman and a splendid companion. Every man counted him his friend and he had never failed us. His fearlessness, his coolness and his intrepidity had made it a foregone conclusion that his career in his chosen Service would have been brilliantly distinguished, and his tragic death is a double loss to us and the Army because he was the possessor of such splendid qualities.

The letter from which the above is quoted was also signed by Lieut. Dix's Commanding Officer, who adds:

> I found him to be a most excellent soldier both on the ground and in the air. He was on his last training flight and was to have received the highest honors of any of my command for his work here. He died while doing work in the air and while holding the position of the first in his class. More glory than this no man can claim for his son.

*EDWIN ARNOLD BROWN

First Lieutenant, A.S., U.S.A., Aerial Gunnery School for Bombers

Died, Nov. 1, 1918

Son of Allan and Minnie (Arnold) Brown; was born Feb. 19, 1893, at Salem, Mass. He was educated in the Salem and Boston public schools; and at the Mechanic Arts High School in Boston, where he was a member of the baseball, football, and basket-ball teams.

He enlisted in the Aviation Service on Dec. 15, 1917, and was sent for training to Kelly Field, San Antonio, Tex.; then to Georgia Technology, at Atlanta; Ellington Field, Houston Tex.; and to San Leon, Houston, Tex.; He was commissioned 1st Lieut. on April 19, 1918; received his sailing orders for overseas, but died in Boston on Nov. 1, 1918, twenty-four hours before the date set for sailing. He was buried in Salem, Mass. Lieut. Brown invented and perfected a more efficient system of sighting machine guns; and wrote a book upon aerial gunnery which is accepted by the War Department as an authority upon the subject. (Portrait on opposite page.)

ROGER THAYER TWITCHELL

Second Lieutenant, A.S.A., U.S.A.

Son of Dr. Edward Thayer and Elizabeth F. (Schuster) Twitchell; was born in Dorchester, Mass., Feb. 10, 1895. He was educated at Milton Academy, and at Harvard University, A.B. 1916. He was a member of the track and cross-country teams at college. He served nine months in France as an ambulance driver, in Section 4, American Ambulance Field Service, on the western front, from Sept., 1916, to June, 1917. In Dec., 1917, he enlisted in the Air Service, at Boston, Mass., and trained at the U.S. Army School of Military Aeronautics, at Cornell University; at Camp Dick, Dallas, Tex., and subsequently at Kelly Field, San Antonio, Tex., at which station he was commissioned 2d Lieut., A.S.A., Aug. 23, 1918. He was then stationed at Wilbur Wright Field, Dayton, Ohio, and later at Payne Field, West Point, Miss. In Jan., 1919, he resigned his commission and was released from service at Payne Field, West Point.

*JOHN S. PFAFFMANN

SECOND LIEUTENANT, A.S.A., U.S.A.

Killed in airplane accident, July 22, 1918

SON of George Eaton and Mabel Abigail (Shaw) Pfaffmann; was born at Quincy, Mass., April 27, 1894. He was educated at the Quincy High School, at Phillips Andover Academy, and at Harvard College. He was a remarkably fine tennis player, and belonged to the Harvard tennis team in 1916 and 1917, and was elected captain in 1917.

He sailed for France in April, 1917, with the Norton-Harjes Ambulance Unit, and served on the Aisne, and about Reims during July, Aug., Sept., 1917. In Oct., 1917, he enlisted in the U.S. Air Service in Paris, and was assigned to Tours, where he remained through Nov. and Dec. He continued his training at St.-Maixent from Jan. to May, 1918, and was transferred to Voves on June 1. He was commissioned 2d Lieut. in June, 1918. On July 22 he was killed at Voves in an airplane accident, when returning from an altitude flight of one hour at 6000 feet, which would have given him his military brevet as Pilot. Watched by his chief and an instructor, he descended to a height of about 200 feet, and banked his plane to come into the wind, and land. The lower wing of the plane was caught in an air-pocket at the same instant that a counter-current hit the upper wing; he crashed, and was instantly killed.

An impressive military funeral was held at Voves, attended by the officers and cadets of the Voves Flying School, veterans of the War of 1870, the Mayor of Voves, and many villagers and children. At the end of the services Lieut. Mayeur, of Headquarters Staff, stepped forward and said:

> Among the first Americans to come to combat the invader upon the soil of France, John Pfaffmann entered the Ambulance Service and distinguished himself at the front by his unflagging energy and his high comprehension of military duty. His desire to do more and yet more for his country and for France soon led him, however, to seek a transfer to the Aviation Service. . . . May the remembrance of his glorious death upon the field of honor be, in some small degree at least, an alleviation of the sorrow of his family, and of all those who have known and loved him.

WILLIAM GRAVES PERRY

CAPTAIN, A.S., U.S.A., HEADQUARTERS AIR SERVICE, FIRST ARMY

SON of Charles French and Georgianna West (Graves) Perry; was born at Boston, Mass., Nov. 8, 1883. He was educated at the Noble and Greenough School; and at Harvard College, A.B. 1905; M.I.T., S.B. 1917, and École des Beaux Arts, Paris, 1913.

He attended the Officers' Training Camp at Plattsburg, in Aug. 1916; served as Capt., Co. M, 13th Reg't., Mass. State Guard. He enlisted Nov. 1, 1917, and was commissioned 1st Lieut., A.S.S.C., reported for duty at Kelly Field, San Antonio, Tex., Nov. 11, 1917, and was put in command of the 65th (later 477th) Aero Squadron.

He sailed overseas March 4, 1918, and was commissioned Capt., A.S.C., Aug. 1, 1918. He was appointed Equipment Officer Air Service, 1st Army, Oct. 14, 1918, and was stationed at Souilly from Oct. 14 until Dec. 24, 1918. From Nov. 21 to 24 he was attached for temporary duty to the 3d Army, to receive airplane and other Air Service material from the enemy. Capt. Perry participated in frequent flights and trips to the lines during the Argonne battle, for the purpose of choosing and preparing airdromes and advanced landing places for the Air Service of the 1st Army.

He was honorably discharged May 31, 1919.

Cited in General Orders as follows:

Captain WILLIAM G. PERRY, A.S., U.S.A., organized and commanded the 477th Aero Construction Squadron which made such an enviable record for itself. Under his direction it built airdromes at Autreville, Amanty, Bicqueley, and St.-Mihiel. At Bicqueley, by superb organization and morale, he was able to build the field in ten days. At these Headquarters, as Equipment Officer during the latter part of the operations west of the Meuse, he successfully and with great tact handled the very difficult proposition of obtaining, and allocating to the units of this command, Air Service material, transportation, and equipment of all kinds.

His extreme conscientiousness was an example which all may well emulate.

By order of Col. MILLING

Married, Aug. 6, 1908, Eleanor Gray.

Brother in Service —

Edward Hale Perry, 1st Lieut., Co. D, 6th Engineers. Killed in action at Warfusée, France, March 30, 1918. Cited for bravery in action.

USR

JOHN ROGERS HURLBURT

CAPTAIN, A.S., U.S.A., ONE HUNDRED SIXTY-THIRD AERO SQUADRON, SECOND DAY BOMBARDMENT GROUP

SON of Henry F. and Fannie E. (Thompson) Hurlburt, of Boston, Mass.; was born at Lynn, Mass., Nov. 8, 1893. He was educated at St. Paul's School, Concord, N.H., and at Harvard College, A.B. 1916. At St. Paul's he was captain of the track team, and member of the Lower School hockey and football teams.

He sailed for France, April 28, 1917, with the American Ambulance Field Service, with which he served until Sept. 18, 1917, when he enlisted as private in the U.S.A., and trained for the Aviation Service at Tours, France. On Jan. 17, 1918, he was commissioned 1st Lieut., and arrived at the front in June, 1918, as Adjutant of 5th Air Dépôt. He was transferred to the 163d Aero Squadron, 2d Day Bombardment Group, with which he served until April, 1919, when he was appointed Aide to Gen. Patrick. On May 30, 1919, he was commissioned Capt., and left France to return to the U.S. on Aug. 18, 1919. He was honorably discharged on Sept. 12, 1919.

Brother in Service —
Paul Hurlburt, Capt., U.S.A., 3d Cavalry.

AUGUSTUS PAGE FARNSWORTH

SECOND LIEUTENANT, A.S.A., U.S.A., ADJUTANT, SIX HUNDRED FORTY-FOURTH AERO SQUADRON

SON of Harrie Clifford and Florence (Gordon) Farnsworth; was born at Hyde Park, Mass., on March 15, 1895. He was educated in the Hyde Park public schools and at Worcester Academy, Worcester, Mass. He graduated from the M.I.T. in 1917. In his freshman and sophomore years he played quarter-back on the M.I.T. football team, and was captain of the football team in his freshman year.

He enlisted in the Air Service on Aug. 11, 1917, in Boston, Mass., and was assigned to the Ground School, M.I.T. On Dec. 3 he was sent to Waco, Tex. He was commissioned 2d Lieut., March 6, 1918, and was ordered to Gerstner Field, Lake Charles, La., for training as a Pursuit Pilot. Subsequently he was sent to the Gunnery School at Taliaferro Field, Hicks, Tex., from which he graduated on June 29, he was then made Gunnery Instructor. Late in Aug., Lieut. Farnsworth received overseas orders; he reported at Hoboken, and on Sept. 4 sailed for Scotland. He went to Paris by way of Glasgow and London, reporting for duty on Oct. 5. He was immediately assigned to the 3d A.I.C. at Issoudun, where he qualified as Pursuit Pilot on Nov. 9, and was made Instructor in Combat on Nov. 11, 1918.

Brother in Service —

Charles Luke Farnsworth, Quartermaster, 1st Class, U.S.N.

GODFREY LOWELL CABOT

LIEUTENANT, U.S.N.R.F., AVIATION AIDE, FIRST NAVAL DISTRICT

SON of Samuel and Hannah Lowell (Jackson) Cabot; was born at Boston, Mass., Feb. 26, 1861. He was educated at the Brimmer, Latin, and Hopkinson schools, Boston; M.I.T., one year; Harvard College, four years; Polytechnic, Zurich, and University of Zurich. He took final honors (*magna cum laude*) in chemistry at Harvard. At college he took one prize in a wrestling match, and won many prizes at tennis.

He was commissioned Ensign, A.D.C., M.V.M., on June 26, 1916. On March 20, 1917, he was commissioned Lieut., U.S.N.R.F., at Cambridge, Mass. He practised flying at Marblehead, May to Dec., 1915; trained at Pensacola, Fla., in April, 1916; Marblehead, May to Dec., 1916; Pensacola, Jan., 1917; Salem Harbor, April, 1917. He first flew as a pilot on April 12, 1917. For over two years he was on active duty, serving from March 20, 1917, to the spring of 1919. He originated and practised the art of picking up burdens in flight, reaching 155 kilometres on Oct. 3, 1919.

Married, June 23, 1890, Maria Moors, of Boston.

Sons in Service —

James Jackson Cabot, 1st Lieut., A.S., U.S.A.

Thomas Dudley Cabot, 2d Lieut., A.S., U.S.A., Instructor at Kelly Field, Tex.

JAMES JACKSON CABOT

FIRST LIEUTENANT, A.S., U.S.A., ONE HUNDRED EIGHTY-SECOND AND EIGHTY-EIGHTH SQUADRONS

SON of Lieut. Godfrey Lowell and Maria (Moors) Cabot; was born at Cambridge, Mass., Sept. 24, 1891. He was educated at the Browne and Nichols Schooi, Cambridge, and at Harvard College, class of 1913. He also took extra courses at M.I.T.

Previous to enlistment he attended the Plattsburg Training Camp for two summers, qualifying as a sharpshooter. He enlisted on Sept. 29, 1917, and trained at the Curtiss School in Buffalo, N.Y., at M.I.T. Ground School, and at Fort Worth, Tex. He was commissioned 1st Lieut. in Jan., 1918. He sailed overseas in May, 1918, and was first attached to Squadron 182; afterwards to Squadron 88. He piloted a number of aeroplanes from England to France, making his headquarters at different aerodromes in England. Six weeks before the Armistice was signed he flew about Verdun and Sedan. He sailed for America the last of Dec., 1918, and was honorably discharged at Garden City, N.Y., in April, 1919.

Married, May 10, 1919, Catharine Rush, daughter of Commandant Rush, of the Navy Yard, Boston.

Father in Service —

Godfrey Lowell Cabot, Lieut., Aviation Aide, First Naval District.

Brother in Service —

Thomas Dudley Cabot, 2d Lieut., A.S., U.S.A.

THOMAS DUDLEY CABOT

SECOND LIEUTENANT, A.S., U.S.A., INSTRUCTOR AT KELLY FIELD TEXAS

SON of Lieut. Godfrey Lowell and Maria (Moors) Cabot; was born at Cambridge, Mass., on May 1, 1898. He was educated at the Browne and Nichols School, Evans School, Arizona, and at Harvard College, class of 1919.

He attended the Plattsburg Training Camp in the summer of 1916 (sharpshooter), and trained with the Harvard Regiment. He took a course in aeronautics at the M.I.T. Ground School, and trained as a flyer at the Curtiss School, Buffalo, N.Y. On Aug. 27, 1917, he enlisted as a private, 1st class, A.S., S.E.R.C., at Ithaca, N.Y. He trained at the M.I.T. Ground School during Oct. and Nov., 1917; was sent to Kelly Field, Tex., on Dec. 1, 1917, where he was attached to the cadet wing for further training as a flyer. He passed the R.M.A. tests on Jan. 17, and was commissioned 2d Lieut., A.S.S.R.C., Jan. 31, 1918. He was in charge of officers' barracks during Feb., March, and April; and at the Instructors' School in May, where he acted as Flying Instructor from June to Oct.; he was sent to Miami, Fla., in Nov., where he trained as a pilot for flying-boats, and as coast patrol pilot. He was sent to Arcadia, Fla., and honorably discharged, at Carlstrom Field, on Dec. 14, 1918.

Father in Service —

Godfrey Lowell Cabot, Lieut., Aviation Aide, First Naval District.

Brother in Service —

James Jackson Cabot, Lieut., A.S., U.S.A.

*ORLANDO MERRITT LORD

SECOND LIEUTENANT, A.S., U.S.A.

Killed in airplane accident, June 24, 1918

SON of John L. and Susan A. Lord, of Rutherford, N.J.; was born at South Boston, Mass., Nov. 9, 1890. He was educated in the public schools of South Boston, and at Cutter's Business School. He was prominent in athletics and played quarter-back on his high school football team. On leaving school he engaged in business, and relinquished a good position to enter the Aviation Service.

He enlisted on Oct. 1, 1917, at Cambridge, Mass., and attended the Ground School, M.I.T. (Squadron A). On Jan. 7, 1918, he was sent to Ellington Field, Houston, Tex., where he remained until May 2, when he was sent to Camp Dick, Dallas, Tex. He was transferred, on May 29, 1918, to Payne Field, West Point, Miss., where he became Instructor in Aviation Acrobatics. He was commissioned 2d Lieut., April 20, 1918.

On June 25, 1918, Lieut. Lord was instructing a pupil, who was directing the plane, when the machine went into an accidental tail-spin, and before the Instructor could obtain control of the plane from the pupil, it had dashed to the ground, killing Lieut. Lord, and severely injuring his companion.

Lieut. Lord was buried at Pine Grove Cemetery, Lynn, Mass. As his body was carried aboard the train at West Point, eight aviators flew overhead, in the form of a cross, and dropped flowers on the casket. Lieut. Lord was exceedingly popular with his associates, and after his death they presented his family with a loving-cup, inscribed: "From his comrades who esteemed him as a soldier, and loved him as a friend."

Lieut. Lord was one of four aviators chosen to make long trips on behalf of the Liberty Loan drives, bombing different cities with Liberty Loan literature. Of this group he was the only one to return without accident to either his plane or himself, and was officially complimented on his flying. It was his one ambition to get across seas and engage in active scout work at the front.

Grandfather in Service —

In Civil War. Lost an arm at battle of Bull Run.

CARLETON SPRAGUE AYER

SECOND LIEUTENANT, A.S., U.S.A., TWENTY-FIFTH SQUADRON

SON of Silas H. and Juliette Butterfield (Davis) Ayer; was born at Boston, Mass., on April 13, 1893. He was educated at the Boston Latin and De Merritt schools, and at M.I.T., where he was a member of Sigma Chi Fraternity. He rowed on the Boston Latin School crew in 1911; and on July 4 of that year received a gold medal, presented by the City of Boston, as stroke of the winning crew in the intermediate eight-oar shell race, Charles River Basin.

He enlisted at Youngstown, Ohio, in the Regular Army, on Sept. 19, 1917, and served one month at Camp Sherman, Chillicothe, Ohio. He received honorable discharge, to enter the Aviation Service. On Jan. 12, 1918, he graduated from the U.S. School of Military Aeronautics, Ohio State University, Columbus. He then trained at Call Field, Wichita Falls, Tex., and was commissioned 2d Lieut., Aviation Section, Signal Reserve Corps, on May 10, 1918.

On May 22, 1918, Lieut. Ayer was assigned to active duty at Camp Dick, Dallas, Tex.; he was transferred on June 29, 1918, to Ellington Field, Houston, Tex., where he completed his work and was ready for overseas duty. He was honorably discharged from the Service in Jan., 1919.

Brothers in Service —

Nathaniel D. Ayer, Lieut., A.D.C., 4th Division, Canadian B.E.F.

Silas H. Ayer, Jr., Bandmaster, U.S.N.R.F.

JAMES GREENLEAF ADAMS

First Lieutenant, A.S., U.S.A., One Hundred Thirty-Eighth Aero Squadron, Fifth Pursuit Group

Son of James M. and Maria (Dame) Adams, of East Lake, Fla.; was born at Nashua, N.H., March 24, 1892. He was educated at the Hackensack, N.J., High School, class of 1909.

In Jan., 1917, he volunteered for the American Ambulance Field Service in France, with Section 8, and served for six months under Major A. Piatt Andrew. In Aug., 1917, he enlisted in the U.S. Air Service, in France. He trained at Tours and Issoudun, receiving a Pilot's license at Tours, and training in acrobacy at Issoudun. He was commissioned 1st Lieut. in Nov., 1917, and has a record of some 800 flights since then.

When the Armistice was signed, Lieut. Adams was flying near the Toul front, piloting observation planes of many types. In June, 1919, he was still in service with the Army of Occupation.

In a letter dated April 21, 1919, Lieut. Adams writes:

Just a word saying we are here on the Rhine. We've all got here now and are comfortably settled at our field near a big German fort, half a mile from Coblenz. I flew up here in my Spad *alone* with my map and compass. Crossed No Man's Land, with its miles of old trenches, near St.-Mihiel, and followed them to Pont-à-Mousson on the Moselle River. Then went right up the river at about 1000 feet altitude to Metz and its circle of unconquerable forts. Then, after about ninety minutes of flying, got to Trèves (Trier), where I landed for gas and oil at a U.S. field, formerly a Zeppelin base, with a huge hangar, big enough for one hundred aeroplanes. . . . Started off again at 3 P.M. up the Moselle. A wonderful valley, but its huge hills, canyons, and mountains made it dangerous flying. But the day was perfect and my motor, too, and I had no trouble at all. Passed over many world-famous Rhine castles and hundreds of towns along the river. A really great experience! Landed at Coblenz O.K., an hour later, where the Rhine and Moselle join, as you can see on a map. Right in the heart of Prussia, and Germans all about us, civilians, children, and militaries. Seems a different world, and impossible for a city like this to be absolutely dominated by an army of khaki!

Brothers in Service —

Leon M. Adams, 2d Class Seaman, U.S.N.

Lincoln D. Adams, 2d Class Seaman, U.S.N.

Grandfather in Service —

James P. Adams, Private, 7th Reg't, N.H. Volunteers, Civil War. Died in Service.

JOHN F. McNAMARA

LIEUTENANT, U.S.N.R.F.

SON of Eugene T. and Mary Agnes (McCarthy) McNamara, of Arlington, Mass.; was born at Somerville, Mass., April 3, 1898. He was educated at the Cambridge High and Latin Schools, and at Boston College. He entered Service at end of freshman year.

He enlisted on April 28, 1917, at Boston, and was sent to Pensacola, Fla., for training. He was commissioned Ensign Dec. 21, 1917, sailed overseas in Jan., 1918, and was stationed for three months at the Royal Naval Air Station at Portland, Eng. While operating there, on scout duty, he bombed and sunk a submarine, being the first American naval aviator to accomplish this feat. He was commissioned Lieut. (j.g.), April 1, 1918. He was transferred to the Royal Air Station at Felixstowe, Eng., where he remained until Aug., when he was attached to the U.S. Air Station, at Killingholme; subsequently he was ordered to the U.S. Air Station at Wexford, Ireland, in command of a squadron of eight seaplanes. On Oct. 1, 1918, he was commissioned Lieut.

He was placed on inactive duty at Bay Shore, N.Y., Jan. 15, 1919.

Married, Oct. 8, 1919, Florence E. Riordan.

To Ensign JOHN F. McNAMARA:

The Department quotes below for your information the report of Vice-Admiral Sims relative to your apparently successful operations while out on scout duty against enemy submarines, on March 25, 1918, under orders from the Commanding Officer of the Royal Naval Air Station, Portland, England, whose report was forwarded by Vice-Admiral Sims: "The attached correspondence relative to the performance of duty of Ensigns —— and John F. McNamara, U.S.N.R.F., reflects credit upon both those officers. It is recommended that adequate recognition of their services be granted."

The Department wishes to avail itself of this opportunity to express to you the very high appreciation felt upon receipt of reports similar to the above. It is strong evidence of the fact that earnest coöperation exists between the Armed Forces of our Allies and the United States Armed Forces. It is work of this character that will impress our enemies with the realization that the United States is a power very much to be considered.

Accordingly, you are hereby highly commended for your valiant and earnest efforts on this particular occasion when your attack on the enemy submarine apparently caused some damage. It is to be hoped that a continuance of such work will be maintained in the future.

JOSEPHUS DANIELS

THEODORE WILLIAM KOCH

First Lieutenant, A.S.A., U.S.A., C.O. Three Hundred Seventy-Second Aero Squadron

Son of Theodore F. and Clara D. Koch; was born at St. Paul, Minn., Aug. 20, 1891. He graduated from the St. Paul High School, and went to the University of Minnesota for one year. He transferred to Harvard College in 1910, and received his degree in 1914. In the meantime his parents moved to Houston, Tex., where after his graduation Lieut. Koch entered business with his father. He enlisted in the Ground Officers' Training School, at Kelly Field, Tex., in July, 1917. He received his commission as 1st Lieut., and was sent to instruct in the Wilbur Wright School of Administration at Dayton, Ohio.

On March 7, 1918, he sailed for England with the 47th Aero Squadron, and was stationed at Cramlington. Later he was assigned as Commanding Officer to the 372d Aero Squadron stationed at Hendon. On Oct. 2, 1918, the Squadron was mobilized at St.-Maixent, France, and fully equipped for service at the front. Then it was sent to the 3d A.I.C. at Issoudun for temporary duty. Late at night on Nov. 10, 1918, orders for the front arrived, but because of the Armistice these were cancelled the following day. Lieut. Koch was Adjutant at Field 10, Issoudun, from Nov. 2, 1918, to Jan. 8, 1919. On April 20 he returned with his Squadron to Mitchel Field, Garden City, N.Y., for demobilization.

WILLIAM M. CONANT, Jr.

Major, A.S.A., U.S.A., School Staff, Third Aviation Instruction Centre

Son of Dr. William M. and Mary B. Conant; was born at Boston, Mass., March 23, 1891. He was educated at the Noble and Greenough School, and at Harvard College, A.B. 1912. In school he was a member of the football, track, and baseball teams; and played on the freshman baseball team at Harvard College.

He served in the 1st Aero Squadron, N.G., of New York, in 1916, and flew at Mineola, N.Y. He enlisted at Mineola in July, 1917, and received his flying training there in Aug. On Oct. 8, 1917, he was commissioned 1st Lieut., and sailed overseas in the same month. He completed his training as "chasse pilote" in Dec., Jan., and Feb., at the 3d A.I.C., Issoudun, France. In Feb., 1918, he was made Tester of Planes, and in April was promoted to be Chief Tester of the School. He was commissioned Capt. on Oct. 3, 1918, and promoted to Major, on Feb. 21, 1919. He is still in the Service at Bolling Field, Washington, D.C.

Married, June 4, 1919, Dinsmore Patrick, of Lexington, Ky.

GEORGE W. BENEDICT, Jr.

First Lieutenant, A.S., U.S.A.

Son of George W. and Anna Louise Benedict, of Cambridge, Mass., was born at Boston, Aug. 14, 1895. He was educated at the Volkmann and at St. George's schools, and at Harvard College, A.B. 1917.

He attended the Plattsburg Training Camp in July, 1916, and the Harvard R.O.T.C., from March to July, 1917. He enlisted at Cambridge on July 7, 1917, in the Signal Enlisted Reserve Corps, and began active service at the Ground School, M.I.T., on Aug. 20, 1917. Graduating on Oct. 13, he was sent to Mineola Embarkation Camp, N.Y.; and on Nov. 14, 1917, sailed overseas. He waited at Tours and St.-Maixent until the end of March, 1918, when he was sent for flying instruction to the French school at Châteauroux. After preliminary training and the French brevet tests, he was stationed at Issoudun for further training, from July 12 to Aug. 17. While at Châteauroux he was commissioned 1st Lieut., May 18, 1918. From Issoudun he was sent to the 2d A.I.C. at Tours, Aug. 17, 1918, to take the course for "Corps d'Armée" Pilots. Shortly afterwards this centre began to train observers exclusively, so that the "Corps d'Armée" Pilots' course was discontinued, and Lieut. Benedict was transferred to the status of Staff Pilot, to fly in coöperation with the observers. He remained on this duty until his discharge in France, April 1, 1919.

WENDELL GAGE REYCROFT

ENSIGN, U.S.N.A.S. NORTHERN BOMBING GROUP, FRANCE

SON of Louis Wendell and Eliza Morgan (Gage) Reycroft, of Arlington, Mass.; was born at Boston on May 11, 1894. He was educated at the Arlington public schools, and at Dartmouth College, A.B. 1917. In high school he was captain of the football team in 1913, and of the hockey team in the same year. At Dartmouth he played on the 'Varsity hockey team for three years.

He enlisted at Arlington, and was trained at the M.I.T. Ground School, Cambridge. On graduation he was ordered to Key West, Fla., where he was commissioned Ensign, and then ordered to Miami, Fla., as Instructor in Flying. He applied for overseas service, and sailed for France in detail Aug. 1, 1918. He saw service with the Northern Bombing Group of Headquarters in Flanders and Belgium. At last reports he was still in Service at Norfolk, Va.

Brothers in Service —

Harlan Long Reycroft, Ensign, U.S.N.A.S.
Harrie Fay Reycroft, Private, 26th Balloon Co., France.
Louis Manning Reycroft, Private, Signal Corps.
George Moulton Reycroft, Qualified Cadet, Officers' School, Camp Frémont.

HARLAN LONG REYCROFT

ENSIGN, U.S.N.A.S.

SON of Louis Wendell and Eliza Morgan (Gage) Reycroft, of Arlington, Mass.; was born at Boston, on Dec. 12, 1892. He was educated at the Arlington public schools, and at Harvard College, A.B. 1915. In high school he ran on the track team, was captain of the football team, 1911, and was on the baseball team, 1911. At Harvard he earned his "H" on the track and hockey teams.

Previous to the war, he served in Mexico with Battery A, 1st Mass. Reg't, F.A., N.G. He enlisted at Arlington, Mass., in 1918; trained at M.I.T. Ground School, from which he graduated, and was ordered to Miami, Fla., on Aug. 3, 1918. Here he was commissioned Ensign, and was appointed Naval Ensign and Instructor in Flying. At last reports he was still in Service.

Married, July 6, 1918, Gladys M. Chamberlain.

Brothers in Service —

Wendell Gage Reycroft, Ensign, U.S.N.A.S., Northern Bombing Group.

Harrie Fay Reycroft, Private, 26th Balloon Co., France.

Louis Manning Reycroft, Private, Signal Corps.

George Moulton Reycroft, Qualified Cadet, Officers' School, Camp Frémont.

CLYDE C. MACKENZIE

SECOND LIEUTENANT, A.S., U.S.A.

SON of Frank E. and Hattie M. Mackenzie; was born at Taunton, Mass., July 17, 1892. He was educated at the Taunton High School and at M.I.T. Prior to his entrance into the U.S. Service he trained with various school and college cadet corps.

On July 2, 1917, he enlisted at the M.I.T., where he attended the Ground School from July 2 to Aug. 23; he continued his training at Wilbur Wright Field, Dayton, Ohio, Aug. 23 to Dec. 30. He was transferred to Ellington Field, Houston, Tex., and stationed there from Dec. 30, 1917, to July 5, 1918 (student and Instructor in day and night bombing). He was commissioned 2d Lieut., Feb. 21, 1918. He was ordered to Taliaferro Field, Fort Worth, Tex., July 5 to Aug. 17, serving as Instructor in Aerial Gunnery.

He sailed overseas and was stationed at the 7th A.I.C., Clermont-Ferrand, France, from Sept. 30 to Oct. 22, 1918, as student and Instructor in Bombing. On Oct. 22, 1918, he was injured in wreck of a D.H. 4. He returned to the U.S. and at last accounts was in the Base Hospital, at Camp Devens, Mass.

Lieut. Mackenzie was the first night-bombing and day-bombing pilot to be trained in the U.S. and sent abroad. He sailed with two others, Lieuts. Jenkins and Nichols; the three being at that time the only completely trained bombing pilots in the U.S.

Married, Aug. 23, 1918, Margaret Traynor.

MARVIN SOMERSETT BOWMAN

SECOND LIEUTENANT, A.S.A., U.S.A., SEVENTH AVIATION INSTRUCTION CENTRE, A.E.F.

SON of Rev. John Elliot and Charly (Root) Bowman; was born at Somerville, Mass., Dec. 30, 1895. He was educated at Vermont Academy, Saxtons River, Vt., and at Harvard College, where he remained for two years with the class of 1916. Prior to his entry into the U.S. Service he was a member of the staff of the *Boston Evening Record.*

He enlisted in Boston, Aug., 1917, as private in the 301st Field Artillery. In Feb., 1918, he was transferred to the Air Service, and trained at the Ground School, Cornell, at Dallas, Tex., and at Selfridge Field, Mich. He sailed overseas in Aug., 1918, and was stationed at Brest, St.-Maixent, and at Clermont-Ferrand. He was commissioned 2d Lieut., A.S.A., July 30, 1918, and was made a member of the instruction staff of the 7th A.I.C., Clermont-Ferrand, France.

In the following communication he has graphically described the spirit of the French toward the American aviators, who have given their lives in France:

> Perhaps you know that a ship always flies overhead to escort the procession to the grave and then drops flowers from the air. There is something very impressive about this, the big ships circling overhead and leading the way to the grave. Seems like the Spirit of the Game welcoming one of its followers. Then a little service by the padre, a flutter of petals from the air as the ships swoop down to ten feet from the ground — three volleys and then "Taps." That bugle call sure gets a man. The point of the story is this: In that pouring rain there were nearly fifty French kids and women hard at work shaping the graves, patting them down, edging them with sod and covering the whole cemetery with flowers from God knows where. There was n't a grave in the place that was n't hidden from sight by blossoms. And they do this every day and have been doing it for months. And believe me, they will keep on doing it for a hundred years. The French never forget. At the cemetery gate they have erected a monument with laurel wreaths and the inscription:
>
> "Aux soldats américains; morts pour la France, pour la Justice, le Droit et l'Honneur du monde; Honneur aux Braves."

Lieut. Bowman was honorably discharged at Garden City, N.Y., Feb. 4, 1919.

Married, Dec. 19, 1916, Helen A. Dodge, of Cambridge, Mass.

GEORGE BEALE EMMONS, Jr.

SECOND LIEUTENANT, A.S.A., U.S.A.

Son of George Beale and Marie (Dupont) Emmons, of Brookline, Mass.; was born at St. Louis, Mo., April 5, 1894. He was educated at the Volkmann School, 1913, and at Harvard University, class of 1917. At Harvard he played on the freshman baseball team in 1914 and on the 'Varsity soccer team, 1916–17. He was a member of Battery A, 1st Mass. Reg't, F.A., N.G., and in 1916 saw four months' service on the Mexican Border. In April, 1917, he enlisted with the 1st Harvard Regiment. He trained at the 1st Officers' Training Camp at Plattsburg, and after finishing the course was transferred to the Air Service. He attended the Ground School, M.I.T., and graduated the high honor man of the Squadron. He then had training in flying at Gerstner Field, La., and at Ellington Field, Houston, Tex. He was appointed Instructor at Baker Field, N.Y., and then at Langley Field, Va.

He was commissioned 2d Lieut., May 3, 1918. At the time of the Armistice he was under overseas orders, at Newport News, being attached to the General Staff, Tours, France.

Upon application, Lieut. Emmons was honorably discharged at Washington, D.C., on Dec. 13, 1918.

Brother in Service —

Arthur B. Emmons, 2d, Capt., Medical Corps, U.S.A.; Evacuation Hospital No. 2; appointed Head of Medical Dep't.

JOHN BROWN PAYSON

SECOND LIEUTENANT, A.S.A., U.S.A.

SON of Herbert and Sally Carroll (Brown) Payson; was born at Portland, Me., Oct. 1, 1897. He attended the public schools of Portland, and the Salisbury School, Salisbury, Conn. He entered Yale College in 1916, leaving to enter the Service in 1917.

He attended the Plattsburg Training Camp in 1916, and was a member of the Yale R.O.T.C. Battery. He enlisted in the Air Service at Boston, Mass., Dec. 11, 1917.

He began his training at the Ground School, Cornell University, Ithaca, N.Y., in Feb., 1918; in March he was transferred to Camp Dick, Dallas, Tex., and from there was sent to Payne Field, West Point, Miss., where he was commissioned 2d Lieut., Aug. 20, 1918. He was assigned to the Armorers' School, Wilbur Wright Field, Dayton, Ohio, in Sept., 1918, and from there he was transferred to Field No. 2, Garden City, N.Y. On Dec. 18, 1918, he was honorably discharged at Garden City, N.Y. (Portrait on opposite page.)

EDWARD TAPPAN BRACKETT

SECOND LIEUTENANT, A.S., U.S.A., FLYING INSTRUCTOR
SELFRIDGE FIELD, MICH.

SON of M. L. and Helen R. (Tappan) Brackett, of Brookline, Mass., was born at Boston, Mass., Jan. 19, 1892. He graduated from Brown University in 1914; he was a member of the 'Varsity swimming and wrestling teams, and of his class baseball and gymnasium teams. In 1915 he served for a few months in the Machine Gun Co., 8th Mass. Volunteer Militia. He enlisted at Plattsburg, N.Y., May 12, 1917, and was attached to the 2d Provisional Training Squadron from May to Aug., 1917. He attended the M.I.T. Ground School during Oct. and Nov., 1917. He received further training at Ellington Field, Houston, Tex., from Dec., 1917, to May, 1918; at Langley Field, Old Point Comfort, Va., through May and June; and at the Aerial Gunnery School, Taliaferro Field, Fort Worth, Tex., during July, 1918. He was commissioned 2d Lieut., April 20, 1918, and from Aug., 1918, to Jan. 30, 1919, was Flying Instructor at Selfridge Field, Mt. Clemens, Mich. He was honorably discharged at Selfridge Field, Jan. 30, 1919.

KARL HARROLD CRAIGIE

SECOND LIEUTENANT, A.S.A., U.S.A.

SON of John H. and Florence C. Craigie, of Stoneham, Mass.; was born Aug. 22, 1898. He was educated at the Stoneham High School, and at Harvard College, member of the class of 1920. At school he won the MacDonald scholarship medal and stood first in his class. He trained for six months with the R.O.T.C., and on Sept. 20, 1917, enlisted at Cambridge, Mass.

He trained at the Ground School, M.I.T.; at Ellington Field, Houston, Tex.; Camp Dick, Dallas, Tex.; Call Field, Wichita Falls, Tex.; and at Wilbur Wright Field, Dayton, Ohio. He was commissioned 2d Lieut., April 3, 1918, and sailed overseas to France, continuing his training at St.-Maixent, then at Issoudun, where he completed Pursuit Pilot training, Nov. 10, 1918. He was transferred to the Concentration Camp at Angers; sailed from Brest, Jan. 15, 1919, and was honorably discharged at Garden City, N.Y., Jan. 28, 1919.

Brothers in Service —

Hugh H. Craigie, Corp., Co. L, 33d U.S.(Reg.) Infantry.
Laurence C. Craigie, Cadet, U.S.M.A., West Point.

JOHN JAY VAN SCHAACK

FIRST LIEUTENANT, A.S.A., U.S.A., ONE HUNDREDTH SQUADRON INDEPENDENT AIR FORCE, B.E.F.

SON of Mr. and Mrs. David Van Schaack, of Hartford, Conn.; was born at Brooklyn, N.Y., July 21, 1894. He was educated at the Pawling School, Pawling, N.Y., and at Williams College.

He left college on April 10, 1917, to train for the Service, and on June 24 joined the Franco-American Flying Corps in New York City, sailing overseas, July 9, 1917. On reaching Paris and finding that his entry into a French flying school would be delayed, he obtained his release from the French Government and enlisted in the U.S. Air Service on Aug. 16, 1917. He trained at Tours from Aug. 19 to Oct. 19, 1917, when he was brevetted as a Pilot by the French Government. He was then assigned to the 3d A.I.C. at Issoudun, where he remained from Oct. 20, 1917, to Feb. 10, 1918, and where he was commissioned 1st Lieut., A.S., U.S.A., on Nov. 20, 1917. In Feb. he trained at Clermont-Ferrand, and on April 16 was sent to England for further training at the First Aerial School of Navigation and Bomb-Dropping at Stonehenge. He was subsequently transferred to Guillons, France, where he joined a French Voissain Group, from June 2 to June 29. He was then detailed to the First Air Dépôt at Colombey-les-Belles. From there he went to join the 100th Squadron, Independent Air Force, B.E.F., with which he remained from July 2 to Aug. 16, 1918.

On the night of Aug. 16, while he was on a night-bombing trip against a German Squadron at Boulay, his motor was struck by machine-gun fire from the ground and he was forced to land. Lieut. Van Schaack and his observer, Capt. John A. King, of Chicago, were captured by the Germans, and held at various prison camps: Saint-Avold, Strasbourg, Karlsruhe, Landshut, Villingen, and Constance. They were released on Nov. 29, 1918, and returned to France by way of Switzerland. Lieut. Van Schaack spent a week in the hospital at Allerey, and on Dec. 20 went to England, where he spent six weeks. On Feb. 5, 1919, he sailed for the U.S., where he was honorably discharged at Garden City, N.Y., on Feb. 28, 1919.

Brother in Service —

Bulkeley Van Schaack, Private, U.S.A., 101st Machine Gun Battalion, 26th Division, A.E.F.

LELAND H. EMERY

SECOND LIEUTENANT, A.S.A., U.S.A., SECOND AVIATION INSTRUCTION CENTRE, TOURS, FRANCE

SON of Frederick L. and Grace L. (Harrington) Emery; was born at Lexington, Mass., March 8, 1896. He was educated at the Volkmann School, Boston, and at Harvard College, class of 1919. He rowed two years on his school crew.

He attended the Harvard R.O.T.C. previous to enlisting. He sailed for France in April, 1917; and entered the American Ambulance Field Service, with the French Army, T.M., Section 526 B, Réserve Mallet, and remained in that service for six months. He then enlisted with the U.S. Army, Aviation Section, Signal Reserve Corps, on Dec. 1, 1917. He trained at Tours, Issoudun, and at St.-Jean-des-Monts, Gunnery School. From Dec. 1, 1917, to June, 1918, he was detained as cadet at St.-Maixent. He was commissioned 2d. Lieut., A.S.A., on June 7, 1918, and from then to the signing of the Armistice was retained as Instructor at Tours and elsewhere, continuing in this capacity until his return to the U.S. He arrived in New York, April 27, 1919, and was honorably discharged May 7, 1919, at Camp Devens.

JOHN LALLEY MORAN

SECOND LIEUTENANT, A.S.A., U.S.A., INSTRUCTOR, LOVE FIELD
DALLAS, TEXAS

SON of Walter Lawrence and Ella E. (Lalley) Moran; was born at Cambridge, Mass., June 30, 1896. He attended the Russell Grammar School and the Rindge Manual Training School, Cambridge. When he was fifteen years old he enlisted in Co. C, 8th Reg't, M.V.M., was made Corporal, and served three years, withdrawing finally because it was necessary for him to work during the evenings.

He enlisted July, 1917, in the Aviation Corps, and entered the Ground School, M.I.T., Dec. 1, 1917. He was transferred to Princeton University, Dec. 29, 1917, and graduated with the class of Feb. 9, 1918. In the same month he was ordered to Love Field, Dallas, Tex., and thence to Kelly Field, and later to San Antonio, Tex. He was commissioned 2d Lieut., May 20, 1918, and appointed Instructor in Gosport System of Advanced Flying, at Love Field, Dallas, a few months later. He was at last account Officer in Charge of Transportation at Love Field.

JOHN FREEMAN BROWN, Jr.

First Lieutenant, A.S.A., U.S.A.

Son of John F. and Alice R. Brown; was born at Milton, Mass., May 27, 1893. He was educated at Phillips Andover Academy, and at Harvard University.

He enlisted March 31, 1917, was appointed Sergeant, and trained for Aviation at Newport News, M.I.T., and Essington, Pa. He was commissioned 1st Lieut., R.M.A., in Nov., 1917. In the same month he sailed overseas for advanced training, which he received at Issoudun and Clermont-Ferrand.

In March, 1918, he was sent to training school at Stonehenge, Eng., for a six weeks' course in night bombing. Returning to Clermont-Ferrand he was put in charge of one of the flying fields and later became Instructor there in Aerial Navigation. After the Armistice he was ordered to the 2d Army of Occupation as Navigation Officer, Dec., 1918. (Portrait on opposite page.)

HAROLD THEODORE RAMSAY

Cadet, A.S.A., U.S.A.

Son of Alexander Theodore and Beda Elizabeth (Boigeson) Ramsay; was born at Cambridge, Mass., Oct. 4, 1897. He was educated at the Huntington Preparatory School, Boston, Mass., and at the Mass. Institute of Technology. At school he played football, baseball, and hockey. He enlisted in the Air Service at Washington, D.C., on Feb. 2, 1918, and was sent to Camp Dick, Dallas, Tex. He was then ordered to Cornell University, Ithaca, N.Y., for ground-school training, and thence to Camp Dick. Subsequently he was assigned to Gerstner Field, Lake Charles, La., for work in flying. He was honorably discharged from the Service on Dec. 21, 1918, at Gerstner Field.

ROBERT LEWIS FISHER

SECOND LIEUTENANT, A.S.A., U.S.A.

SON of Samuel H. and Margaret (Sargent) Fisher; was born at New Haven, Conn., June 22, 1898. He was educated at the Taft School, Watertown, Conn.; the Thacher School, Ojai, Cal.; and at Yale College.

He enlisted in the Air Service at New Haven, Conn., on Jan. 19, 1918, and was assigned to the U.S. School of Military Aeronautics at Princeton, N.J.; after completing the course there he was sent to Payne Field, West Point, Miss., for flying instruction. Subsequently he was ordered to Wilbur Wright Field, Dayton, Ohio, for a course in Pursuit Pilot's gunnery. He was commissioned 2d Lieut. on Aug. 20, 1918. He was discharged from the Service at Garden City, N.Y., Dec. 12, 1918.

JOHN W. CRAIG

Second Lieutenant, A.S.A., U.S.A.

Son of Arthur E. and Adelaide May (Starbird) Craig; was born at Portland, Me., July 9, 1895. He was educated at the Portland Grammar and High Schools, M.I.T., and at Cornell University. He enlisted from Cornell in June, 1917, and was sent to the Officers' Training Camp at Plattsburg, N.Y. Later he transferred to Aviation, and was assigned to M.I.T., Cambridge, Mass., for ground-school work. He was trained in primary flying at Park Field, Memphis, Tenn., where he remained from Jan. 1 to June 1, 1918; and in advanced flying at Ellington Field, Houston, Tex., where he remained from June, 1918, to March, 1919. On completing the course at Ellington Field he was commissioned 2d Lieut. in April, 1918, and held as Instructor in Night Bomb Raiding.

Lieut. Craig had several narrow escapes from death. On July 9, 1918, while flying a new ship at Ellington Field, the engine refused to function at an altitude of 9000 feet. Fortunately he was able to plane to earth in safety, although his machine was badly smashed in colliding with a barbed-wire fence. On Dec. 9, 1918, he and another instructor had barely left Ellington Field when their engine stopped. In the forced landing which followed the plane was smashed and his companion was killed. Lieut. Craig escaped unhurt. He was honorably discharged at Ellington Field in March, 1919, and returned to Cornell to finish his college course.

CHARLES HENRY SMITH

SECOND LIEUTENANT, A.S., U.S.A., NINTH AERO SQUADRON

SON of Charles E. and Albertine (Flanders) Smith; was born at Nashua, N.H., April 26, 1895. He was educated at Florida Military Academy, Green Cove Springs, Fla., and at Andover Academy, Andover, Mass.

He enlisted in the U.S. Service on May 2, 1917, at Plattsburg, N.Y.; trained at Plattsburg, and at the M.I.T., where he finished his course on Dec. 18, 1917. He continued his training at Ellington Field, Houston, Tex., where he was commissioned 2d Lieut., A.S., U.S.A., on April 15, 1918, remaining there until he was sent overseas, May 15, 1918. He trained at Tours, France, and at Clermont-Ferrand during which period trouble with his eyes necessitated his transference to a bombing squadron. After some weeks of this training it was evident that his previous experience in night flying, acquired at Ellington Field, had made him available for that branch of the Service, and he was sent as a replacement to the 9th Aero Squadron, which was doing night reconnoitring for the American Aviation Headquarters.

From Aug. 1 to Nov. 11, 1918, Lieut. Smith was at the front engaged in night-patrol work, flying as Pilot with the 3d Army Corps. After the signing of the Armistice he was sent into Germany with the Army of Occupation, and has since been doing photographic work with the 9th Squadron.

Married, May 8, 1917, Marrion P. Gould.

SAMUEL GARDINER JARVIS

SECOND LIEUTENANT, A.S.A., U.S.A., ASSISTANT O.I.C.
GUNNERY DEPARTMENT, GERSTNER FIELD, LOUISIANA

SON of Leonard Jarvis, M.D., and Mabel (Howard) Jarvis; was born at Claremont, N.H., Jan. 6, 1896. He was educated at St. Paul's School, Concord, N.H., and at Trinity College, Hartford, Conn., class of 1919. He was a member of Psi Upsilon Fraternity and of the Senior Honorary Society. He played on the 'Varsity football team two years; 'Varsity track, two years; 'Varsity hockey team, one year. He left college in the middle of his senior year and enlisted on April 3, 1917.

He served in Troop B, Hartford, Conn.; then in U.S. Ambulance Corps. He was sent to M.I.T. Ground School on Nov. 3, 1917, then to Cornell, where he remained until Jan. 12, 1918. He was then transferred to Gerstner Field, La., where he qualified as Pilot, and was commissioned 2d Lieut., May 6, 1918. On May 7 he was made Instructor in Aerial Gunnery, Flying Combat, and Martin Gun. He was ordered to Dayton, Ohio, Aug. 1918, and returned to Gerstner Field in Oct. as assistant O.I.C., Aerial Gunnery. In Nov. he was attached to the French and English Commission at Camp Beauregard. He was honorably discharged at Gerstner Field, Lake Charles, La., Jan. 7, 1919.

Great-uncle in Service —

Charles Jarvis, Major, U.S.A., 9th Vermont Regiment; killed in action in Civil War.

ROGER COOLIDGE

First Lieutenant, A.S.A., U.S.A., Instructor, Third Aviation Centre, Issoudun, France

Son of Herbert and Phila E. Coolidge; was born at Watertown, Mass., Feb. 23, 1897. He was educated at St. George's School, Newport, R.I., and at Harvard College, class of 1919.

He enlisted at Cambridge, Mass., in July, 1917, and had three months' training at the M.I.T. Ground School. He was commissioned 1st Lieut. in Oct., 1917, and sailed overseas in that month. About Jan. 1, 1918, he was appointed Instructor in Bombing at Headquarters Detachment, 3d A.I.C, at Issoudun, France.

Certain extracts from Lieut. Coolidge's letters are of interest:

January 28, 1918

I have been appointed an instructor in bombing for this camp, and have had to do some intensive studying before beginning my lectures. I find your honorable professor a very busy one, for besides giving four lectures a day, I have begun flying myself, in consequence of being a member of the Training Department, and this naturally is the best part of it all. However, having taken this position, I shall remain in camp after the other fellows go, perhaps for several months.

March 23, 1918

Am back at my old job, but I certainly wish I could get into active flying work, especially now that the big German offensive is on, and while the work here is interesting, I don't intend to be a school teacher for the rest of the war. If I don't get to service flying soon, I shall try to get to the front as a bomber.

November 16, 1918

Everybody here is thinking up alibis for, "Why I did not get to the front." It is n't our fault the war stopped. The only difference to us caused by the Armistice is that we are not to fly on Sundays, which perhaps is just as well, as Sunday has been the day for getting killed . . . four last Sunday.

Quentin Roosevelt and Hamilton Coolidge were here a long time, and I knew them very well. They were in my class at college, as you may remember. They were fine fellows. Ham had gotten several Boches, I understand, and had been made a Captain.

We continue flying, when weather permits, and I am glad that I changed over from Nieuports to the de Haviland machines. The latter are easy to learn, but give one more work to manœuvre at high speed. Have just led a formation in a cross-country trip, and that keeps one busy every minute.

HERBERT FRANKLIN COMSTOCK

Second Lieutenant, A.S.A., U.S.A.

Son of John Moore and Persis (Dearborn) Comstock; was born at Chelsea, Vt., Feb. 12, 1893. He was educated at the Chelsea, Vt., High School; Manual Training High School, New Haven, Conn.; Kimball Union Academy, Meriden, N.H.; and at Dartmouth College, one year, class of 1915. He took part in track athletics, and played baseball and basket-ball.

He enlisted in the U.S. Air Service in Aug., 1917, at Sandusky, Ohio. He trained at the M.I.T. Ground School, and sailed overseas in Nov., 1917. He spent the following winter in camp at St.-Maixent; training being hindered by lack of planes. In the spring and summer of 1918 he completed his training at Châteauroux, and Issoudun. He was commissioned 2d Lieut. on May 18, 1918. For a month he was assigned to motor transport service; and he served for some time as Instructor at the Issoudun training field. While so engaged he met with a serious accident which incapacitated him from active service for some weeks. He returned to America in March, and was honorably discharged on March 17, 1919.

LELAND V. CLARK

First Lieutenant, A.S.A., U.S.A.

Son of Frederick W. and Carrie E. (Vining) Clark; was born at North Abington, Mass., June 3, 1893. He was educated in the Abington public schools, and at the M.I.T. He played on his school football team; and at Technology was a member of the tug-of-war team.

He enlisted on June 18, 1917, at M.I.T. Ground School, where he spent two months. He was then transferred to Belleville, Ill., on Aug. 18, 1917, where he made his first flight from Scott Field on Sept. 11, 1917. He was commissioned 1st Lieut. in Jan., 1918, and sailed for overseas service on the ill-fated *Tuscania,* which was torpedoed off the Irish coast on Feb. 7, 1918.

Lieut. Clark was in active service in France until the end of the war. (Portrait on opposite page.)

Grandfather in Service —

A. Elliot Vining, served in the Civil War.

THOMAS R. TARRANT

Second Lieutenant, A.S., U.S.A.

Son of Mr. and Mrs. Thomas R. Tarrant, of Brookline, Mass. He entered Dartmouth College in the class of 1918. In June, 1917, he enlisted in the American Ambulance Field Service, and sailed for France with the Dartmouth College unit. He was in the Camion Service for five months; was appointed Corporal by the French, and placed in charge of cars taking ammunition to the front. In Dec., 1917, he transferred to the Aviation Service, and trained with the French, receiving a French brevet. On May 18, 1918, he was commissioned 2d Lieut. in the U.S. Aviation Service, and served as an Instructor until the end of the war.

GELSTON TYLER KING

Second Lieutenant, A.S., U.S.A.

Son of Samuel Gelston and Alice (Tyler) King; was born at Boston, Mass., July 20, 1894. He was educated at the Noble and Greenough School, Boston, class of 1912, and Harvard College, A.B. 1916.

He attended the Officers' Training Camp at Plattsburg, in the summer of 1917, and the M.I.T. Ground School in the fall of 1917, leaving there in Dec. to continue his training at Ellington Field, Houston, Tex. He was commissioned 2d Lieut. and sent to Taliaferro Field, Fort Worth, Tex., where he completed a course in advanced flying, as Bombing Pilot. He was sent overseas in the fall of 1918, and remained at Clermont-Ferrand until after the Armistice was signed, when he was sent to pilot some of the ships, that our American aviators had left at the front, back to their bases. He returned to the U.S. in Feb., 1919. (Portrait on opposite page.)

HARRY W. SEELEY

First Lieutenant, A.S., U.S.A.

He was one of the original members of the First Aeronautical Division, called out on April 6, 1917. He received an honorable discharge from this organization to join the Lafayette Escadrille in France. He trained at Tours from Sept., 1917, to March, 1918. and at Issoudun from March to Aug., 1918. From Aug., 1918, to Nov. 11 he was employed as Ferry Pilot, flying machines to the squadrons at the front, from Orly, France. In Dec., 1918, he was assigned to the 28th Aero Squadron in the 3d Army of Occupation.

HENRY GOLDSBOROUGH MacLURE

First Lieutenant, A.S., U.S.A., One Hundred Thirty-Ninth Aero Squadron

Son of Rev. Laurens and Ella T. MacLure, of Newton, Mass.; was born at Oakhurst, Pa., Nov. 7, 1892. He attended the Newton High School, and graduated from Harvard College in 1915. At school he was captain of the track team, and at college a member of the track team and captain of the cross-country team.

In May, 1917, he attended the Officers' Training Camp at Plattsburg, and while there volunteered for the Air Service, and was one of twenty-five accepted by the Government and sent to the Royal Flying Corps School at Toronto, Can., in Aug., 1917. On Dec. 1 he was transferred to Fort Worth, Tex., to continue his training, and in Feb., 1918, he was commissioned 1st Lieut., and sent overseas, where he was attached to the 139th Aero Squadron.

On July 17, 1918, he volunteered to protect a photographic plane going from the Marne back to the Aisne, some twenty miles behind the German lines; his engine failed as they started to return and he was overtaken by an enemy plane and forced to descend. Lieut. MacLure, who was badly injured, was captured and taken to a German prison hospital at Stuttgart, Wurtemberg, where he remained until Oct. 20, when he was able to be transferred to the prison camp at Landshut, Bavaria. He was sent from there to Villingen, from which camp he was liberated with other American officers on Nov. 29, 1918. Lieut. MacLure was repeatedly asked by the Germans during his imprisonment, "How many Americans are there in France?" And he always replied, "At least five millions." He was returned through Switzerland, and sailed from Brest in Feb. 1919. He was honorably discharged at Mineola, N.Y., early in March, 1919.

HIRAM BINGHAM

LIEUTENANT-COLONEL, A.S.A., U.S.A.; COMMANDING OFFICER
THIRD AVIATION INSTRUCTION CENTRE, ISSOUDUN, FRANCE

SON of Rev. Hiram Bingham, D.D., and Clarissa (Brewster) Bingham; was born at Honolulu, Hawaii, Nov. 19, 1875. He was educated at Punahou and Andover Academy, graduated from Yale College with the degree B.A. in 1898, took an M.A. at the University of California in 1900, an M.A. at Harvard University in 1901, and a Ph.D. at Harvard in 1905. He received the degree of Litt.D. from the University of Cusco, Peru. He was Capt. of Headquarters Co. of the 10th Militia, F.A. (Yale Batteries), from June to Oct., 1916; at Tobyhanna from July to Sept., 1916.

He enlisted in the Air Service at Washington, D. C., on May 3, 1917, from New Haven, Conn. He was trained at the Curtiss Flying School, Miami, Fla., in March and April, and passed his brevet test on April 30, 1917, when he was stationed at Washington, D.C., in charge of all ground schools, from May to Nov., 1917. He took his R.M.A. at Mineola in Aug., 1917. From Nov., 1917, until March, 1918, he was in charge of the Air Personnel. He was then ordered overseas.

He was in charge of Air Personnel at Tours, France, from April to Aug., 1918. During this time he made one trip to the front on a tour of inspection to the 1st Pursuit Group, the 1st Observation Group, and the 1st Balloon Co., during the battle of Épieds, north of Château-Thierry, July 23 and 24, 1918. He was subsequently transferred to the 3d A.I.C., at Issoudun, France, where he was Commanding Officer from Aug. 27 to Dec. 26, 1918. During this time he flew Nieuport 23's and Auros. At the termination of his command at Issoudun, Lieut.-Col. Bingham received the following letter from the Chief of the Air Service of the A.E.F.:

LIEUTENANT-COLONEL HIRAM BINGHAM *December* 17, 1918
Commanding Officer
Issoudun

MY DEAR COLONEL BINGHAM:

As the school at Issoudun is about to close you will soon be relieved from your present duty as its Commanding Officer and returned to the United States. Before your departure I desire to place on record my hearty appreciation of the excellent work you did while in command of this, our largest training-centre in France. The results achieved speak for themselves and evidence the interest you took in your work and your power to inspire those who were working with you.

May I add that I was just about to recommend your promotion when the Armistice came and all advancement was stopped. While it was thus impossible to bestow upon you this well earned evidence of work well done, I want you to be assured that in my opinion it was your due.

Very truly yours
(*Signed*) MASON M. PATRICK
Major-General, U.S.A.
Chief of the Air Service

Col. Bingham returned to the U.S., and from Jan. to March, 1919, was stationed in Washington, D.C., where he was honorably discharged, March 8, 1919.

He was commissioned Capt., F.A., July 3, 1916. He was made Major, A.S., S.O.R.C., on June 6, 1917, and was promoted to the rank of Lieut.-Col., A.S.A., on Oct. 23, 1917.

Married, Nov. 20, 1900, Alfreda Mitchell. He has seven sons.

PHILIP SIMMONS YORK

SECOND LIEUTENANT, A.S., U.S.A.

SON of James M. and Emily L. York; was born at South Portland, Me., May 24, 1891. He was educated at the Mt. Herman School, and at Harvard College, class of 1918. He trained with the Harvard R.O.T.C., and was a member of Troop A, Cavalry, M.V.M. He attended the First Officers' Training Camp at Plattsburg, and enlisted there, May 14, 1917. In July, 1917, he transferred to the Aviation Section, and from Oct. to Dec., 1917, trained at the M.I.T.; from there he went to Cornell University, completing the course Jan. 19, 1918, when he was sent to Ellington Field, Houston, Tex., Jan. to May. He trained at Camp Dick, Dallas, Call Field, Wichita Falls, Tex., Wilbur Wright Field, Fort Sill, Okla., and finally at Taliaferro Field, Fort Worth, Tex., where he was stationed from Aug., 1918, to Jan., 1919. He was commissioned 2d Lieut., R.M.A., May 14, 1918. On Jan. 19, 1919, he was honorably discharged at Taliaferro Field.

HAROLD COHEN

First Lieutenant, A.S.A., U.S.A., Eighty-Fifth Aero Squadron, Fourth Observation Group

Son of Adolph and Rachel Cohen; was born at Pawtucket, R.I., Sept. 12, 1891. He was educated at Phillips Andover Academy; Sheffield Scientific School, Yale; and at the Mass. Institute of Technology.

He enlisted at Boston, Mass., on June 15, 1917; and attended the Ground School, M.I.T., from June to Aug., 1917, when he was sent to the Flying School at Belleville, Ill., in the first Squadron there trained. He was commissioned 1st Lieut., Dec. 12, 1917, and sailed overseas, to France. He trained at Issoudun from Feb. to July; was attached to the 85th Aero Squadron at St.-Jean-des-Monts, Hill 402, in Sept. and Oct., 1918; at Toul Aerodrome from Oct., 1918, to Jan., 1919. On Sept. 15, 1918, he made his first flight alone. He was honorably discharged at Garden City, N.Y., on Feb. 21, 1919.

Lieut. Cohen was the originator of the "Soldiers and Sailors Day" idea, which was carried out on July 4, 1918. On the stated day every one in Rhode Island was, at the request of the Governor, expected to write to friends in service overseas. (Portrait on opposite page.)

Brother in Service —
Dr. Bernhard Cohen, Lieut. (j.g.), U.S. Navy.

CHARLES E. LITTLE

Sergeant, A.S., U.S.A.

Son of Charles H. and Catherine H. (Wilson) Little; was born at Melrose, Mass., Jan. 6, 1896. He attended the public schools of Melrose, and entered the M.I.T., class of 1919, leaving at the end of his junior year. He enlisted on Dec. 8, 1917, and trained at the M.I.T. Ground School, at Princeton, N.J., and at Chanute Field, Rantoul, Ill., where he was appointed Sergeant. He sailed overseas in July, 1918, and was stationed near Dover, Eng., until after the signing of the Armistice. He returned to the U.S. on Dec. 3, 1918, and was honorably discharged.

WINTHROP WHEELER SPENCER

FIRST LIEUTENANT, A.S., U.S.A., TWO HUNDRED TWENTY-SECOND AERO SQUADRON; ONE HUNDRED FOURTH AERO SQUADRON, FIRST OBSERVATION GROUP

SON of Charles W. and Ethel M. (Wheeler) Spencer; was born at Cambridge, Mass., Jan. 29, 1897. He was educated at the Cambridge Latin School, the Noble and Greenough School, and at Harvard College, class of 1918.

Previous to entering the Air Service, he served for two years in the 8th Mass. Reg't, N.G., and attended the First Officer's Training Camp at Plattsburg.

He enlisted on May 12, 1917, at Boston, and had preliminary training at Selfridge Field, Mt. Clemens, Mich. During Oct., 1917, he was stationed at Mineola, N.Y. He was commissioned 1st Lieut., Oct. 5, 1917, and was ordered overseas on Nov. 2, 1917, attached to the 104th Aero Squadron. On reaching England he was transferred to the Royal Flying Corps, and from Dec., 1917, to Aug., 1918, trained at Yatesbury and Salisbury, England. From May to Aug., 1918, he was attached to the Staff, S.W. Area, R.A.F. He acted as a test pilot at No. 5 A.A.P., Bristol. He left England for France attached to the 222d Aero Pursuit Squadron, and in Sept., Oct., and Nov. was in active service in the Toul sector.

Lieut. Spencer was recommended for promotion to Capt. by the Commanding Officer of the 1st Air Dépôt, France, on Jan. 2, 1919. He returned to the U.S. in the spring of 1919; was honorably discharged from the Service, and is now engaged in business in South America.

Married, Nov. 12, 1917, Henrietta Brooks Faxon.

*CARLTON MERRILL BLISS

Second Lieutenant, A.S., U.S.A., Ninety-Second Aero Squadron

Killed in airplane accident, Nov. 14, 1918

Son of Francis Walker and Lina (Coe) Bliss; was born at Attleboro, Mass., June 9, 1895. He was educated at the Attleboro High School, and at Colby and Brown Universities. At school he played on the baseball team, track, and football teams; he was two years captain of basket-ball, the last year winning sixteen out of seventeen games played by the school. At Colby he played one year on the football team.

On May 12, 1917, he attended the Officers' Training Camp at Plattsburg. From there he was assigned to the Ground School, at the M.I.T., graduating Dec. 22, 1917. On Jan. 2, 1918, he was sent to the Flying School at Kelly Field, Tex.; and on March 9, 1918, he was commissioned 2d Lieut. in the Aviation Service. He completed his course at Ellington Field, Houston, Tex., where in Aug. he received his overseas orders, sailing Sept. 2, 1918.

On Nov. 14, 1918, Lieut. Bliss was killed while instructing a pupil, at Ford Junction Airdrome, Sussex, Eng. He was buried at Morn Hill Cemetery, Winchester, Eng.

Brother in Service —

Earle F. Bliss, Capt., 331st Reg't, F.A.; served with the 86th Division.

HAROLD TOWLE HAMBLETON

SECOND LIEUTENANT, A.S.A., U.S.A.

SON of William G. and Harriet (Towle) Hambleton, of West Newton, Mass.; was born at Plympton, Mass., June 11, 1894. He was educated in the public schools of Newton, and at Boston University. He left college after three years, to enter the theatrical profession, in which he continued until his entry into the U.S. Service.

He enlisted at Cambridge, Mass., in May, 1917, and began his training at the M.I.T. Ground School. In Nov., 1917, he sailed overseas and completed his training at Tours, Gondrecourt, and at Cazaux, France. On May 16, 1918, he was commissioned 2d Lieut. and saw active service on the western front until July, 1918. From July until the signing of the Armistice, Lieut. Hambleton was Instructor in Aerial Gunnery at the French Aviation School at Cazaux. He was brevetted by the French Government, and made an honorary member of the Aero Club of France. He returned to the U.S., and was honorably discharged at Garden City, N.Y., on Feb. 12, 1919.

Married, March 26, 1919, Marion S. Bowen.

STEDMAN HANKS

Major, A.S., U.S.A., Commanding Officer, Air Service Concentration Brigade

Son of Charles Stedman and Clarina Bartow (Shumway) Hanks; was born at Manchester, Mass., July 17, 1889. He was educated at Groton School, Groton, Mass., and at Harvard College, A.B. 1912. He played on his class baseball team, and was a member of the 'Varsity track team.

Prior to the declaration of war he trained as civilian aviator, and received Pilot's certificate from the Aero Club of America, Aug. 16, 1916; he had preliminary training at Governors Island, and at Mineola, N.Y. He enlisted May 26, 1917, at New York City, and was commissioned Captain, Signal Officers' Reserve Corps, May 26, 1917. He served as Aide to Maj.-General Geo. O. Squier, Chief Signal Officer, War Department, and subsequently, as Liaison Officer for Air Service with French, British, and Italian Aviation Missions. On Aug. 15, 1917, he was promoted to grade of Major, U.S.A., and later transferred to A.S.M.A. On Jan. 11, 1918, he passed his R.M.A. tests, at San Diego, Cal., where he was Commanding Officer of the 18th Aero Squadron. Major Hanks inspected many aviation fields, both by aeroplane and with Gen. Squier; was Commanding Officer of 2d Wing, Concentration Brigade, Aug. 19, 1918; commanded Concentration Brigade, Aug. 30, 1918, and was officer in charge of review of 6000 troops, Air Service. He was also President of Special Court-Martial; and officer in charge of demobilization of Air Service, at Kelly Field, Tex., where he was discharged under special orders from the War Department, Jan. 7, 1919.

Married, Feb. 11, 1919, Margery Hancock.

Relatives in Service —

Seven cousins in Army: 2 Major-Generals; 2 Colonels; 1 Lieut.-Colonel (flying status); 1 Captain; 1 Lieutenant, killed in action.

US

RAY A. BARNES

First Lieutenant, A.S., U.S.A.

Son of Mr. and Mrs. F. A. Barnes, of Whiting, Vt.; was born at New York City, Aug. 10, 1888. He was educated in the public schools, and at Bryant and Stratton Business College, Boston.

He enlisted at Boston on July 19, 1917, and received his ground and flying training at Mineola, N.Y., Lake Charles, La., and Ellington Field, Houston, Tex. He was commissioned 1st Lieut., Dec. 20, 1917, and has been recommended for promotion several times. While in flying service he acted in several capacities; was Officer in Charge of Officers' Club, at Gerstner Field, for nearly eight months; was Mess Officer, Cadet Mess Officer, and Tactical Officer for Cadets, at Gerstner Field. At this station he was on the overseas list at the time of the big storm that nearly wrecked the field. The Commanding Officer removed Lieut. Barnes from the overseas list to help reconstruct the field. He had charge also of all transportation to town, during the influenza epidemic in the fall of 1918, and of food supplies at Gerstner Field.

Lieut. Barnes was at last accounts still in service at Ellington Field, Houston, Tex.

RALPH D. McLAUGHLIN

Second Lieutenant, A.S.A., U.S.A., C.O. Six Hundred Thirty-Seventh Aero Squadron

Son of John Joseph and Annie Agnes (Brennan) McLaughlin; was born at Worcester, Mass., July 22, 1893. He prepared for college at St. John's High School, Worcester, and attended Holy Cross for three years.

He enlisted at Boston on June 26, 1917. He attended the Ground School of the Univ. of Texas, graduating in Sept.; he continued his training at Rockwell Field, Sept. 22 to Dec. 12, and at Kelly Field, Dec. 15 to Jan. 6, when the school was discontinued. He served as Barracks Officer, S.M.A., at Georgia Tech., Atlanta, Ga., and was subsequently assigned to the 83d Aero Squadron at Rantoul, Ill. After graduating from the Armament and Gunnery School at Fairfield, O., he was commissioned 2d Lieut. in Feb., 1918. He sailed overseas in June, 1918.

From June 15, 1918, to Jan. 22, 1919, he was at the 1st Air Dépôt, and C.O. 637th Aero Squadron. Though ordered to finish training as gunner and bomber on Aug. 3, 1918, Lieut. McLaughlin could not be spared from his duties as C.O., on account of the scarcity of Officers. When relieved from flying, he served for some time as Instructor in Engines at San Diego, Cal.

JOHN HOPKINSON BAKER

FIRST LIEUTENANT, A.S., U.S.A., COMMANDING OFFICER, THIRD AERO SQUADRON, FORT SILL, OKLAHOMA

SON of George Pierce and Christina (Hopkinson) Baker; was born at Cambridge, Mass., June 30, 1894. He was educated in the Cambridge public schools, and graduated from Harvard College in 1915. At school he played on the hockey team and rowed on the crew; at college he was on the soccer team.

He enlisted on April 23, 1917, at Washington, D.C. He was trained for Aviation at Mineola, N.Y., and was commissioned 1st Lieut. on July 30, 1917. At different periods he acted as instructor in flying, liaison with artillery, liaison with infantry, and aerial gunnery, at Mt. Clemens and Fort Sill. He was Commanding Officer of the 3d Aero Squadron, Fort Sill, Okla; went overseas in Aug., 1918, and was officer in charge of Field 1, for Biplace Machines, at the Aerial Gunnery School St.-Jean-des-Monts, Vendée, France. He returned to the U.S. and was honorably discharged.

Brothers in Service —

Edwin O. Baker, Assistant Paymaster, U.S.N.
Myles P. Baker, Harvard R.O.T.C.

PHILIP L. CARRET

First Lieutenant, A.S., U.S.A.

Son of James R. and Hannah T. Carret, of Cambridge, Mass.; was born on Nov. 29, 1896, at Lynn, Mass. He was educated at the Cambridge High and Latin School, and at Harvard College, graduating in 1917, A.B. *cum laude.* He completed one year at Harvard Graduate School of Business Administration during his senior year at college.

He trained with the Harvard R.O.T.C., Feb. 1 to July 7, 1917, and enlisted in the Aviation Service, July 7, 1917. He attended the M.I.T. Ground School for eight weeks, to Oct. 6, 1917, and sailed overseas on Oct. 26. He trained in flying at Tours and Issoudun; and had three weeks at the Gunnery School at Cazaux. On May 13, 1918, he was commissioned 1st Lieut. Having completed the full course of training for an Aviator, and having passed all tests for Chasse Pilot, he was sent to the front, 5th Air Dépôt, on Sept. 19, 1918, and was engaged in ferrying planes (binets) until Oct. 20, 1918. He returned to the U.S., and at his request he was honorably discharged on March 5, 1919, at Garden City, N.Y.

WILLARD PERRIN FULLER

CAPTAIN, A.S., U.S.A.

HE graduated from the Milton High School, Milton, Mass., in 1906, and from Harvard College in 1910. On Sept. 12, 1917, he was commissioned 1st Lieut., Aviation Section, Signal Reserve Corps. He was on duty, Personnel Section, Air Service, at Washington, D.C., and was promoted to Capt., Signal Corps, Regular Army (temp.), Feb. 19, 1918. On May 27, 1918, he was appointed Executive Officer at Mather Aviation School, Sacramento, Cal., and was stationed there until Nov. 1, 1918. Reserve Military Aviator, Oct. 28, 1918. He was appointed Assistant Executive Officer, on flying duty, at Kelly Field, San Antonio, Tex., serving from Nov. 4 to Dec. 5, 1918. On Dec. 12, 1918, he was chosen to serve on Peace Organization Committee for the Air Service, at Washington, D.C. (Portrait on opposite page.)

LAURENCE L. SHEA

SECOND LIEUTENANT, U.S. MARINE CORPS, SQUADRON 9
NORTHERN BOMBING GROUP

SON of John F. and Mary A. (Sullivan) Shea, of Somerville, Mass.; was born at Springfield, Mass., Nov. 25, 1896. He was educated at the Somerville High School and at Boston College.

He went to the Mexican Border with the National Guard in 1916, and served with that body until his transfer to Naval Aviation in July, 1917. He was assigned to the Ground School, M.I.T., in Oct., and on graduation, Nov. 20, was sent to Hampton Roads, Va., where he remained until Jan. 1, 1918. He was then ordered to Pensacola, Fla., where he qualified as Naval Aviator. On May 5, 1918, he was transferred to Miami, Fla., where he was commissioned 2d Lieut., U.S. Marine Corps, June 1, 1918. He sailed overseas July 1, and saw active service with the British First Army from Aug., 1918, to the close of the war. He was attached to Squadron 9 of the Northern Bombing Group, operating in Flanders.

Brothers in Service —

Joseph A. Shea, Sergeant-Major, 1st Division, A.E.F.
Edwin P. Shea, Private, Base Hospital 7, A.E.F.

MELVIN W. COLE

First Lieutenant, A.S., U.S.A., One Hundred Fourth Aero Squadron, Fifth Corps, Observation Group

Son of William S. and Mary A. (Wilson) Cole; was born at Boston, Mass., Feb. 28, 1893. He was educated at the Boston Latin School and at Harvard University.

He enlisted at Boston in Aug., 1917, and was sent to M.I.T. Ground School, graduating with the class of Oct. 13, 1917. He sailed overseas, and trained at Issoudun, France, 3d A.I.C., from Nov., 1917, till March, 1918; he was attached to the 2d A.I.C. at Tours, France, from March until June, 1918, and was commissioned 1st Lieut. on May 18, 1918. Lieut. Cole was again at Issoudun from June till July, 1918, and again at Tours 2d A.I.C. in July and Aug. From Sept. 7, 1918, until Dec. 31, 1918, he was attached to the 104th Aero Squadron, 5th Observation Group.

Returning to America, Lieut. Cole was discharged at Garden City, N.Y., on Feb. 19, 1919.

GARDINER FRANK GREENE

First Lieutenant, A.S.A., U.S.A.

Son of Frank Eugene and Mary A. Greene, of Monson, Mass.; was born Nov. 10, 1884. He was educated at the Volkmann School, Brookline, Mass., and at Harvard College, graduating A.B. 1907. He pitched on the 'Varsity baseball team.

He enlisted on June 17, 1917, and attended the M.I.T. Ground School from June 17 to Aug. 11, 1917. He went for further training to the Flying School at Mt. Clemens, Mich.; to Mineola, N.Y.; and to Kelly Field, Texas. He was commissioned 1st Lieut. Jan. 3, 1918, and in Feb. sailed overseas. On July 25, 1918, he graduated at the 3d Aviation Instruction Centre, Issoudun, France. At Orly he acted as Ferry Pilot and was in charge of testing machines.

Married, Sept. 10, 1910, Gladys Gibbs; has one child, Gardiner Gibbs Greene, born Sept. 16, 1914.

Brother in Service —

Robert R. Greene, Sergeant-Major, A.S., U.S.A.

DUNCAN DANA

CAPTAIN, A.S.A., U.S.A., THIRTY-SECOND AERO SQUADRON

SON of Mr. and Mrs. Paul Dana; was born Nov. 17, 1892, at New York, N.Y. He was educated at Groton School, Groton, Mass., and at Harvard College, graduating in 1914. He played end on the 'Varsity football team in 1914–15.

He was a member of Battery A, M.V.M., in 1912 and 1913. He enlisted on July 10, 1917, and received preliminary training at the M.I.T. Ground School. He sailed overseas on Oct. 26, 1917. He was stationed at Issoudun for the remainder of the war as commanding officer in charge of the shop for repairing, testing, and improving planes. He was commissioned 1st Lieut., May 16, 1918; Capt., on Sept. 30, 1918, 32d Aero Squadron. He is still in Service.

Married, June 10, 1916.

Brother in Service —

Anderson Dana, Capt., Battery A, 305th Reg't.

EDWIN THAYER MacBRIDE

First Lieutenant, A.S.A., U.S.A.

Son of Edwin Plympton and Carrie (Thayer) MacBride, of South Weymouth, Mass.; was born at South Weymouth, June 11, 1893. He was educated at Chauncy Hall School, and at the M.I.T.

He enlisted in the Harvard R.O.T.C., May, 1917. He was trained at the Cornell Ground School for two months prior to going overseas. He was assigned to the 3d A.I.C. at Issoudun, where he remained for a year and three months. He was commissioned 1st Lieut., May 16, 1918, and served as Staff Officer and Flying Officer at Issoudun, France. (Portrait on opposite page.)

ADOLPH A. KUEHL

Second Lieutenant, A.S.A., U.S.A.

Son of Adolph Alexander and Louise Marie (Pinkert) Kuehl; was born at Medford, Mass., June 29, 1894. He graduated from the Medford High School and from the electrical engineering course at Northeastern College. He enlisted in the Air Service at Boston, Mass., Nov. 8, 1917, and received his ground school training at M.I.T. and at Princeton University. He was then transferred to Camp Dick, Dallas, Tex., to Concentration Camp, and thence to the flying field at Taliaferro Field, Hicks, Tex. He was commissioned 2d Lieut. at Barron Field, Everman, Tex., on June 22, 1918, and began instructing there. After reassignment to Camp Dick, he was ordered to Payne Field, West Point, Miss., and finally to Love Field, Dallas, Tex., where he was honorably discharged, Dec. 13, 1918.

Brothers in Service —

Herman A. Kuehl; served at the Mexican Border.

Otto E. Kuehl, Supply Co. 334, Q.M.C., Army of Occupation.

LEON P. TUCK

First Lieutenant, A.S., U.S.A.

Son of Whitfield L. and Susan E. Tuck; was born at Winchester, Mass., May 25, 1891. He was educated in the Winchester public schools, and at Dartmouth College, B.S. 1915. He played football and hockey at school and college.

He enlisted at Boston, on May 2, 1917, attended the First R.O.T.C. at Sackett's Harbor, and the Cornell Ground School. Receiving overseas orders, he sailed for France in Oct., 1917, and had flying training at the 3d A.I.C. and at A.A.A.P. No. 1, in France.

In May, 1918, he was commissioned 1st Lieut., and up to Nov. 10 was on duty taking planes from England to the front. After the signing of the Armistice he was ordered back to America and was honorably discharged at Camp Devens, Mass., on May 28, 1919. (Portrait on opposite page.)

ROBERT WHITNEY

First Lieutenant, A.S., U.S.A.

Son of Mr. and Mrs. A. C. Whitney, of Lexington, Mass.; was born Dec. 8, 1895. He enlisted in the American Ambulance Field Service and sailed for France June 9, 1917. He served until Oct. 1, 1917, when he transferred to the U.S. Aviation Service, in France. He was commissioned 1st Lieut. in June, 1918, and continued in the Aviation Service in France until after the signing of the Armistice.

EVERETT PRESTON WELCH

Ensign, U.S.N.R.F.

Son of Martin L. and Margaret (Arnold) Welch, of Gloucester, Mass.; was born at Salem, Mass., on Feb. 10, 1891. He was educated at the Gloucester High School and at St. John's Preparatory School, Danvers, Mass. At school he was a member of the football, baseball, and basket-ball teams.

He enlisted in Aug., 1917, and was trained at Pensacola, Fla.; at Miami, and at M.I.T. He sailed overseas and continued his training at various stations in France and England. On Aug. 13, 1918, he was commissioned Ensign; and was still in Service at the U.S. Naval Air Station, Chatham, Mass., at last accounts. (Portrait on opposite page.)

Brother in Service —

Martin L. Welch, Private, U.S. Marine Corps; killed in action at Belleau Wood, France, June 13, 1918.

ISIDOR RICHMOND

Ensign, U.S.N.R.F.

Son of Hyman and Lena (Tanzer) Richmond; was born at Chelsea, Mass., Dec. 2, 1893. He was educated at the Revere High School and at the Mass. Institute of Technology, from which he graduated in 1916. He enlisted in the U.S.N.R.F. at Boston, Mass., July 24, 1917. From July 24 to Nov., 1917, he was held at the Boston Navy Yard, and from Feb. 18 to May 1, 1918, he was trained with the Naval Aviation Detachment at the M.I.T. He was then sent to the Naval Air Station at Pensacola, Fla., where he remained for flight training from May 4 to Aug. 17, 1918. He was transferred to the Naval Air Station, Chatham, Mass., for patrol and convoy duty, Aug. 20, 1918. He was commissioned Ensign, Aug. 6, 1918.

CHARLES RICHARD STEEDMAN

SECOND LIEUTENANT, A.S.A., U.S.A.

SON of Charles John and Mary B. (Lippitt) Steedman, of Providence, R.I.; was born at San Francisco, Cal., July 31, 1897. He was educated at St. Mark's School, Southboro, Mass., and Harvard College, class of 1920. He attended the 2d Officers' Training Camp at Plattsburg, in July, 1916, and trained with the Harvard R.O.T.C. from May 8 to Aug. 15, 1917. He enlisted in the Aviation Service on Sept. 18, 1917, at M.I.T., Cambridge, Mass. He attended the Ground School at Princeton, N.J., graduating with honor, Feb. 9, 1918, and was then sent successively to Camp Dick, Dallas, Tex., and Kelly Field, San Antonio, Tex. He was commissioned 2d Lieut., A.S., on June 5, 1918, and transferred to Camp Dick on June 10; to Payne Field, West Point, Mississippi, on July 25. He was transferred to Air Service Dépôt, Garden City, N.Y., on Oct. 3, 1918, for overseas duty; but the Armistice intervened. He was honorably discharged at Garden City, N.Y., on Dec. 11, 1918, and returned to Harvard College to finish his course.

FREDERICK H. WARNER, Jr.

First Lieutenant, A.S.A., U.S.A.

Son of Frederick H. and Eleanor (Skinner) Warner; was born at Boston in 1885. He was educated at the Volkmann School, Boston, and graduated from Harvard College, A.B. 1907. He trained with the Harvard R.O.T.C. in 1917, and attended the 2d Plattsburg Training Camp in 1917, where he was commissioned 1st Lieut. on Nov. 28, 1917. He was assigned to the Aviation Corps, University of Illinois; was transferred to Columbus, Ohio; then to Waco, Tex.; and later to Camp Greene, Charlotte, N.C., remaining about three months in each place. He was next transferred to Garden City, N.Y., for a short time, then assigned as Instructor in the Students' Army Training Corps, University of New York. (Portrait on opposite page.)

PAUL EDWIN FENTON

Second Lieutenant, A.S.A., U.S.A., One Hundred Twenty-Ninth Aero Squadron

Son of Mr. and Mrs. Edwin Wilbur Fenton; was born at Thomaston, Conn., Jan. 23, 1895. He graduated from the Thomaston High School, and from Trinity College, class of 1917. On Nov. 10, 1917, he enlisted at Boston, Mass., and after completing the ground courses at M.I.T., and at Princeton University, he was ordered to Camp Dick, Dallas, Tex. He was transferred to Scott Field, Belleville, Ill., where he was commissioned 2d Lieut., A.S.A., June 15, 1918, and passed his R.M.A. flying tests. After further training at Brooks Field, San Antonio, Tex., he acted as Flying Instructor at Taylor Field, Ala., from Aug. to Dec., 1918. He was honorably discharged at Taylor Field, Montgomery, Ala., Dec. 16, 1918.

JUNIUS ALEXANDER RICHARDS

First Lieutenant, A.S., U.S.A., Ninth Aero Squadron

Son of Reuben Francis Richards (deceased) and Maria Louisa Alexander (now Mrs. Charles Frost Aldrich); was born at Cambridge, Mass., Oct. 7, 1892. He was educated at St. Mark's School, Southboro, Mass., graduating in 1911, and at Harvard College, graduating in 1915. At St. Mark's he played on the football team. At Harvard he was one of the authors of the 1915 Hasty Pudding play. He was a member of the 1st Corps of Cadets, M.V.M., 1911–14; served with them on strike duty in Lawrence, Mass., in 1911.

He enlisted in the Aviation Service, on April 16, 1917, and trained in the first Government Aviation class at Mineola, N.Y. On July 16, 1917, he was commissioned 1st Lieut. (R.M.A.), A.S.S.R.C., and stationed as Instructor and Supply Officer, 9th Aero Squadron, at Selfridge Field, Mt. Clemens, Mich. On Nov. 20, 1917, he sailed for England, where he organized and commanded two American Aviation sections of several squadrons each, serving in conjunction with the Royal Air Force; at Grantham and Spittlegate. After five months of service at these fields, he was transferred to the American Air Service Headquarters, at London, in charge of the technical training of all enlisted men in the American Army Air Service in Great Britain. In July, 1918, Lieut. Richards was ordered to Scotland to command all American Army Aviation units there; squadrons being trained under his direction for service at the front. He was three times recommended for promotion to a Captaincy, but the promotion did not go through. He was honorably discharged at Garden City, N.Y., Dec. 23, 1918.

Recommendation for Promotion by Major Fitzgerald

Headquarters Base Section 3, Service of Supply, A.E.F.
London, *March* 27, 1918

This is to certify that 1st Lieut. J. A. Richards, Sig. R.C., A.S., is now on duty in charge of several squadrons of the U.S. Aviation Section, Signal Corps, at Spittlegate, Grantham, Eng. This officer has been under my personal observation since September, 1917. He has given every satisfaction, is a fine disciplinarian, and has his command under excellent control. He gets along exceptionally well with the British authorities, and it is my belief that he should be promoted.

I, therefore, take great pleasure in recommending that 1st Lieut. J. A. Richards, Sig. R.C., A.S., be promoted to Captain, Sig. R.C., A.S., believing that such promotion will be for the best interests of the Service.

Commendations

To Officer Commanding 24th Wing, R.A.F.

SPITTLEGATE, *May* 11, 1918

I have the honour to bring to your notice the assistance I have had from Lieut. J. A. RICHARDS, U.S.A., Aviation Section, from the date I took over this Squadron.

Owing to his ready coöperation and tact, difficulties incident to the amalgamation of British and American Sections have been successfully overcome.

I have never had occasion to take disciplinary action against any of the N.C.O.'s or men under his administration.

(*Signed*) H. S. LEES-SMITH, *Captain*
Commanding No. 37 T.S.
Royal Flying Corps

HEADQUARTERS, 24TH WING, R.A.F.
GRANTHAM, *May* 14, 1918

DEAR COLONEL MORROW:

Lieut. RICHARDS has left my Wing to report at your Headquarters, and I wish to express to you how much I and everybody have appreciated his services.

As you know four Squadrons and a Flight of Americans are in my Wing, and to get this party settled in, presented no small task, yet it was attained, and my thanks are in a great part due to the extraordinary ability and powers of coöperation of Lieut. Richards. I am

Yours sincerely

A. B. BURDETT

From Officers' Record

December 4, 1918

Lieut. RICHARDS has shown marked ability in the execution of various duties requiring executive ability and tact in connection with the U.S. Air Service Units stationed in England.

December 5, 1918

Lieut. J. A. RICHARDS has been on duty under my supervision for almost a year. He has initiative, energy, ability, and is an excellent leader of men. As C.O. of a large post, he discharges his duties most efficiently.

PAUL RICE DOOLIN

SECOND LIEUTENANT, A.S.A., U.S.A.

SON of Mr. and Mrs. William Doolin; was born at St. Albans, Vt., July 24, 1897. He was educated at St. Albans High School, at Phillips Andover Academy, graduating in 1916, and at Harvard College, class of 1920. On graduating from Andover he was made a member of the Cum Laude Society, and received the John Harvard Scholarship in the first class (1917); Detur (1917). At Phillips Academy he was a member of the track team in 1916.

He attended the R.O.T.C. at Plattsburg from July 5 to Aug. 8, 1916, and the R.O.T.C. at Harvard in April and May, 1917. He served with the American Ambulance Field Service in France, T.M. 526, from June 25 to Oct. 1, 1917, sailing with the Phillips Andover Unit.

On Oct. 1, 1917, he enlisted in the U.S. Army, at Jouaignes, France, applying for entrance to an Aviation training school. As the schools were at that time full, he was not admitted until the following spring, serving in the meantime at Field Service Headquarters, part of the time as interpreter. On March 19, 1918, he was transferred from Division Motor Transportation to the 496th Aero Squadron; and assigned to Air Service Concentration Barracks No. 3, at St.-Maixent, on March 29, as Cadet. He attended the French Flying School at Voves from May 29 to July 22, and was brevetted by the French on July 21. He had Sopwith training at the French School in Avord from Aug. 1 to Sept. 3; and Nieuport training at Issoudun, until Dec. 16, 1918. On Sept. 25, 1918, he was commissioned 2d Lieut., dating from Aug. 26, 1918. Lieut. Doolin's training was interrupted for about six weeks by ground-glass poisoning, followed by influenza. At the time of the Armistice he was just completing his training as a Combat Aviator.

Lieut. Doolin was honorably discharged at Garden City, N.Y., March 27, 1919.

ERROLD BANKS THOMAS

Second Lieutenant, A.S., U.S.A.

Son of Frank Henry and Alice Lucy (Stearns) Thomas, of Newton, Mass.; was born at Cambridge, Mass., Feb. 16, 1893. He graduated from the Cambridge Latin School in 1912, and from Harvard College in 1916. He was assistant manager of the *Harvard Crimson*, 1914–16.

He enlisted on May 12, 1917, at Plattsburg Barracks, N.Y., in the 1st Provisional Training Regiment, Battery 3. On Aug. 14, 1917, he transferred to the Aviation Section, Signal Corps, and entered active service as Flying Cadet, at the M.I.T. Ground School. He was assigned to Ellington Field, Tex., where he received primary and advanced flying instruction. He was commissioned 2d Lieut., A.S., U.S.A., April 6, 1918, and classed as Bombing Pilot, continuing his advanced training until he received overseas orders, Aug. 23, 1918. He sailed on Sept. 8, and continued his training in England. Lieut. Thomas was assigned to the 92d Squadron, at Field 1, Ford Junction, Sussex, for night bombing, and was engaged in this training at the time of the signing of the Armistice. He sailed for the U.S. on Dec. 4, 1918, and was honorably discharged at Mineola, N.Y., Jan. 4, 1919. (Portrait on opposite page.)

Married, Feb. 14, 1919, Louise Ames Smith, of Newton Centre, Mass.

ROYCE B. CRIMMIN

Cadet, A.S., U.S.A.

Son of C. Hollis and Gertrude Ethel Crimmin, of Bradford, Mass.; was born at Haverhill, Mass., Feb. 9, 1896. He was educated at the Haverhill High School, where he played basket-ball, and was a member of the track team; and at the Mass. Agricultural College, Amherst, Mass. He entered the Air Service on May 25, 1918, at Cambridge, Mass. After finishing the course at the M.I.T. Ground School he was sent to the concentration camp at Camp Dick, Dallas, Tex., with Squadron 11. From there he was ordered to Kelly Field No. 2, San Antonio, Tex.

*GEORGE W. KILLORIN

SECOND LIEUTENANT, A.S., U.S.A.

Killed in airplane accident, Sept. 27, 1918

SON of Mr. and Mrs. G. W. Killorin, of Wakefield, Mass. He graduated from Holy Cross College in 1917. In June, 1917, he enlisted in the Air Service, and attended the M.I.T. Ground School. He continued his training at Ellington Field, Houston, Tex. In April, 1918, he was commissioned 2d Lieut., and appointed Instructor of Aerial Gunnery at Taliaferro Field, Fort Worth, Tex. While acting in this capacity he was killed in an airplane accident at Taliaferro Field, on Sept. 27, 1918. (Portrait on opposite page.)

BRICE S. EVANS

PRIVATE, FIRST CLASS, A.S., U.S.A.

SON of Charles R. and Henrietta (Thompson) Evans, of Watertown, Mass.; was born at Boston, Mass., March 16, 1888. He was educated at the Boston Latin, the Volkmann, and the De Meritte Schools; and at Amherst College. In 1906 he was runner-up in the Canadian Golf Championship, and Schoolboy Golf Champion. He enlisted at Boston, Mass., on Jan. 24, 1918. From June 1 to July 3 he was in training at Camp Dick, Dallas, Tex., and from July 5 to Sept. 7 at the M.I.T., Cambridge, Mass. He was assigned to the Ground School at Cornell University, where he remained from Sept. 8 to Nov. 6, 1918. He was transferred to Camp Dick, Dallas, Tex., on Nov. 8, and was honorably discharged from the Service there, Dec. 4, 1918.

Married, March 5, 1919, Dorothy Ruggles.

FRANK EMMONS ALEXANDER

First Lieutenant, A.S., U.S.A.

Educated at St. George's School, Concord, N.H., and at Harvard College, class of 1919. He enlisted in the Aviation Corps in June, 1917, and was sent to the M.I.T. Ground School. He finished his training at Belleville, Ill., and was commissioned 1st Lieut., A.S., U.S.A. He was appointed Instructor, first at Gerstner Field, Lake Charles, La., then at Call Field, Wichita Falls, Tex. In Sept., 1918, he sailed overseas, and was in training for a Pursuit Pilot, at Issoudun, France, when the Armistice was signed. (Portrait on opposite page.)

DWIGHT FLETCHER BARNES

Second Lieutenant, A.S., U.S.A.

Son of J. Fletcher and Anna E. (Baldwin) Barnes, of Bedford, Mass.; was born at Hubbardston, Mass., Jan. 23, 1890. He was educated at Mt. Hermon School, Mass., and at the Mass. Agricultural College, Amherst.

He enlisted, Nov. 3, 1917, and attended the M.I.T. Ground School; going from there to Cornell University. He trained in flying at Gerstner Field, Lake Charles, La.; and had advanced training at Call Field, Wichita Falls, Tex.; at Wilbur Wright Field, Dayton, Ohio; at Post Field, Fort Sill, Okla.; and at Taliaferro Field, Fort Worth, Tex. He was commissioned 2d Lieut., May 14, 1918. He sailed for France, and was stationed at Issoudun for final training. He was attached to the 186th Aero Squadron, 1st Army Observation Group. After the signing of the Armistice he was sent into Germany with the 3d Army of Occupation.

Married, Dec. 23, 1916, Mary Baker.

HAROLD ARTEMAS PACKARD

First Lieutenant, A.S., U.S.A.

Son of Frederick C. and Mary (Winchester) Packard; was born at Roslindale, Mass., Aug. 10, 1894. He graduated from the Boston Latin School, and from Harvard College (with honors) in 1915. He enlisted in the U.S.A. in April, 1917, and was sent to Fort Monroe, Va., and commissioned 2d Lieut. (provisionally), on Oct. 26, 1917. In Jan., 1918, he was commissioned 2d Lieut., and in March, 1st Lieut. He volunteered for the Air Service in May, 1918, and trained at Langley Field, Old Point Comfort, Va., and at Selfridge Field, Mt. Clemens, Mich. On Sept. 1 he was ordered overseas, and continued his training at Tours, France; he was later attached to the 88th Squadron, and ordered to the front just at the time of the signing of the Armistice. Lieut. Packard was then assigned to the Army of Occupation. Subsequently he spent three months at the University of Poitiers, France, after which he served in the Department of Rents, Requisition, and Claims. Lieut. Packard had two brothers also in the Service. (Portrait on opposite page.)

LAWRENCE EARLY

Second Lieutenant, A.S., U.S.A.

Son of Bernard and M. Alice Early; was born at Newton, Mass., July 27, 1896. He was educated at the Newton High School, and at Holy Cross College. He enlisted in the Air Service at Boston, Aug. 20, 1917. He attended the Ground Schools at the M.I.T., and at Princeton University. He trained in flying at Taliaferro Field, Fort Worth, Tex., and at the Gunnery Schools, Taliaferro Field, and Wilbur Wright Field, Dayton, Ohio. He then proceeded overseas, and was assigned to the 3d A.I.C. at Issoudun, France, for advanced training. He was subsequently transferred to the school at St.-Jean-des-Monts. He was then detailed as Staff Pilot to the 4th Artillery Aerial Observers' School at Meucon, France. He was commissioned 2d Lieut., June 17, 1918, and was honorably discharged at Garden City, N.Y., Feb. 8, 1919.

*LEROY AMOS SWAN

Second Lieutenant, A.S., U.S.A.

Killed in airplane accident, June 19, 1918

Born at Norwich, Conn., June 5, 1894. He was educated at the Norwich Free Academy, and at the Mass. Institute of Technology, class of 1917. He entered the Service at the M.I.T., Oct., 1917, and attended the Army Aviation School. He trained at Wilbur Wright Field, Dayton, Ohio, and was there commissioned 2d Lieut., A.S., Signal Corps. On June 19, 1918, he was killed at Wilbur Wright Field, when his machine collapsed. (Portrait on opposite page.)

DAVID W. GORDON

Second Lieutenant, A.S., S.C., Second Provisional Squadron, Ellington Field, Houston, Texas

Son of William W. and Harriet (Covil) Gordon; was born at Hazardsville, Conn., May 31, 1894. He attended the Central High School, Springfield, Mass., where he was president of the senior debating society and captain of the crew. He graduated from Wesleyan University, Middletown, Conn., where he was a member of the football and track teams. He enlisted at Boston, Mass., May 11, 1917, with the Medical Corps, Ambulance Section, and transferred from the station at Allentown, Pa., to Army Aviation, at Mineola, N.Y., Aug. 29. He attended the Ground School at the M.I.T., from Nov. 3, 1917, to Jan. 12, 1918. He continued his training at Kelly Field, San Antonio, Tex., from Jan. 18 to April 5; there he was commissioned 2d Lieut. on April 5, 1918, and was sent to Camp Dick, Dallas, Tex. He was stationed at Hoboken, N.J., awaiting overseas orders, from May 5 to May 29, and then sent to Ellington Field, Houston, Tex., for advanced training in bombing. He remained there from June, 1918, to Jan. 11, 1919, when he was honorably discharged.

Married, Sept. 2, 1918, Doris Clark.

Grandfather in Service —

Andrew Gordon, served in the Civil War.

JOSEPH V. HUGHES

Second Lieutenant, A.S., U.S.A.

Son of John L. and Mary E. (Ford) Hughes; was born at Brighton, Mass., July 15, 1894. He was educated in the public schools of Brighton, and at Boston College. He enlisted on July 2, 1917, at the M.I.T. In Sept., 1917, he continued his training at Wilbur Wright Field, Dayton, Ohio; he was transferred to Ellington Field, Houston, Tex., in Jan., 1918. He served as Instructor at Camp Dick, Dallas, Tex., at Call Field, Wichita Falls, and at Love Field, Dallas. He was commissioned 2d Lieut. in April, 1918. In Sept., 1918, he sailed overseas and continued his training in France. He returned to the U.S. in May, 1919, and was honorably discharged in June, 1919. (Portrait on opposite page.)

CHARLES LESTER MORSE

Second Lieutenant, A.S.A., U.S.A.

Son of Mr. and Mrs. Charles Morse, of Lancaster, N.H.; was born at Colebrook, N.H., June 2, 1893. He was educated in the public schools of Lancaster, N.H., at the Lancaster Academy, and at the Mass. Institute of Technology. At the Lancaster Academy he belonged to the baseball, basket-ball, football, and track teams, making a record in the 100-yard dash, and in a high jump, of five feet, three inches. At the M.I.T. he was a member of the class baseball, football, basket-ball, and track teams, and of the 'Varsity basket-ball team. He enlisted in the Air Service, July 17, 1917, at Mineola, N.Y. He was assigned to the Cornell University Ground School, whence he proceeded to Gerstner Field, Lake Charles, La., and then to Camp Dick, Dallas, Tex. He was subsequently transferred to Taliaferro Field, Fort Worth, Tex., where he was detailed as Instructor in Aerial Gunnery. He was then ordered to the School of Aeronautical Engineering at the M.I.T., and later to McCook Field, Dayton, Ohio.

EDWIN LAWRENCE NOBLE

SECOND LIEUTENANT, A.S., U.S.A.

SON of William F. and Sarah (Savage) Noble, of Newton Centre, Mass.; was born Aug. 23, 1891. He was educated at Andover Academy, graduating in 1912, and at Yale University, graduating in 1915. He enlisted in the Air Service in 1917, and trained at the Ground School at Columbus, Ohio. In Nov., 1917, he sailed for France and continued his training at Issoudun. He was commissioned 2d Lieut. in May, 1918. Lieut. Noble was taken ill with influenza, which for a long period prevented him from flying, and kept him from seeing active service at the front. He was attached to the Requisition and Claims Department, and after the signing of the Armistice was stationed at Tours, and at Villel, France. He was honorably discharged in Sept., 1919. He has since joined the Kosciusko Escadrille in Poland, as pilot, and is engaged in fighting the Bolsheviki forces. (Portrait on opposite page.)

Brother in Service —

Arthur W. Noble, Corp., 302d Inf., 76th Division, A.E.F.

ROBERT A. SLATER

SECOND LIEUTENANT, A.S.A., U.S.A.

SON of Robert and Martha (McLennon) Slater, of South Royalton, Vt.; was born at Charlestown, Mass., Aug. 24, 1895. After graduating from the South Royalton High School, he attended Denison University, Granville, Ohio, for one year. At both institutions he played baseball, basket-ball, and football. He enlisted in the Aviation Service at Boston, Mass., Oct. 14, 1917, and reported for active duty Dec. 15, 1917, at the M.I.T. He was transferred to the Ground School at Cornell University, Ithaca, N.Y., on Jan. 7, 1918, and was ordered to Dallas, Tex., March 22, 1918. He was sent to Kelly Field, San Antonio, Tex., April 23, and after completing his training there, was commissioned 2d Lieut., Oct. 18, 1918. He was subsequently assigned to North Island, San Diego, Cal., for scout flying. On Nov. 28 he took part in a flight in which 212 planes were in the air at one time. He was honorably discharged at San Diego, Cal., Jan. 8, 1919.

*WOLDEMAR E. CROSSCUP

ENSIGN, U.S.N.R.F.

Killed in seaplane accident, July 6, 1918

BORN Dec. 30, 1895. He attended the Quincy (Wollaston) Grammar School, and Wilbraham Academy. He was later associated with his father in the printing business. Following the declaration of war, he enlisted in the Aviation Service, and was assigned to the Squantum Aviation Field, in May, 1917. After the breaking-up of the Squantum Field he was transferred to Pensacola, Fla. He was ordered overseas in Feb., 1918, and served in France until July, 1918. He was killed in a seaplane crash, on July 6, 1918, at Moutchic-Lacanau. He was buried at Lacanau, Gironde, France. (Portrait on opposite page.)

WESLEY L. KEOUGH

SECOND LIEUTENANT, A.S., U.S.A.

SON of Henry Edward and Charlotte Adaline (Rogers) Keough of Lowell, Mass.; was born at Chelsea, Mass., Jan. 23, 1891. He graduated from the Winthrop High School, Winthrop, Mass., and from the Lowell Textile School in 1910. From 1911 to 1915 he served in K Co., 6th Inf., Mass. N.G. He enlisted at Plattsburg, N.Y., May 14, 1917, and attended the 1st Officers' Training Camp. He was then transferred to the M.I.T. Ground School, and subsequently served as a cadet at Kelly Field, San Antonio, Tex. He was commissioned 2d Lieut. on Feb. 14, 1918. He served as Instructor in flying at Kelly Field, and later at South Field, Americus, Ga. He was ordered to Garden City, N.Y., for overseas service, but was prevented from sailing by the signing of the Armistice. He was then ordered to duty at Rockwell Field, San Diego, Cal., where at his own request he was discharged, Jan. 9, 1919.

*HENRY SOUTHER

MAJOR, A.S., U.S.A., SIGNAL OFFICERS' RESERVE CORPS

Died in Service, Aug. 15, 1917

BORN at Boston, Mass., Sept. 11, 1865. He was educated in the Boston public schools, and at the Mass. Institute of Technology, graduating in 1887. After leaving the M.I.T. he took post-graduate work in metallurgy in Germany, and was subsequently associated with the Pennsylvania Steel Co., at Steelton, Pa. He established a testing laboratory at Hartford, Conn., for commercial work. He enlisted in the U.S. Service, in 1917, and was commissioned Major in the Signal Officers' Reserve Corps, and was appointed Assistant Chief of Division of Aviation.

Major Souther died at Fort Monroe, Va., Aug. 15, 1917, after a surgical operation. (Portrait on opposite page.)

FRANK NICHOLS FERRONE

ENSIGN, U.S.N.R.F.

SON of Michael A. and Annie A. Ferrone, of Jamaica Plain, Mass.; was born at East Boston, Aug. 21, 1889. He was educated at the Mechanic Arts High School, Boston, and at the Thomson Houston Engineering School.

He enlisted in the Naval Air Service at Boston, April 24, 1917, and was assigned to the Ground School, M.I.T. For flight training, he was sent to Pensacola, Fla. He was commissioned Ensign, Aug. 27, 1918, and was subsequently attached to the Naval Air Service Headquarters, London, Eng.

Ensign Ferrone was placed on inactive duty at Boston, June 15, 1919.

ARTHUR PARKER TEULON

LIEUTENANT (*j.g.*), U.S.N.R.F., ATTACHED TO TWO HUNDRED TWENTY-EIGHTH SQUADRON, SEVENTY-THIRD WING, R.A.F.

SON of Arthur Mitchell and Ruth (Leavitt) Teulon, of West Newton, Mass.; was born at Dorchester, Mass., Sept. 3, 1893. He graduated from the Newton High School, where he was a member of the track and hockey teams; he was also a member of the swimming team of the Newton Y.M.C.A.

He enlisted in the U. S. Naval Aviation Service, at the Boston Navy Yard, on May 23, 1917, and received his ground training at the M.I.T., when he was sent to Pensacola, Fla., for flying training. He was commissioned Ensign, Dec. 27, 1917. In Jan., 1918, he sailed overseas, and was stationed at Great Yarmouth, Eng., where he was attached to the 228th Squadron, 73d Wing, R.A.F., and engaged in patrolling and scouting over the North Sea from Jan. to July 1, 1918. For some time he was detained in the Naval Hospital with an attack of influenza.

On Aug. 1 he was detached from the British Service and sent to the U.S. Naval Air Station at Lough Foyle, Ireland, where he remained as Squadron Commander until Jan. 1919. He was commissioned Lieut. (j.g.), Oct. 1, 1918. On April 7, 1919, Lieut. Teulon was placed on the inactive service list at Washington, D.C. He was cited for bravery while stationed at Pensacola, for risking his life by swimming out into the bay to rescue some Government property. In April, 1918, he was recommended for promotion for the good work performed in hunting the German submarines in the North Sea.

A DETACHMENT OF FIFTEEN AVIATORS

UNITED STATES NAVAL RESERVE FLYING CORPS
AT ROEHAMPTON, LONDON, ENGLAND
DECEMBER, 1, 1917

THESE fifteen Americans (the officer in the centre is an Englishman) entered the U.S. Service as Seamen, 2d Class, U.S. Naval Reserve, early in 1917.

Standing — Left to right

EUGENE I. WOLFE, *Baltimore, Maryland*
ALFRED GARDNER, *Garden City, New York*
RALPH HAWTHORNE NORRIS, *Chelsea, Massachusetts*
MAX J. BAEHR, *St. Louis, Missouri*
DONALD H. MERRILL, *Cambridge, Massachusetts*
R. L. PIPER, JR., *Tyrone, Pennsylvania*
GEORGE DANA ANDERSON, *Somerville, Massachusetts*
ALBERT A. BAILEY, *Norfolk, Virginia*
THOMAS R. PUNNETT, *New York, New York*

Seated — Left to right

ADDISON C. BURNHAM, JR., *Newton Centre, Massachusetts*
THOMAS E. MCCRACKEN, *Brooklyn, New York*
PHILIP J. BARNES, *Minneapolis, Minnesota*
ENGLISH OFFICER, *London, England*
N. J. LEARNED, *Elmira, New York*
JOSEPH WARREN HOMER, JR., *Brookline, Massachusetts*
HARRISON S. GOODSPEED, *Grand Rapids, Michigan*

August 20th, 1917, they were enrolled in the Naval Aviation Detachment Corps, Massachusetts Institute of Technology, Cambridge, Massachusetts, at that time a Ground School for Aviators. In October, 1917, they were sent to England, some of them going voluntarily to "learn to fly 'blimps'" (dirigibles).

They left Boston October 15, and New York, October 27, 1917.

They were the first U.S. Aviators who went in a body to England to become pilots and assist the Royal Naval Air Service in observation and convoy work off the English coast.

(This photograph was taken December 1, 1917, by F. N. Birkett, London.)

WINGED FORCES OF THE U.S. NAVY

By Lieutenant Clifford A. Tinker

The building-up, from a small nucleus, of a Naval Aviation Corps with a personnel, in service and training, almost as large as was the entire Navy before the war; the building of scores of stations in Europe as well as in America; the exploits of naval aviators in the war zone, make up one of the most interesting chapters of America's part in the war.

Previous to the declaration of war, the United States Navy maintained the Naval Air Station at Pensacola, Florida, with a complement of thirty-eight naval aviators and one hundred and sixty-three enlisted men, with twenty-two seaplanes, five kites, and two free balloons. A certain amount of flight training and mechanical training was given at this station, but, in a word, Pensacola with its small personnel and material summed up most of the aviation activities of the United States Navy.

The remarkable growth of the Service from April, 1917, to Armistice Day, in November, 1918, reflects the greatest credit on the officers in charge of Naval Aviation.

Captain Irwin gathered around him as his aides and executives a group of enthusiastic naval aviators, selected from those at Pensacola, who handled the departments over which they had charge with extraordinary ability, and pushed the work with untiring energy, so much so that at the close of hostilities there had been enrolled and trained over fifteen hundred naval aviators, over thirteen hundred ground officers, and over thirty-five thousand enlisted men; and there were in training four thousand flight officers and ten thousand enlisted men. There were in commission, in round numbers, fourteen hundred seaplanes and airplanes and about three hundred lighter-than-air craft. There had been sent abroad over twelve hundred officers and nineteen thousand enlisted men for aviation, together with three hundred and eighty-eight seaplanes, one hundred and forty airplanes, and forty-two kite balloons. At the close of hostilities there was, either in Europe or *en route*, a sufficient number of seaplanes to supply all our stations abroad, and to replace losses and crashes which might occur during the year 1919.

It is a fact worth recalling that the Aviation Detachment which left the United States in May, 1917, in charge of Commander Kenneth Whiting, U.S.N., was the first detachment of any American armed force to set foot in Europe after the United States entered the war. Closely following the arrival of Commander Whiting and his organization, Captain Hutch I. Cone and a board of officers reached France for the purpose of studying the types of planes in use by our allies and formulating methods of coöperation with the Naval Aviation Forces of England, France, and Italy, and our policy abroad was based upon the report of this board.

At the end of the fighting the number of stations in this country had increased from one to seven training stations, ten patrol stations, nine rest and refuelling stations, two experimental stations, and a number of additional stations for various purposes had been authorized and were under construction. These stations extended from North Sydney, Nova Scotia, to Coco Solo, Canal Zone, and a large station was located at San Diego, on the Pacific Coast. In Europe there had been established and were in commission twenty-eight stations, two training stations, and twelve bombing squadrons located in England, Ireland, France, and Italy, including a Marine Aviation station at the Azores.

To the flyers themselves too much praise cannot be given. They are the men who, by the very nature of their duty, were called upon to exhibit not only the highest qualities as naval officers, but the utmost skill and daring as aviators. They were in competition with the world's best, but they did not suffer in the least by the comparison. Aside from the dogged, monotonous work of patrol, they proved themselves heroes in action. Many of them were decorated by the Allied Powers of Great Britain, France, Belgium, and Italy.

Admiral Sims sums up the place held by our naval aviators in the war in the following despatch sent to Washington at the cessation of hostilities:

> Please express to the Naval Aviators of America my most sincere appreciation of their courageous and loyal performance of duty at home and abroad throughout the war. Their brilliant exploits, their determination to win, will ever remain one of the highest tributes to American manhood. The performance of duty of these young Naval Aviators under my command has not only been in keeping with the very best traditions of our Naval Service, but has in addition won for America the enthusiastic praise of her allies.

The real measure of success of Naval Aviation was, of course, its ability to engage in actual war operations. This was done on a large scale. In home waters new stations were put into commission in order to cover by patrol all the waters threatened by the enemy submarines. These patrols covered all the important harbors and most of the coast from the north of Nova Scotia to the waters at the mouth of the Rio Grande. Each seaplane on patrol covered an area of three thousand square miles, and it is interesting to note that the total distance covered by naval coastal patrols in American waters during the month of August, 1918, was 360,000 miles; in September, 480,000 miles were covered, and in October, 465,000 miles.

The seaplane patrols and convoys were especially successful. After the installation of our seaplane patrols and during thousands of miles of convoy, only one ship in such convoys was ever successfully attacked by enemy submarines. Prior to our patrols on the French coast the sinkings by the enemy submarines averaged one Allied ship each day, but in the ten months our patrols were active, only three ships were lost on the patrol area between Penmarch and Ile d'Yeu, a ninety-nine per cent reduction. Credit is given us by the British, French, and Italians of attacking ninety-five per cent of all submarines sighted on our patrols, of damaging forty-five per cent, and sinking twenty-five per cent of those attacked. Many mines were also sighted and destroyed, which is another important part of the work performed by our seaplanes in the war zone.

During the Great War, in the North Sea sector, "lighter than air" was one of the most important fleet adjuncts in use by the British, and on more than one occasion their use by the Germans baffled the best-laid plans of the Admiralty. No less an authority than Admiral Jellicoe gives to the airship the credit of the German escape at Dogger Bank; or, if not the entire credit, then the most important place in the scheme of observation and intelligence used by the Hun in that epoch-making battle.

The German Zeppelin was in no sense a failure. Scouting and observation for the High Seas Fleet was only a part of its function. They maintained regular patrols over the North Sea and kept a very close watch of the Allied navies. They made possible the destroyer raids on Yarmouth and other English coastal towns, working in close touch with the Hun flotillas, giving ample information regarding the location of the British in order that the attacks could be made and a get-away successfully accomplished before the possible arrival of the Allied ships.

The frightful Zeppelin raids over London were a side issue with the German airship fleet. As soon as the British developed sufficient anti-aircraft defence to push the "Zepps" up to a high ceiling and make inland raids particularly dangerous, the giant airships were recalled to their main duty with the fleet; the Germans being sensible in this respect that they could not afford to lose their supremacy in naval observation, however enticing other activities might be. Before the installation of the London aerial defences, Zeppelins were able to fly as low as 9000 feet above the city and plant bombs with astonishing accuracy.

The British, early in the war, began a systematic development of the lighter-than-air section of the Royal Air Force. The coast of Scotland and England, being the most exposed portion of the British Isles, and also the gathering-place of the major portion of the Allied fleets, naturally provided the location for the large air stations to which airships were assigned. And at these stations were posted our own airship pilots, first as students, and then, as they progressed in skill, as pilots and captains.

Free balloons, kite balloons, dirigibles, both non-rigid and semi-rigid, and the right type of airship were among the list of ships and lighter-than-air craft with which our pilots became experts. Parachute jumping, bombing, patrolling, scout duty, convoying, navigation and signalling, and squadron manœuvres were among the arduous tasks which these young men were obliged to perform, and they became so skilful as to excite the admiration of their commanding officers as well as their comrades.

Letter after letter of commendation and citations with decorations were won by the American lighter-than-air pilots, although their exploits have seemingly never come to light, but have been overshadowed by the speedier and more spectacular heavier-than-air craft. In a letter to Admiral Sims, dated June 22, 1918, Brigadier-General E. M. Maitland, Superintendent of Airships, writes:

It is desired to bring before your notice the most excellent work which has been done by the United States officers who are lent for training. Since their graduation all these officers have done very useful patrol work. . . . The work done by Ensign Barnes has been specially noticeable; the officer, besides being the Captain of his ship, is also in charge of a mooring-out station, which is run very efficiently and to the present station's entire satisfaction, and it is suggested that its officer deserves to receive special recognition.

Below is given the actual number of hours flown by each of these officers, including the times as pilot and passenger, for your information:

	Hours	*Min.*
Ensign G. D. Anderson	368	0
Ensign H. E. Goodspeed	114	41
Ensign P. J. Barnes	254	20
Ensign L. A. Pope	30	30
Ensign R. L. Piper	245	35
Ensign N. J. Learned	214	40
Ensign J. W. Homer	301	10
Ensign D. H. Merrill	90	45
Ensign R. H. Norris	143	15

Yours faithfully

E. H. MAITLAND

With about half the complement strength, Barnes (in May and June, 1918) operated the Royal Air Station at Lowthrope, Yorkshire, to the utmost satisfaction of the Royal Air Force, for which success he was named to command His Majesty's airship C-Star-9, and after a brilliant series of exploits with this ship he was further honored by the Admiralty.

During this time Barnes was the first pilot to fly a single-engine airship for a period of more than twenty-four hours, winning the world's record by a non-stop flight of twenty-five hours and forty minutes. Shortly after, not being content with this record, he increased it by making a sustained flight of thirty hours and eighteen minutes, a feat which brought a special commendation from the Commanding General. While convoying ships, in which he was engaged for a total of more than two hundred hours without the loss of a single ship from any cause, Barnes destroyed nine enemy mines which had been planted in the ship-lanes off the British coast.

[It is of interest to note in the above record of hours flown that Ensign G. D. Anderson heads the list, and that Ensign J. W. Homer ranks second in the list. *Ed.*]

*JOSEPH WARREN HOMER, Jr.

ENSIGN, U.S.N.R.F.C.

Died of pneumonia, Nov. 9, 1918

SON of Joseph Warren and Constance (Smith) Homer; was born at Roxbury, Mass., April 11, 1897. He attended the Brookline public schools; the Stone School, Boston; entered the Mass. Institute of Technology in the class of 1919; played on his class football team, rowed on his class crew, was associate editor of *The Tech*, and member of S.A.E.Fraternity. On Aug. 14, 1916, he enrolled in the Civilian Naval Training Cruise on U.S.S. *Virginia*, returning to M.I.T. in Sept. to remain until Dec., when he left to enter the Potomska (Cotton) Mills, New Bedford.

On June 26, 1917, he enlisted in the U.S. Naval Reserve; on Aug. 20 he joined the Aviation Detachment at M.I.T., and in Oct. was one of fifteen men who volunteered to go to England to learn to fly "blimps" (dirigibles), sailing Oct. 27, 1917. He and his associates were the first U.S. aviators to land in a body in England to become pilots, and assist the Royal Naval Airship Service. During Nov. and Dec. he trained at Aviation Ground Schools at Roehampton and Cranwell. In March, 1918, he received his Pilot's license and was ordered to the Royal Air Force Station, Polegate, Sussex, for "active duty," and engaged in observation and convoy work over the English Channel. He was twice lost in fog, once blown sixty miles north of his course, his airship being damaged after landing, and again blown eighty miles south, landing "for a few minutes" on the north coast of France. May 16, 1918, he was commissioned Ensign.

On Aug. 13 he was ordered to the R.A.F. Station at Portsmouth, then to Howden, East Yorks, and on Aug. 23 to East Fortune, Scotland, flying over the North Sea. In Oct. he returned to London, and engaged in studying the design and construction of airships. While there he was taken ill with influenza, and died of broncho-pneumonia at the U.S. Naval Hospital, London, on Nov. 9, 1918. On Dec. 24, 1918, he was buried at Mount Auburn, Cambridge, Mass., following an impressive memorial service conducted by the Rev. Abbot Peterson at Brookline, Mass.

The following extracts from Ensign Homer's letters give an excellent idea of the dirigible pilot's training in England:

London, *Sunday, Dec.* 9, 1917

We have made our solo balloon flights, and are now ready for balloon pilot's licenses. It was a lot of fun going up in a balloon all alone, 'way up over the clouds 4000 or 5000 feet where you can't see the earth or anything. That is n't high, but the balloons we use are n't much good except for training. From now on we will be using the real blimps.

The other night we went up for a night flight, and went over London. We got home about midnight, and about three hours later the air raid of twenty-five gophs started. . . .

Our job will be to escort transports and supply ships through the danger zone into port, we going out to meet the ships in our airships. . . .

The real front is only about eighty miles from here, and yesterday we heard the guns thundering all day. . . . But you would never know there was a war here — it's *so* peaceful. . . .

And beyond the hills the War, in all its horror of the latest enormous Hun offensive — I don't feel a *bit* like killing any one, but in a few minutes an orderly will report my ship ready, and I'll slide over the hills and away to the Channel to hunt for U-boats.

Polegate, *May* 12, 1918

Yesterday, I went on patrol at 6 A.M. and got into the fog (we are almost always out of sight of land) and flew around for about four hours. I was just going to lay a course for home when I sighted land to the south where it ought *not be*. On investigation it was Cape Barfleur. So I flew inland until I reached a French Airship Station and landed for a few minutes. . . . Then I went home (about eighty miles, arriving at 7 P.M. thirteen hours over the water). It was just a matter of sticking to it. . . . Coming home I laid a course, and arrived within two miles of the place I headed for, steering seventy miles out of the eighty by compass only, so you see you can get along pretty well without seeing land. . . . Am Captain of a ship of my own now, her name is "Sea Scout Zero 39" and she has "S S Z 39" in enormous letters on the envelope. . . .

Have been for five hours without seeing anything except gray sea below and gray fog all around — and have come home when it was so thick that I could n't see the station a *quarter* of a mile off — just had to find the beach, then find the town I knew, then follow roads and railways about a hundred feet off the ground until I got to the station.

On Sept. 8, 1918, he wrote from East Fortune, where he had been made 3d Officer of the R 29:

Skipped all intervening types of ships and have gone from the smallest to the largest ship in the service. The C.O. of my ship is a peach of a boy and I'm all happy. It seems funny to go to bed a thousand feet up in the air! But very nice. . . . We do patrols of one or two days usually. . . .

Previous to this, his Commanding Officer had written on Aug. 17:

GROUP HEADQUARTERS, ROYAL AIR FORCE
WARSASH, HANTS

MY DEAR ENSIGN HOMER,

It is with much regret that you leave this Command to go to bigger ships. However, it is all for your good, and that is the only consolation that I have personally. During the time you have been under my command at Polegate and the Mooring-out Stations you have set a very high example in all-round efficiency in anti-submarine patrols and you are destined to do big things, I think, before this war is over. Au revoir, and the best of good luck go with you. I am

Yours very sincerely

FRASER
Lt.-Col., R.A.F.

On Sept. 20, Homer wrote from East Fortune to Lieut. W. A. Edwards, U.S.N., Aide for Aviation, Grosvenor Gardens, London, saying:

I am getting a good deal of experience in the handling of the Rigid, but Major Thomas thinks that I could learn more of the construction by going for short periods to other stations devoted entirely to constructional work; especially to Barlow, where the new R 34 is building, and to White City where the fabric work is done.

On Oct. 8 he was ordered to Wormwood Scrubbs, London, where he had an opportunity to follow the construction of the R 34, destined to make the famous trans-Atlantic flight. And it is of interest to note that when this British airship landed at Roosevelt Field, one of its officers conveyed a message of sympathy to the parents of Ensign Homer, testifying to the appreciation of those that had trained with their son in England.

The final extract is Ensign Homer's description of a sunrise viewed from the air:

The sunrise over the clouds is gorgeous — sublime — incomparable — untellable. One does n't feel very poetic after one has been out in the darkness and fog all night — but when the sun rises and lights up the tops of the mist one forgets the war, the cold, the cramped legs, and glories in the beauty of the scene. The sun comes up out of its cloud of gray, turning it to a shell-pink. Then, as it climbs higher, it sets the whole sea of clouds sparkling and seething — a myriad of rainbows, a mass of majestic, rolling, heaving beauty. There is no use in my trying to explain it — one must be in it and surrounded by it — the only bit of humanity in all the vast firmament — then only can it be appreciated.

DONALD T. HOOD

LIEUTENANT, U.S.N.R.F.

SON of Frederic C. and Myra (Tucker) Hood; was born at Brookline, Mass., Feb. 13, 1893. He was fitted for college at St. George's School, Newport, R.I., and in 1914 graduated from Harvard College, where he had acted as manager of the Harvard baseball team. He attended the Officers' Training Camp at Plattsburg, N.Y., in Aug., 1916.

He enrolled at Washington, D.C., on Nov. 20, 1917, as Lieut. (j.g.). He was ordered to Akron, Ohio, where he was put in charge of the construction and testing of lighter-than-air craft for the Navy. He qualified as a Naval Aviator on June 28, 1918, and was a member of the first crew to make the flight from Akron to the Atlantic Coast. He was promoted to Lieut. on Oct. 1, 1918, and was released from active service on March 4, 1919.

Lieut. Hood has kindly written the account of the lighter-than-air construction which follows:

LIGHTER-THAN-AIR CONSTRUCTION IN THE UNITED STATES

Lighter-than-air construction in this country previous to the war had consisted, as far as the Navy was concerned, in one non-rigid dirigible balloon, the DN 1, which was built about 1914, and used at the Naval Air Station, Pensacola, Florida, and several kite and free balloons.

When the United States entered the war it had had practically no experience with lighter-than-air craft, whereas Germany had developed it to a very marked degree with their rigid airships previous to the war, and England had led the Allies in development during the war, with France and Italy following.

The first dirigibles built during the war were approximately 160 feet long by 35 feet in diameter, having a capacity of 77,000 cubic feet, and a displacement of about 5400 pounds. The fuselage used in these first dirigibles was taken from a standard Navy training seaplane, using a single 100-horse-power Curtiss motor, which gave the dirigible speed of about forty-eight miles an hour, an endurance of about ten hours at full speed, and a ceiling of about 6000 feet.

During the war about twenty of these dirigibles were built, and all used in this country at our Naval Air Stations for patrol purposes. At first, due to lack of experience both in construction and operation, many difficulties were encountered, but as the manufacturers had more experience in the construction of dirigibles and the Navy more experience in their operation this first type of dirigibles became very successful and was used to great advantage.

The main objection to the first dirigibles was their almost certain loss if serious motor trouble developed, since they had only one motor, and at most of our coastal stations on the Atlantic Coast there is a prevailing westerly wind which would drive them out to sea in case the motor stopped.

Early in 1918 plans for a twin-engine dirigible were got out and the first dirigible was flown successfully in the late summer of the same year. This dirigible was about 192 feet long, 41 feet in diameter, had a capacity of approximately 180,000 cubic feet, and a displacement of about 12,600 pounds; a maximum speed of about 60 miles an hour; a cruising speed of about 45 miles an hour, carrying two 150-horse-power motors, and had considerable bomb equipment and complete wireless installation. The car was especially built for dirigibles, being about 40 feet long, and provided space for five to seven men with available space which could be used for bunks or storage. The two motors were mounted on outriggers amidships of the car.

The first dirigible C 1 was built and tried out at Akron, and after being successfully tested was flown from Akron to the Naval Air Station at Rockaway Beach, N.Y., with a stop at Washington. This was the first successful long flight over land made in a dirigible in this country, although this same flight had been twice attempted before. This same dirigible was used at the Naval Air Station at Rockaway for several months, and was then flown by three stages to the Naval Air Station, Key West, Florida. Several duplicates of the C 1 were built and it was planned to fly one of them, the C 5, across the ocean.

Kite balloons, which were built in large numbers, and used for observation purposes from battleships, destroyers, and smaller craft, formed a most important part of the Navy's lighter-than-air programme.

Free balloons, which were built in small quantities, were used in elementary flight training by all lighter-than-air officers in order to instruct them in the effects of varying atmospheric conditions upon a balloon. The free balloon consists of a spherical envelope around which a net is placed which supports a basket, and the balloon having no propelling forces, moves with the wind, and can only be controlled up or down by throwing over ballast or valving gas. Training in free balloons was essential, as the effects of varying atmospheric conditions on the gas in the envelope are the largest factors in the operation of lighter-than-air craft. Also, when the motor of a dirigible stops or a kite balloon breaks away, they both become essentially free balloons and must be treated as such.

Akron was really the centre of balloon manufacturing and development because of the rubber companies situated there. The companies were the logical manufacturers of lighter-than-air craft, because a balloon envelope is made of a rubberized light-weight cloth or silk, and the development of this fabric is of utmost importance.

The Navy purchased and built a station near by Akron for test and construction purposes where the dirigibles were assembled and tested.

GEORGE DANA ANDERSON

LIEUTENANT (*j.g.*), U.S.N.R.F.

SON of James Robb and Katharine Dana Anderson, of Somerville, Mass.; was born at Denver, Col., June 6, 1895. He attended the Somerville public schools, and entered the Mass. Institute of Technology, where he remained for two years. He took three years at Boston University, being granted leave of absence in May, 1917, to enlist. He trained with the R.O.T.C., and on June 30, 1917, enrolled as seaman, second class, in the U.S.N.R.F., and was ordered to the Naval Aviation Ground School at M.I.T., where he trained until ordered overseas Oct. 20, 1917.

On reaching London he was sent to Roehampton, for kite balloon and dirigible training, and from there, on Dec. 10, he was ordered to the Royal Naval Air Station, Cranwell, Lincolnshire. On Feb. 20, 1918, he was sent to the Royal Naval Air Station at East Fortune, Scotland, where his duties consisted of fleet reconnaissance, anti-submarine work, and convoy duty. He was commissioned Ensign, with Pilot's license, in March, 1918.

After a few weeks as Second Officer, at East Fortune, he acted as Captain of one of the ships at this station, where he remained for seven months. In Oct., 1918, he was commissioned Lieut. (j.g.), and was ordered to the Royal Naval Construction Station, at Kingsnorth, for a course in designs and the rigging of airships. On Nov. 15 he was sent to the U.S. Naval Aviation Headquarters, London, and attached to the Bureau of Construction; there he did special work on repairs and testing, and on parachutes, being one of two men who volunteered for, and actually made two daring parachute jumps.

On April 1, 1919, Lieut. Anderson was ordered to Washington, D.C., for duty in the Office of Naval Operations. On Sept. 1, 1919, he was appointed Aide for Aviation Recruiting. He performed approximately 500 hours of patrol duty during the war. He is still in the Service.

RALPH H. NORRIS

Lieutenant (*j.g.*), U.S.N.R.F.C.

Son of Charles H. and Elizabeth M. Norris; was born at Chelsea, Mass., March 29, 1892. He attended the Chelsea public schools and Sanborn Seminary, and graduated from Dartmouth College.

He enlisted in May, 1917, in the U.S.N.R.F.C. at Boston, Mass., and was assigned to the Naval Aviation School at M.I.T., where he received instruction in the main rudiments of dirigible and balloon work. Upon completing this course he was ordered overseas to London, Oct. 20, 1917, and thence to Roehampton for kite balloon and dirigible training with the Royal Naval Air Service, where he qualified as a Free Balloon Pilot. On Dec. 10, 1918, he was assigned to the Royal Naval Air Station at Cranwell, Lincolnshire, to qualify as a Dirigible Pilot. He was commissioned Ensign, March, 1918, and Lieut. (j.g.) in Sept., 1918.

He was assigned to the Royal Naval Air Service Station at Tembroke, Wales; from there he went to Mullion, Cornwall, and thence to the U.S. Naval Air Station at Paimbœuf, France, for dirigible duty in connection with the location of enemy submarines. He is credited with two Hun submarines.

Lieut. Norris returned to the U.S. on Dec. 15, 1918, being assigned duty at Montauk Point, N.Y., in charge of the C 4 and two smaller dirigibles. He represented the Naval Air Service at Mineola, during the landing of the British trans-Atlantic dirigible R 34. He has been assigned to the North Island Naval Air Station, Cal., where he is still in Service.

Married, June 25, 1917, Erdine L. Gay.

Brother in Service —

Clarence W. Norris, Sergeant, U.S.A., Permanent Detachment, Overseas Casual, Oct. 5, 1917, to March, 1919.

ARTHUR DOUGLAS BREWER

LIEUTENANT, U.S.N.R.F.

SON of Clifford M. and Harriette W. Brewer; was born at Medford, Mass., May 4, 1896. He was educated at Medford High School, Phillips Exeter Academy, and at Harvard College, class of 1919.

He enlisted on May 21, 1917, at the Charlestown Navy Yard, in U.S.N.R.F. From June to Sept., 1917, he studied at the Goodyear Balloon School, Akron, Ohio. He was commissioned Ensign on Oct. 27, 1917, and ordered to overseas duty. In France he trained at U.S.N. Air Station, Paimbœuf, France, from Nov., 1917, to Oct. 31, 1918, where he did excellent convoy and patrol work in a zone mined and patrolled by the enemy. He was attached to the Naval Air Station at Guipavas, from Nov. 1 to Nov. 23, 1918. He was commissioned Lieut. (j.g) on March 23, 1918, and Lieut. on Oct. 1, 1918. He was ordered back to the U.S. and stationed at Bay Shore, N.Y., from Dec. 6, 1918, to Jan. 8, 1919. He was then sent to U.S. Naval Air Station at Chatham, on Jan. 11, 1919, as Dirigible Officer.

Lieut. Brewer was cited by the French Government, and by the U.S. Government.

Citations

(*From copy of French citation*)

I have the honor to inform you that following the ascension of twenty-five hours and forty-three minutes made on the 27th of April, 1918, by Dirigible AT 1, at the American Dirigible Centre at Paimbœuf, during a wind of five to twelve metres, and in a zone mined and patrolled, I have decided to record an official statement of satisfaction to:

Lieutenant CULBERT, Commanding
Ensign DELENO
Ensign BREWER
Ensign MACCRACKEN, and to the crew of the AT 1

with the following motive:

Have given proof, during the course of an ascension of twenty-five hours and forty-three minutes, which constitutes by its duration a remarkable performance, of the most excellent qualities of endurance, of energy, of sang-froid, and technical ability.

(*Signed*) *Vice-Admiral* SALAUN
Director-General of Submarine Warfare

(From Bureau of Navigation, Washington, D.C.)

To Lieut. (j.g.) A. D. Brewer, U.S.N.R.F.

The Bureau is pleased to quote below a communication received from Vice-Admiral Salaun, Director-General Submarine Warfare, French Republic, commending you for the performance of the Dirigible AT 1, following the ascension made on April 27, 1918. (Then follows quotation of French citation.) A copy of this letter will be filed with your official efficiency record.

(*Signed*) Hanis Laning
Chief of Bureau

DONALD HERSEY MERRILL

Lieutenant (*j.g.*), U.S.N.R.F.

Son of Ernest W. and Helen L. (Hersey) Merrill; was born at Somerville, Mass., Jan. 22, 1896. He attended the public schools of Somerville, and in the fall of 1916 entered Tufts College, taking an engineering course. Early in 1917 he enlisted in the U.S. Naval Reserve, and during the summer was engaged in road construction at Camp Devens, and also worked for the Mass. Highway Commission. About Aug. 20 he entered the Naval Aviation Ground School at M.I.T., as a member of Flight C, and on graduation in Oct., 1917, was one of fifteen men sent to England for training.

He was in active service in England, engaged in patrolling the west coast in search of submarines, until July, 1918, when he was sent to France and stationed at Paimbœuf. He was commissioned Ensign while in England, and Lieut. (j.g.) after his arrival in France. He returned to the U.S., June 22, 1919, and after a short furlough was sent to Norfolk, Va. In the middle of Aug. he was transferred to Panama, where he was stationed at last accounts.

Married, Aug. 9, 1919, Marion Roop, of Arlington, Mass.

* KENNETH MacLEISH

Lieutenant, U.S.N.R.F.C., Northern Bombing Group

Killed in action, Oct. 14, 1918

Son of Andrew and Martha (Hillard) MacLeish; was born in Glencoe, Ill., Sept. 19, 1894, of distinguished New England ancestry. He prepared for college at the Hotchkiss School, Lakeville, Conn., and at Treat's Tutoring School, Helenwood, Tenn. He entered Yale College in the class of 1918. He was a member of the freshman and 'Varsity track teams, and of the 'Varsity water polo team.

Before the U.S. entered the war, he associated himself with a group of Yale men whose purpose was to establish a naval flying corps to be placed at the service of the Government in case of war. He enlisted in the Naval Reserve Flying Corps, as an electrician, second class, on March 24, 1917, and late in March left college for West Palm Beach, Fla., for training in the use of hydroplanes. In June he finished his training at Huntington, N.Y., where he was commissioned Ensign in Aug. 1917, and served as Officer Instructor at Langley Field, Norfolk, Va. He sailed overseas in Oct., 1917, to France, and was detailed for a brief time as Instructor; then assigned to important inspection work at the Navy Assembly and Repair Bases. From the middle of Dec., 1917, to the middle of March, 1918, he trained at Moutchic-Lacanau, France, Eastleigh and Gosport, Eng., and at Turnberry and Ayr, Scotland. He was ordered to the front, March 27, 1918, on a chasse machine attached to the British Naval Air Service. He received a commission as Lieut. (j.g.) on June 23, 1918, and was promoted to Lieut. in Aug., 1919. From April 20 to May 24, 1918, he was attached to the U.S. Naval Air Station at Dunkirk. Most of his flights at this time were made with the British Royal Air Force, against the enemy submarine bases at Zeebrugge and Ostend, the object being not only to damage the mole and harbor works, but also to catch the submarines as they came out at high tide. On May 24 he was transferred to the 7th A.I.C. at Clermont-Ferrand for a course at the U.S. Aviation Bombing School. In the middle of July Lieut. MacLeish returned to Flanders and flew a two-seater bombing machine with the British R.A.F. in raids upon Zeebrugge, Bruges, and other points behind the enemy lines. Early in Sept. he returned to Eastleigh, Eng., where he became the First Flight Officer. Early in Oct.,

1918, he declined a furlough to return for a few weeks to the U.S., and applied for the opportunity to go to the front with the famous British Combat Squadron No. 213, R.A.F., in the great offensive which the Allies were just beginning in Flanders. On Oct. 13 he was given permission to join this Squadron, and on the morning of Oct. 14, 1918, he went out over the lines bringing down an enemy plane. In the afternoon of the same day he went out, and was seen to bring down a second enemy plane, and then, with assistance, a third enemy plane. At this juncture he and his British companions were attacked by Germans in numbers three to one. MacLeish headed right into the enemy and was heavily engaged, when his five comrades, seeing his desperate position, turned to help him. Four of the British were brought down immediately, but Lieut. MacLeish and the Flight Commander fought off the Germans in a running fight of sixteen miles, at the conclusion of which the Commander was brought down in flames and MacLeish killed in the air, over Schoorl, Belgium. Not until Dec. 26, 1918, was his body found by the owner of the Belgian farm in Leffinghe, where he fell. He is buried where he fell, his grave marked by a headstone brought over by his comrades of the U.S.N.R.F.C. The Royal Air Force has planned a permanent memorial to mark the spot.

The night before he left for the front Lieut. McLeish wrote:

> If I find it necessary to make the supreme sacrifice, always remember this — I am so firmly convinced that the ideals I am going to fight for are right and splendid that I am happy to be able to give so much for them. I could not have any self-respect, I could not consider myself a man, if I saw these ideals defeated when it lies in my power to defend them. So I have no fears; I have no regrets; I have only to thank God for such a wonderful opportunity to serve Him and the world. No, if I must make the supreme sacrifice I will do it gladly and I will do it honorably and bravely, as your son should, and the life that I lay down will be my preparation for the grander, finer life that I shall take up. I shall live! You must not grieve. I shall be supremely happy — so must you — not that I have "gone West," but that I have bought such a wonderful life at so small a price and paid for it gladly.

Brothers in Service —

Norman Hillard MacLeish, 2d Lieut., 53d F.A.
Archibald MacLeish, Capt., 146th F.A.

RICHARD L. COOLEY

LIEUTENANT (*j.g.*), U.S.N.R.F.

SON of Levi and Agnes (Stimson) Cooley; was born at Newtonville, Mass., Aug. 10, 1895. He fitted for college at the Mitchell Military School, and at Phillips Exeter Academy, and entered Dartmouth with the class of 1918.

On May 5, 1917, he left college to enter the American Ambulance Field Service, sailing for France with the first Dartmouth Unit. He returned to this country in Oct., 1917, and enlisted in Naval Aviation, Nov. 20, 1917, at Boston, Mass. He was called to active duty Feb. 18, 1918.

While training at the Ground School, M.I.T., he was drafted for lighter-than-air service, and sent to the Naval Air Station, Akron, Ohio, April 27, 1918. After a preliminary course in lighter-than-air work, he was assigned to Pensacola, Fla., for dirigible training, June 20, 1918. He received his commission as Ensign, Aug. 22, 1918, and acted as an Instructor at Pensacola. In Oct., 1918, he was placed in charge of bombing instruction in the lighter-than-air section. At the end of Oct., he was recommended for junior lieutenancy.

He was returned to inactive duty, Dec. 9, 1918. He received promotion to Lieut. (j.g.), March 1, 1919; commission to date back to Jan. 1, 1919.

*CLYDE NORTON PALMER

ENSIGN, U.S.N.R.F., NORTHERN BOMBING GROUP

Killed in accident, Sept. 14, 1918

SON of Winfield H. and Mary E. (McGrath) Palmer; was born at Malden, Mass., May 17, 1897. He was educated at the Malden High School, and at the Wentworth Institute, graduating in 1917. He attended the Plattsburg Training Camp in July, 1916.

In Aug., 1917, he enlisted in the U.S.N.R.F. at Boston, Mass.; trained at M.I.T., and later at Pensacola, Fla. He was sent overseas in April, 1918, having received his commission as Ensign in Feb., 1918. He trained in France until June, at Moutchic-Lacanau, Gironde. He was then sent to Italy to train for night bombing with Caproni machines, at Malpensa. Ensign Palmer was brevetted in Italy in July, 1918, and was made First Pilot in the same month. After finishing his training, he was sent on a special mission, to test out and pilot a new 600-horse-power Caproni bombing-machine, ordered by the U.S. In this machine he flew from Milan over the Alps to Paris. The flight was made in seven hours, actual flying time, with landings at Turin, Lyons, Dijon, and Paris. From Paris he was ordered to the Northern Bombing Group, Field A.

He was killed in an accident at St.-Inglevert, France, on Sept. 14, 1918, and was buried in the Military Cemetery at Calais, France.

Married, March 23, 1918, Dorothy Keniston.

WILLIAM PENN WHITEHOUSE, Second Lieutenant, U.S.N.A.F.; Chief Pilot, U.S. Naval Air Station, Paimbœuf, France

Son of Robert Treat and Florence (Brooks) Whitehouse; was born in Portland, Me., on Aug. 9, 1895. He graduated from Harvard College in 1917.

He volunteered for Naval Aviation at the Charlestown Navy Yard on April 16, 1917, and was at once assigned to the Dirigible Training Camp at Akron, Ohio. After six months' training, he was graduated as a balloonist and Dirigible Pilot, being among the first six officers qualified for that service in America. He received his commission as Ensign on Oct. 31, and in Nov., 1917, was ordered overseas.

He was stationed at Rochfort-sur-Mer, France, where he remained for two months, and from there he was transferred to Paimbœuf on the south side of the Loire River, where the largest lighter-than-air station on the coast of France was situated. There he organized the first meteorological weather bureau station for air service on the coast of France. Subsequently he was sent to England to make a special study of aviation gunnery at the leading English stations. On his return to Paimbœuf, he was detailed to patrol the coast for submarines and convoy the transports to the port of St.-Nazaire. He was one of the officers on the dirigible ordered to convoy the *George Washington* with President Wilson on board, into the port of Brest. He was promoted to Lieut. (j.g.) on March 29, 1918, and to Lieut. on Oct. 1, 1918. For the last four months of the war Lieut. Whitehouse was Chief Pilot at Paimbœuf. Before he left for the U.S., he was appointed to compile the history of all the American Naval Air Stations in France.

Lieut. Whitehouse was given his inactive service papers at the U.S.N. Air Station, Bay Shore, N.Y., on March 28, 1919.

Brother in Service —

Robert Treat Whitehouse, Jr., Ensign, U.S.N.R.F.C., U.S.N. Air Station, Le Croisic, France.

ROBERT TREAT WHITEHOUSE, Jr.

Ensign, U.S.N.R.F.C., U.S.N. Air Station, Le Croisic, France

Son of Robert Treat and Florence (Brooks) Whitehouse; was born at Portland, Me., Jan. 10, 1897. He was educated at Phillips Exeter Academy, and at Harvard College. At college he was a member of the 1919 cross-country team, and belonged to the Harvard R.O.T.C. During his sophomore year he enlisted at Newport, R.I., on May 11, 1917, in the U.S. Naval Reserve, for active duty on patrol boats. On Oct. 1, 1917, he was transferred to Naval Aviation, and assigned to the Ground School, M.I.T., with Flight 6. On Dec. 1, 1917, he was sent to the Naval Air Station, at Hampton Roads, Va., for flying instruction. He was later ordered to Pensacola, Fla., for further training.

He was commissioned Ensign, N.R.F.C., on Feb. 12, 1918, and sailed overseas in March. He was then assigned to the Naval Air Station at Moutchic-Lacanau, France, for a four months' course on seaplane piloting and bombing. Subsequently he was transferred to the Naval Air Station at Le Croisic, on the northwest coast of France, at the mouth of the Loire River, near St.-Nazaire, the port at which a large portion of the American troops disembarked. Here he was on active submarine patrol duty from July 11 to Dec. 12, 1918, as seaplane pilot, flying the (French) Tellier type of seaplane, convoying Allied ships, patrolling, and bombing submarines. He returned to the U.S. on Dec. 24, 1918, and was placed on inactive duty in the U.S. Naval Air Force, Jan. 9, 1919. He then completed his course at Harvard College.

Brother in Service —

William Penn Whitehouse, 2d Lieut. U.S.N.A.F., Chief Pilot, U.S. Naval Air Station, Paimbœuf, France.

ALBERT CUSHING READ

LIEUTENANT-COMMANDER, NC 4, A.S., U.S.N.

SON of the Rev. and Mrs. Joseph B. Read; was born at Lyme, N.H., in 1887. He attended the public schools at Lyme and later the Whitman High School, Whitman, Mass., from which he graduated in 1903. He was immediately appointed to the Naval Academy at Annapolis, and graduated with high honors.

As an Ensign, he saw considerable service on various battleships and cruisers. In 1908 he was sent to the Pacific Station, serving there until 1911, when he was ordered home from Nagasaki, Japan. In July, 1915, when interest in Aviation was being stimulated by the Great War, he was sent to the aeronautical station at Pensacola, Fla., for a course in Aviation. At that time he held the rank of Lieut. In May, 1916, he was detached from the Aviation Service and sent to the battleship *North Carolina*, but he was ordered back to air work again in June, 1917, when he was placed in charge of the Air Station at Bay Shore, N.Y.; he was then a Lieut.-Commander. When the battleship *North Carolina* was equipped with hydroplanes for experimental flights from the decks, Lieut.-Commander Read and Lieut.-Commander Bellinger were assigned, with others, for special service, and visited the Navy Yard at Portsmouth, N.H. While he was there, Lieut.-Commander Read had an accident: his plane fell, and he was thrown into the water, but escaped injury. Subsequently, he served at several naval air stations, including those at Rockaway Beach, Montauk, Garden City, and Port Washington, N.Y.

While he was stationed on Long Island during the war, he was in charge of a number of important tactical air manœuvres, and made many flights offshore while the German submarines menaced the coast. At this time he was also on the staff of the Chief of Naval Operations at Washington, and was detached for temporary duty in connection with the camouflaging of seaplanes at Hampton Roads, Va.

In March, 1919, he was selected to command one of the three NC planes in the first trans-Atlantic flight, and joined Commander John Henry Towers and Lieut.-Commander Patrick Nelson Lynch Bellinger at Rockaway. On May 8 he left Rockaway at 10.04 A.M. in the NC 4 for Halifax, N.S., but was forced down off Chatham,

Mass., by motor trouble. His plane rode the sea all night, and put in at Chatham Bay in the morning. On May 14 he left Chatham for Halifax at 9.05 A.M., arriving at 1.15 P.M., flying 340 miles in 4 hours and 10 minutes. On May 15 he left Halifax for Trepassey at 9.52 A.M., but was compelled to land on the water thirty minutes later, at Storey Head. The NC 4 arose again at 11.47, and arrived at Trepassey at 5.37 P.M., having made a flight of 461 miles in 8 hours and 45 minutes elapsed time, or 6 hours and 20 minutes actual flying time. On May 16 he left Trepassey for Ponta Delgada, Azores, at 6.07 P.M., arriving at Horta, Azores, at 9.25 A.M., on May 17, and completing a journey of 1200 miles in 15 hours and 18 minutes. On May 20 he left Horta for Ponta Delgada at 8.40 A.M., arriving at 10.24 A.M., and making the trip of 150 miles in 1 hour and 45 minutes. He was held up for a week by bad weather, but on May 27 left Ponta Delgada for Lisbon at 6.18 A.M., arriving at 4.01 P.M., flying 800 miles in 9 hours and 43 minutes. On May 30 he left Lisbon for England at 1.24 A.M., but, after flying 100 miles, was forced to land at the mouth of the Mondego River on account of engine trouble. He resumed flight at 9.38 A.M., and arrived at Ferrol, Spain, at 12.45 P.M., having travelled 330 miles in 11 hours and 21 minutes elapsed time. On May 31 he left Ferrol at 2.27 A.M., arriving at Plymouth, Eng., at 9.26 A.M., flying 475 miles in 6 hours and 59 minutes, and completing the trans-Atlantic voyage, the first successful venture of its kind in the world's history.

GEORGE CHURCH

CHIEF QUARTERMASTER, U.S.N.R.F., BALLOON SECTION

SON of Mr. and Mrs. John H. C. Church; was born at Great Barrington, Mass., Nov. 26, 1896. He graduated from the Berkshire School, Sheffield, Mass., in 1915, and attended the Sheffield Scientific School, Yale, class of 1918.

He enlisted on April 16, 1917, at Newport, R.I. Until Oct. 29, 1917, he was in active service with the Naval Reserve, driving a car for a medical officer. From Feb. 18, 1918, to April 29, 1918, he trained at the Naval Aviation Ground School, M.I.T. From April 30, 1918, to May 2, 1918, he trained at Akron, Ohio. On May 2, 1918, on his first balloon flight, he was thrown from the car when it struck a tree, and his back was broken. He was on sick-leave from May 2 to June 12, 1918, at the hospital in Warren, Ohio, and was honorably discharged on Oct. 25, 1918. He is still living, but helpless, at his home in Great Barrington, Mass., being paralyzed from the waist down. (Portrait on opposite page.)

EDWARD ROGERS HASTINGS, JR.

SECOND LIEUTENANT, A.S.A., U.S.A.

SON of Edward Rogers and Caroline Bartlett (Tirrell) Hastings, of Milton, Mass.; was born at South Weymouth, Mass., June 19, 1893. He was educated at Milton Academy and at Harvard College. He enlisted at Cambridge, Mass., on Nov. 12, 1917, and was assigned to the M.I.T. Ground School, where he remained from Nov. 24, 1917, to Jan. 6, 1918. He was then transferred to Princeton, N.J., where he was stationed from Jan. 6 to Feb. 2, 1918. He received further training at Camp Dick, Dallas, Tex., from Feb. 2 to April 1; at Chanute Field, Rantoul, Ill., from April 1 to July 2; and at Brooks Field, San Antonio, Tex., from July 20 to Sept. 7. He was subsequently ordered to Call Field, Wichita Falls, Tex., where he remained from Sept. 7, 1918, until Jan. 3, 1919, instructing, and transporting aerial mail. He was commissioned 2d Lieut. at Chanute Field, June 12, 1918, and appointed Instructor. He was honorably discharged on Jan. 3, 1919, at Call Field.

GEORGE RICHMOND FEARING, Jr.

Lieutenant-Commander, U.S.N.R.F.

Son of George R. and Harriet (Graves) Fearing, of Boston, Mass.; was born in New York City, Feb. 20, 1871. He attended the Cutler Preparatory School, N.Y., graduated from Harvard College, A.B. 1893, and from the Harvard Law School. He was a member of the Harvard track team four years, football team one year, crew one year, and was once U.S. champion in court tennis, and five times at racquets (doubles).

He attended the First Officers' Training Camp at Plattsburg, and in Feb., 1916, enlisted in the Mass. Naval Militia, Aviation Section, and trained at Marblehead, Mass., receiving instruction in Aviation at Misery Island for two weeks in Sept., 1916.

Early in 1917 he was elected to the Mass. Public Safety Committee, as head of Aviation Section of Committee on Naval Affairs. This committee examined about 1000 candidates for U.S. Naval Aviation, accepting about 350, who entered the Naval Reserve Flying Corps. On May 7, 1917, he enrolled in U.S.N.R.F. as Ensign, having resigned from the Mass. Naval Militia on the same day.

He was ordered overseas Aug. 16, 1917, to Paris; from there he was ordered to Houstin, Gironde, a French flying school, and placed in charge of the American aviators in training there. About Nov. 1 he was transferred to Paris to the U.S. Naval Aviation Headquarters.

He was commissioned Lieut. (j.g.) as of Feb. 1, 1918; and Lieut. as of March 23, 1918. Lieut. Fearing was made liaison officer with U.S. Air Service; also one of executive committee of five of Naval Aviation; in addition, he served as a Naval member of the Foreign Committee of Aircraft Production Board while it functioned; he was subsequently made Chief of Aviation, U.S. Naval Aviation Foreign Service. He removed to London when the U.S. Naval Aviation Headquarters was transferred, and acted as head of the Planning Section there. He was promoted to Lieut.-Commander, as of Sept. 30, 1918. Returning to the U.S., Lieut.-Com. Fearing was placed on inactive duty, Jan. 14, 1919.

Married, March, 1897, Hester Sullivan Cochrane.

HENRY FORSTER

Ensign, U.S.N.R.F., Northern Bombing Group

Son of Frederick Prentiss and Edith (Allen) Forster, of Milton, Mass.; was born in New York City, March 21, 1889. He was educated at Groton School, Groton, Mass., and at Harvard College, A.B. 1911. At Harvard he rowed on the freshman eight-oared crew in 1908, and on the 'Varsity foar-oared crew in 1909 and 1910. Previous to the war he served two and a half years in Squadron A, Cavalry, National Guard, N.Y., and six months in the 2d Battalion, Naval Militia, N.Y.

He enlisted in the French Army Aviation Service on June 21, 1917, and was assigned to the Lafayette Flying Corps. He trained at Avord, France, from June 22 to Nov. 24, 1917, graduating as "Caporal Pilote" on Nov. 1, 1917. He was then ordered to Pau, where he remained from Nov. 27 to Dec. 17, 1917. On Dec. 19 he was transferred to the Aviation Dépôt at Plessis-Belleville and stayed there until Jan. 27, 1918. From April to July, 1918, he served at the front on patrol duty. After he had spent the required number of hours over the enemy's lines, he was promoted to "Sergent Pilote" on May 16, 1918. He worked with Division Nieuport and Spad, and on June 1, 1918, was attached to Escadrille, C 74, Section Spad, Br. 224, Section Spad, Spa 102, and Spa 15, G.C. 13.

He was transferred to the U.S.N.R.F., with an Ensign's commission, on July 19, 1918. He served at the Dunkirk Station from Aug. 8 to 24, 1918, and then attended the Bombing School at Boscombe, Devon, Eng., from Sept. 7 to Oct. 22, 1918, learning to fly big machines. He was then ordered to Calais, France, with the Northern Bombing Group. He was honorably discharged at Boston, Mass., on Feb. 26, 1919.

Brothers in Service —

Frederick A. Forster, 2d Lieut., U.S.A., 305th Infantry; killed in accident.

Horace W. Forster, Capt., U.S.A., Troop K, 2d Cavalry, A.E.F.

Reginald Forster, Private, U.S.A., 11th Field Artillery, A.E.F.

Gardner Forster, Driver, Italian Ambulance Field Service.

*BRADSTREET PARKER

CADET, U.S.N. AVIATION DETACHMENT

Died of pneumonia, Sept. 21, 1918

SON of George S. and Grace M. Parker; was born at Salem, Mass., April 13, 1897. He attended the public and private schools of Salem; graduated as president of his class, from the Hackley School, Tarrytown, N.Y., and entered Harvard College, class of 1919, where he remained until the end of his sophomore year, when he left to enter business with his father, in Parker Bros. Inc., of Salem and New York. At college he played football, baseball, and hockey.

He attended the Officers' Training Camp at Plattsburg in the summer of 1916, receiving his diploma on Aug 8. On June 18, 1918, he enlisted in the U.S. Naval Aviation Detachment at M.I.T., Cambridge, Mass., attached to Co. 28, which graduated on Oct. 7, 1918. After three months of training, he died of pneumonic-influenza on Sept. 21, 1918, before finishing this course. His record called forth high praise from his Commanding Officer, who wrote to Parker's family regarding his admirable work.

> Pr. Parker's record here was excellent, both in academic work and in his aptitude for the Service, and there is no doubt that he would have proved a great credit to our school and the Navy at large had his life been spared.

Married, Dec. 15, 1916, Ruth Comfort Mansfield, of Brookline, Mass.

*RALPH ROBY McCORMACK

Ensign, U.S.N.R.F.

Killed in seaplane accident, Feb. 7, 1919

Son of Thomas and Mary J. McCormack; was born at East Boston, Mass., Jan. 8, 1897. He was educated in the public schools of East Boston, the High School of Commerce, Boston, and at the Mass. Agricultural College. He was coxswain in his junior year at the High School of Commerce, and won medal for high jump at interscholastic meet in 1912.

He enlisted in the Naval Aviation Detachment at M.I.T., on May 29, 1918, and after ten weeks' training there, was sent to Key West, Fla.; then to Miami, and subsequently to Pensacola, where he was commissioned Ensign on Dec. 11, 1918.

On Feb. 7, 1919, he was killed with two other naval aviators, when the seaplane in which they were flying fell into Pensacola Bay. The machine was seen in a nose-dive over the channel, but nothing was thought of it until the men failed to return; then an alarm was sounded and the wreckage was discovered. The bodies were later recovered, and Ensign McCormack was buried at Winthrop, Mass.

Ensign McCormack wrote home enthusiastically of his work:

Flying is wonderful! I had my first "hop" on Tuesday, just at sundown, and I really cannot do it justice. After climbing to 2000 feet, spiralled down to 1500, nose-dived to 1000, and then glided, long and easily, to the water with the "stick" (propeller) purposely dead. It only lasted nine minutes, but in that time we covered fifteen miles. I was n't at all afraid, and all my senses were alive to new sensations.

"Taking-off," leaving the water for the air, was far different than I expected. Just a deliciously free sensation, accompanied by great speed, excessive wind pressure, the roar of the exhaust, and the slight tilting and bucking of the plane as she first takes the air. You climb steadily and gradually higher and higher, taking care all the time to keep on the course. Soon the harbor unfolds beneath you. We are now approaching the fort and soon pass directly over it and on and out over the ships. Our air speed has varied from 85 to 95 miles an hour, but our tachometer and thermometer indicate a healthy engine condition.

We now bank and turn sharply to the right; the floor of the ocean is plainly seen and several sharks and porpoises are easily seen. We dart through a low-hanging cloud and glimpse on the far horizon several white sails. Directly before us stretch the Keys for miles and miles, and in the west a large red sun is sinking.

The cloud effects are wonderful, and we do some tall thinking.

PHILIP DUDLEY MOSSER

ENSIGN, U.S.N.R.F.

ENLISTED in April, 1917, at which time he was a senior at Cornell University. He entered the coast patrol, and served on a patrol boat in Long Island Sound. In Oct., 1917, he transferred to the Naval Aviation Service, and was sent to the M.I.T. Naval Aviation Ground School. Upon completion of the course there, he was transferred to the Naval Air Station, at Bay Shore, N.Y. He was commissioned Ensign, U.S.N.R.F. On May 4, 1918, he fell in his hydroplane, and his skull was fractured. He recovered from this accident, although the injury to one eye prevented him from further flying. He was subsequently appointed a ground officer, and stationed at Pensacola, Fla. (Portrait on opposite page.)

CHARLES B. MILLER

SECOND LIEUTENANT, A.S., U.S.A.

SON of Nathan and Emma F. Miller; was born at Fall River, Mass., May 14, 1889. He was educated at the Durfee High School and at Phillips Exeter Academy. He enlisted in the Air Service at Boston, Mass., on Jan. 16, 1918, and was assigned to the M.I.T. Ground School. He received further training at Camp Dick, Dallas, Tex.; at Carruthers Field, Benbrook, Tex., and at Barron Field, Everman, Tex. He was commissioned 2d Lieut., March 10, 1919, and honorably discharged from the Service at Barron Field, Everman, Tex. March 12, 1919.

*RALPH TUPPER ROGERS

ENSIGN, U.S.N.A.S., EIGHTH SQUADRON

Died in Service, Jan. 8, 1919

SON of George F. and Ida M. Rogers, of Roslindale, Mass.; was born at Cambridge, Mass., Oct. 9, 1893. He was educated at the Medford High School and at the Mass. Institute of Technology. At the high school he won honors in French. Previous to enlisting he took a course in Aviation at the M.I.T. He was a sergeant in the Boys' Brigade at Medford, and was attached to the Church Cadets in high school.

On May 25, 1918, he enlisted in U.S. Aviation, at Cambridge, Mass. He was trained at Miami, Fla., being attached to the 8th Squadron. He was then sent to Pensacola, Fla., to finish his flying courses. He was commissioned Ensign, and had just completed his training when he was taken ill and died at Pensacola, on Jan. 8, 1919. He is buried at Forest Hills Cemetery, Mass.

Ensign Rogers worked very hard and with great enthusiasm for the Service that he loved. He had intended remaining in Aviation after the war, had he lived. (Portrait on opposite page.)

PHILIP L. CHENEY

ENSIGN, U.S.N.R.F.

SON of Charles Willie and Flora (Hutchinson) Cheney; was born at Brookline, Mass., Dec. 29, 1897. He was educated at the Mohegan Lake School, the Volkmann School, and at Harvard College, where he trained with the Harvard R.O.T.C. On May 29, 1918, he enlisted at the Boston Navy Yard, and was assigned to Co. 24, at the M.I.T., for the ground school course, from May 31 to Aug. 20, 1918. He was sent to Miami, Fla., where he was trained, from Aug. 23 to Oct. 26, in elementary flying. For advanced work in flying he was ordered to Pensacola, Fla., where he remained from Oct. 28 to Dec. 28. He was then transferred to Hampton Roads, Va., for work in aerial navigation. He was stationed there from Dec. 30, 1918, to March 6, 1919, and was commissioned Ensign, U.S.N.R.F., Jan. 13, 1919. He was relieved of all active duty at Hampton Roads, March 8, 1919.

*JOHN SQUIRE BUCHANAN, Second

Lieutenant (*j.g.*), U.S.N.R.F.

Drowned in seaplane accident, April 25, 1919

Son of Neil Ellsworth and Ella J. Buchanan; was born at Boston, Mass., Oct. 31, 1895. He was educated at the Rice Grammar, Mechanic Arts High School, and at the Mass. Institute of Technology.

He served at the Mexican Border from July 2 to Oct 28, 1916, with Battery F, 1st Mass. Regiment, F.A., N.G.

On June 13, 1917, he enlisted in the U.S.N.R.F., for Aviation, at Boston, and was trained with the U.S. Naval Aviation Detachment, M.I.T., from Aug. 9 to Sept 29, 1917; and at Pensacola, Fla., Oct. 4 to Dec. 22, 1917. On Dec. 22, 1917, he was appointed Naval Aviator, No. 276, at Pensacola; and served at Pensacola in that capacity until Feb. 9, 1918. On Jan. 17, 1918, he was commissioned Ensign, U.S.N.R.F., and was ordered overseas to France, Feb. 7, 1918.

Lieut. Buchanan saw service in France at U.S.N.A.S., Moutchic-Lacanau, Gironde; Panillac; Le Croisic, Loire; and St.-Trojan, Charente-Inférieure. He won the Croix de Guerre for a number of rescues made in the Bay of Biscay, famous for its perilous winds and waves, and for many other attempted rescues in near-by regions. He was commissioned Lieut. (j.g.) on Aug. 5, 1918.

He sailed for the U.S. on Dec. 22, 1918, and was detailed to the U.S.N.A.S. at Chatham, Mass., where he remained up to the time of his death.

Lieut. Buchanan was drowned in Cape Cod Bay on April 25, 1919, the day of the parade in honor of the 26th Division. With him were Ensign John G. Howard, of Rochester, N.Y., and Electrician Bernard Tornes. The plane was one of a patrol which had been performing in the air above the parade, and was returning to Chatham Air Station, with a heavy gale blowing. Carrier pigeons brought back the news that their engine was disabled, and rescuers searched in vain for them. The plane was wrecked and the three aviators drowned.

One of the last things Lieut. Buchanan did after the parade, before leaving for Chatham, was to circle the house in Boston where his family were watching him, and as he made a turn to the south he waved them a last greeting.

*CHARLES L. OSTRIDGE

LIEUTENANT (*j.g.*), U.S.N.R.F.

Drowned in seaplane accident, May 19, 1919

SON of Anselm Arthur and Elizabeth A. (Bradlee) Ostridge; was born at Watertown, Mass., April 18, 1893. He attended the public schools of Watertown, and graduated from Boston College in 1917; at college he played on the football team, and during vacation time was for two years Life Guard, at the Metropolitan Parkway, at Watertown.

On May 14, 1917, he enlisted at Boston, Mass., and on June 26 was sent to Pensacola, Fla., for training; there he was commissioned Ensign, Dec. 21, 1917, and ordered overseas. Arriving in England he was stationed at Calshot and Benbridge, and subsequently at Wight, and at Lough Foyle, Londonderry, Ireland; later he was transferred to Queenstown, Ireland. On Oct. 1, 1918, he was commissioned Lieut. (j.g.). He returned to the U.S. and was stationed at Hampton Roads, Va., and then at Chatham, Mass. He had been but about three weeks stationed at Chatham, when he was lost in a seaplane accident, on May 19, 1919

Lieut. Ostridge was present at the garden-party given in London on June 27, 1918, for the American officers, and was one of a group to be photographed on that occasion, with the King and Queen of England. Since his death his memory has been especially honored by the Town of Watertown.

*ERIC LINGARD

Ensign, U.S.N.R.F.

Died of pneumonia, Oct. 29, 1918

Son of Adrian Alexander and Adele Randolf (Liberick) Lingard; was born at Boston, Mass., Nov. 7, 1891. He attended the Middlesex School, Concord, Mass., where he rowed on the crew and played on the football team. He graduated from Harvard College in 1913, and entered the Law School, leaving there in the middle of his second year. At Harvard he played on the 'Varsity football team, and was rated the second strongest man in college.

In the spring of 1917 he worked at the Fore River Ship Yards, where he remained until his enlistment, Sept. 12, 1917, at Washington, D.C. On Oct. 1 he entered the Naval Aviation Ground School at the M.I.T., and, after completing the course, he finished his training at Pensacola, Fla. In April, 1918, he was commissioned Ensign, and on April 20 was detailed to the station at Chatham, Mass., for patrol duty, pending foreign orders; soon after his arrival he was made Ordnance Officer, in addition to his other duties, and was in charge of this department up to the time of his death.

For six weeks during the U-boat trouble, Chatham, the only Air Station on the coast from Cape Cod to Canada, had only eight pilots available for a patrol of 12,000 square miles, covered from daylight to dark. Most of these pilots (including Lingard) flew seven or more hours daily.

Lingard's participation in the U-boat attack off Orleans, Mass., is described in the following extract from the Service Record issued by the Commanding Officer of the U.S. Naval Air Station, Chatham, Mass. Jan. 3, 1919:

> Ensign Eric Lingard . . . *was the first aviator to ever engage an enemy vessel on this side of the Atlantic.* This was on July 21, 1918, when a German submarine shelled a tug and four barges off Orleans, Mass. Lingard was the first pilot to reach the scene, flying one of the H.S. boats, and Special Mechanic Howard,[1] who was his observer on that flight, said: "Lingard is the most wonderful pilot I ever rode with. He flew exactly over the centre of the submarine." The bomb dropped within a few feet of the

[1] "Special Mechanic Howard," an expert on Liberty motors (which he tested as they were installed), had flown with pilots of every Air Station on the Atlantic Coast. Howard was later assigned to the NC IV as Engineer for the first trans-Atlantic flight, but a few hours before the start his hand was cut off by the propeller.

submarine. If the bomb had functioned, the submarine would have been done for.

(*Signed*) P. B. Eaton
Captain of Engineers, U.S.C.G.
Commanding

Lingard, with Ensign E. M. Shields, assistant pilot, and E. H. Howard, observer, was over the U-boat fourteen minutes after being ordered out for combat, and flew as low as 400 feet into the enemy's gunfire, facing destruction from his own bomb which was designed for altitude of 1500 feet. The U-boat, 250 x 30 feet, used six-inch and anti-aircraft guns. After Lingard had spent his one bomb, he "stood by" without amunition of any kind, and with a shaky plane, circled low over the U-boat to mark the place, and keep the U-boat firing at him and therefore "awash," until the arrival of Captain Eaton, whose bomb also failed to function. Although the U-boat was not destroyed, yet the Chatham Air Patrol accomplished its purpose, as shown by the following extract from affidavit made by Lieut. E. E. Williams, then Executive Officer of the Chatham Naval Air Station, and initialled by the Commanding Officer:

> The enemy was attacked and driven away and never again appeared so near the shores of the United States. It is reasonably certain that had the U-boat not been attacked from the air, she would have destroyed Chatham and Orleans (both towns less than four miles away), not because of any possible military value, but for the decided moral effect that such destruction would have had — just as the English coast-towns were shelled.

This was the only engagement of the Great War on this side of the Atlantic. Several shells from the U-boat struck land, about three miles away. Because *Seaplane H.S.I.L.* 1695, commanded by Lingard, was the first aircraft ever to defend the shores of the United States from direct enemy attack, this plane became of historical interest. At the request of the City of Gloucester, and by order of the Navy Department, the hull was turned over to the city officials, on July 3, 1919, so that, in accordance with a letter from Secretary Daniels, "it may be set up in the Marine Park as a historical relic of the war."

On Sept. 27, while searching for a lost aviator, Lingard and his crew were wrecked at sea and taken to New York by a Quebec steamer. The following is an extract from "Officers' Fitness Report," Sept. 30, 1918:

Very high sea running. Picked up by S.S. *Parima* after four hours. Lingard swam from Parima to wrecked flying boat with line through heavy sea. Made line fast around engine. Liberty motor saved through his efforts.

Recommended that he be promoted to next higher rank.

(*Signed*) P. B. Eaton, *Commanding*

On Oct. 10, in response to an S.O.S. from a South American steamer reporting U-boat attack, Lingard volunteered as gunner, eager to use the Davis machine gun, just arrived at the station. The wind was blowing forty miles an hour, and his plane was forced down with engine trouble. In order to lessen resistance to the waves, the fabric had to be stripped from the wings. One wing was battered to pieces, and to keep the plane from sinking, Lingard and the assistant pilot lay all day and night stretched on the bare framework of the other wing with the sea breaking over them — too cold and weak to touch food or water. Lingard's companion soon became unconscious, and had to be held on to the wing. After tossing for twenty-seven hours, the flyers were rescued by an S.P. boat, and although the storm made it almost impossible to transfer them, Lingard and Ensign Shields, pilot, insisted on saving the machine gun. This long exposure resulted in Lingard's death from influenza-pneumonia on Oct. 29, 1918. He was buried at Annisquam, Mass., with full military honors, seaplanes flying over from Chatham to drop flowers.

Dr. Henry van Dyke, then Chaplain, Lieutenant-Commander, U.S.N.R.F., in an address to the officers and men of the Chatham Naval Air Station, said of Lingard:

Early this morning one of your best comrades, a brave youth, a faithful officer, a daring and skilful aviator, passed out of this life. His death was the immediate consequence of injury and exposure which came to him in the course of duty as an air scout guarding the shores of our country.

Hon. Franklin D. Roosevelt, then Acting Secretary of the Navy, in a letter of June 24, 1919 (initialled by the Chief of the Ordnance Department and the Director of Naval Aviation), wrote to Lingard's sister, his only surviving relative, as follows:

Your brother lived up to the best traditions of the Navy and I cannot speak too highly of his gallant work.

THOMAS DURFEE

LIEUTENANT (*j.g.*), U.S.N.R.F.

SON of Samuel Slater and Eliza (Weeden) Durfee; was born at Providence, R.I., June 3, 1899. He was educated at the Middlesex School, and at Harvard College, member of class of 1921. At Middlesex he played on the baseball and football teams.

Prior to entering the Service, he trained at the Fort Perry Training Camp, in 1916. On July 2, 1917, he enlisted in the U.S.N.R.F.C. at the Boston Navy Yard, and trained at the Naval Aviation Ground School, M.I.T., beginning Oct. 1, 1917; he continued training at the Naval Air Station, Hampton Roads, Nov. 25, 1917, and at the Naval Air Station, Pensacola, Fla., Jan. 12, 1918. He was commissioned Ensign, Feb. 28, 1918, and on March 8, 1918, was stationed at the Naval Air Station, Chatham, Mass., as Patrol Pilot. There he discharged the duties of Lieut., March 15 to June 1; Squadron Commander, June 1 to July 30; Flight Commander, July 30 to Oct. 1. From Nov. 15 to April 19, 1919, he served as Flight Commander, and for three months as Assistant Executive Officer.

Ensign Durfee's report of the submarine engagement in which he took part off Orleans, Mass., follows:

On July 21, 1918, at 10.48, word was received that a submarine was shelling a tug and four barges off Nauset Harbor, about five miles from the station. I immediately had bombs put on two planes which were on the point of leaving for Portland. At 10.50 the first plane left the beach with Durfee and Hicks as pilots, and Cleary as observer. Due to spark-plug trouble we were unable to take off, and returned to the beach. Two minutes after we left, the second plane, with Lingard and Shields, pilots, and Howard, observer, shoved off. They arrived on the scene while the submarine was still on the surface. The first bomb was then dropped, landing within forty feet of the submarine, but did not function. After firing a few shots at the plane, it submerged, but came up shortly, and Lingard dropped his second bomb. In the meantime Capt. Eaton and Ensign Brown arrived in two monoplanes and both dropped a bomb. Finally, my plane was fixed and we got there after the submarine had submerged a second time, but it was still visible, and we dropped a bomb, which fell about thirty feet from it. All the bombs failed to function owing to two reasons: too many safety devices, and too small a detonator and booster charge. In all, five bombs were dropped, four of which would have probably totally disabled it. All the planes made the attack from a height

of under four hundred feet. About a dozen shots were fired at the first two planes, several passing within a few feet of their target.

On Oct. 4, 1918, four planes left Chatham at 6 A.M., en route for the Philadelphia Navy Yard. The pilots were Ensign Durfee, Flight Commander, Ensigns Hudson, Shields, and Walker. At 9.30 they reached Bay Shore, completing the first leg of the trip, 168 miles. They left Bay Shore for Cape May at 12 M. arriving at 4 P.M., 180 miles. Then after re-fuelling and a slight rest, they left for Philadelphia, arriving without mishap. This was set down as a record distance for a single day, and especially remarkable as the planes were being taken down for overhauling as unfit for further patrol duty. Ensign Durfee holds the altitude record for H.S. 2 with full fighting equipment. He was commissioned Lieut. (j.g), dating from April 1, 1919, and was placed on inactive duty at the Navy Yard, Boston, April 19, 1919.

DUDLEY BOWLES MURPHY

Ensign, U.S.N.R.F.

Son of H. Dudley and Caroline Hutchinson (Bowles) Murphy, of Lexington, Mass.; was born at Winchester, Mass., July 10, 1897. He was educated at Milton Academy, Milton, and at the Mass. Institute of Technology. Prior to the declaration of war he spent one year at an Army training camp at Monterey, Cal. He enlisted in the Air Service, April 29, 1917, at Cambridge, Mass. He was trained at Squantum, Mass., and then at Norfolk, Va., from May 10, 1917, till Jan. 1, 1918. He was commissioned Ensign, Dec. 26, 1917. Ensign Murphy went overseas, Jan. 25, 1918. He was stationed at Killingholm, Eng., for nine months, and spent one month with the Royal Navy, at East Fortune, Scotland. He did 250 hours of enemy submarine patrol in the North Sea from Feb. 10 to Nov. 20, 1918. He was credited with one enemy submarine by Commander Kenneth Whiting.

He received inactive duty orders at Bay Shore, N.Y., Feb. 18, 1919.

NUGENT FALLON

LIEUTENANT-COMMANDER, U.S.N.R.F.

SON of John B. and Jennie E. (Murphy) Fallon; was born at Boston, Mass., March 22, 1884. He was educated in the Boston public schools, and at the Mass. Institute of Technology. In school he won the Franklin Medal; and at Tech. he was a member of the crew and of the track team. In 1916 he went on the civilian cruise of the U.S.S. *Kearsarge*, as a preparation for enlistment. On May 9, 1917, he enlisted at New York, in the U.S.N.R., Class 5 (A.). He began training with the N.A. Detachment, Newport News, Va., at the Curtiss Co. School. He then moved to Naval Operating Base, Norfolk, Va.

He was commissioned Ensign in May, 1917; was ordered overseas and stationed at Headquarters, London; then at Headquarters, Paris. He was ordered in turn to U.S.N. Aviation Base, Moutchic-Lacanau; French Flying Corps, at Hourtin, Gironde; and Royal Naval Air Station, Felixstowe, Eng. He engaged in numerous bombing raids over Germany, and in exciting engagements in the North Sea.

On Nov. 24, 1917, he was recommended for a British medal for gallant conduct during an encounter with a German submarine, but was not allowed to accept such an honor from a foreign Government.

On March 12, 1918, while he was attached to the Royal Naval Air Fleet at Felixstowe, Eng., he engaged in two air fights over the North Sea, and was commended to the British Admiralty by the Admiral at the base. He was flying at the time in a British hydroplane, and his wireless operator was shot and wounded seriously in the neck. Ensign Fallon left his seat, climbed over the wounded man, administered first aid, and returned to his place, bringing the plane safely to landing. It was in reference to this deed that Lieut. Edwards, Aide for Aviation, U.S.A., wrote to him in part as follows:

> Accept my hearty congratulations on the splendid fight which you put up against the Huns. I think I may safely say that in consequence your promotion is assured, and that you will be sent a very strong letter of commendation on the fine work which you have accomplished.

He was commissioned Lieut. (j.g.) in March, 1918; Lieut. in June, 1918; and Lieut.-Commander in Oct., 1918.

In recognition of his service Lieut.-Commander Fallon was ordered back to the U.S. and appointed Aide to the Commanding Officer at Pensacola, Fla. Later he was ordered to Washington, D.C., in charge of the Ground School, and following that to the Naval Detachment, M.I.T., Boston, as Executive Officer. He was put on inactive duty at Boston, Mass., Feb. 1, 1919.

Married, June 26, 1918, Elizabeth S. Fitzpatrick, of Boston.

Brother in Service —

Robert M. Fallon, Capt., Q.M.C., A.E.F.

(*From a Commendation, dated April* 24, 1918, *signed Franklin D. Roosevelt*)

1. The Department is pleased to quote below for your information an extract from the report of J. C. Porte, Wing Commander, R.N., dated March 9, 1918, which is concurred in by Rear Admiral G. C. Gayley, R.N., both officers attached to the Royal Naval Air Station, Felixstowe, England:

"I have the honour to bring to your notice the name of Ensign N. Fallon, who acted as second pilot in Seaplane N 4582 during the engagement of two of our machines against five enemy seaplanes, which took place on the 12th inst. Ever since this officer has been on the Station he has done excellent work and always shown the greatest courage and resource. During the present engagement he handled his machine gun with great skill and it was very largely due to him that our machines did so well."

And follows an Extract from the report of Vice-Admiral Sims, transmitting the above to the Department: "Ensign Nugent Fallon, U.S.N.R.F., has conducted himself in a manner which has reflected great credit upon the U.S. Naval Service, and has proven himself to be a gallant officer under fire."

2. The Department avails itself of this opportunity to highly commend you for the splendid work performed during the engagement described above. It is work of this character that will tend toward the successful prosecution of the war, and the Department cannot express itself too warmly in terms of praise for such exemplary work. Coöperation between our personnel and that of our allies is very greatly to be desired, especially during the present urgent emergency; and acts such as you have performed denote very clearly that such coöperation is very much in evidence. It is hoped that a continuance of this good and effective work will be maintained.

SAMUEL ABBOT SMITH

LIEUTENANT (*j.g.*), U.S.N.R.F., SQUADRON COMMANDER AT U.S.N. AIR STATION, CAPE MAY, N.J.

SON of George A. and Anna (Putnam) Smith; was born at Arlington, Mass., Dec. 9, 1895. He graduated from Milton Academy, Milton, and entered Harvard College with the class of 1918. He left college at the end of his junior year to enter the U.S. Service, having never received lower than honor grade during the three years of his attendance; was awarded Harvard College Scholarship, 1915–16, and 1918–19, and the John Harvard Scholarship, 1916–17; he was awarded Detur in his junior year, and elected member of Phi Beta Kappa. He played football, and held Harvard championship in wrestling (145 lb. class), in 1915.

On July 16, 1917, he enrolled in U.S.N.R.F. (Aviation) at the Charlestown Navy Yard, and attended the Ground School, M.I.T. On Nov. 24, he was sent to the Naval Air Station at Hampton Roads, Va., and on Jan. 10, 1918, was transferred to the Naval Air Station, at Pensacola, Fla.

He was commissioned Ensign, March 11, 1918, and Lieut. (j.g.), to rank from Oct. 1, 1918. Lieut. Smith was sent to the Coast Patrol Station at Cape May, in Aug., 1918, where he was Squadron Commander engaged in active service hunting submarines. He was one of the aviators to meet and welcome the fleet on its return to New York, Dec. 26, 1918. On Dec. 30, 1918, he was ordered to inactive duty at Cape May, returning to Harvard, Jan. 2, 1919, to complete his college course. He holds Pilot's licenses for land and seaplanes from the Aero Club of America; also U.S. Naval Pilot's license.

Brother in Service —

Charles Putnam Smith, 2d Lieut., U.S.A., Infantry.

Grandfather in Service —

Charles Putnam, Ensign, U.S.N., under Farragut, in Civil War.

ERNEST F. HENDERSON, Jr.

LIEUTENANT (*j.g.*), U.S.N.R.F., SQUADRON A, NORTHERN BOMBING GROUP

SON of Ernest F. and Bertha Henderson; was born at Chestnut Hill, Mass., March 7, 1897. He was educated at the Noble and Greenough School, and at Harvard College, A.B. 1918 (war degree). He rowed on the freshman inter-dormitory crew.

He enlisted at Cambridge, Mass., on April 3, 1917, as Radio Operator, U.S.N.R.F., and on April 28 was called to active duty; after two months he asked to be transferred to the Aviation Service. He trained at the Naval Aviation Ground School, M.I.T.; at Hampton Roads, Va.; and at Pensacola, Fla. He sailed overseas, March 29, 1918, and was stationed for three months at U.S.N. Seaplane Station, Moutchic-Lacanau, Gironde, France, when he was sent to Italy to fly Caproni biplanes back to France. The first machine in which he was sent out caught fire while flying over Turin, Italy, but with the flames streaming about him he succeeded in making a safe landing. The planes were imperfectly constructed, and five of the nineteen aviators who attempted to fly them to France lost their lives on the way. Lieut. Henderson finally accomplished his flight over the Alps and reached Lyons on Sept. 21, his time from Turin being three hours and five minutes. He was subsequently stationed at St.-Englevert, France, with the Northern Bombing Squadron, which was preparing to begin operations when the Armistice was signed. Lieut. Henderson had a second narrow escape when his machine was wrecked on landing, owing to defective gear.

He was commissioned Ensign, U.S.N.R.F., Feb. 28, 1918; Lieut. (j.g.), Oct. 1, 1918. He returned to the U.S. on Feb. 9, 1919, and was placed on inactive duty, March 15, 1919.

Brother in Service —

George B. Henderson, 1st Lieut., U.S.A., A.E.F.

CHARLES PRESCOTT STEWART

ENSIGN, U.S.N.R.F.

SON of Charles M. and Nettie (Prescott) Stewart; was born at Worcester, Mass., July 10, 1895. He was educated at the Bancroft School, Worcester; Worcester Classical High School; Milton Academy, Milton; and at Harvard College, class of 1917. At Milton he was monitor and baseball manager in 1913, playing second base on the team. At Harvard he was a member of the Delphic Club, Hasty Pudding, D.K.E., and Institute of 1770; and was on the staff of the *Lampoon*. He trained with the Harvard R.O.T.C. from Feb. to May, 1916. When war was declared he left college, and on April 30, 1917, enlisted in U.S.N.R.F., at the Brooklyn, N.Y., Navy Yard. From May 8 to Oct. 25, 1917, he served as Quartermaster on board the U.S.S. *Tarantula* (S.P. 124), guarding the entrance to New York Harbor. From Feb. 18 to May 1, 1918, he studied at the Aviation Ground School, M.I.T., acting as C.Q.M. (Aviation). From May 4 to July 14 he had elementary training at U.S.N.A. Station, Miami, Fla. From July 17 to Sept. 25 he took advanced training at Pensacola, Fla. He was commissioned Ensign, Sept. 14, 1918, and was ordered to England. From Nov. 4 to Dec. 1, 1918, he was attached to the U.S.N.A. Station, at Moutchic-Lacanau, France. He returned to the U.S. and received inactive duty orders, Jan. 13, 1919, at Bay Shore, N.Y.

CARL ELLIOT SHUMWAY

Lieutenant (*j.g.*), U.S.N.R.F., First Naval Kite Balloon Unit

Son of Mr. and Mrs. Franklin P. Shumway; was born at Melrose, Mass., June 30, 1890. He graduated from the Melrose High School, and from Dartmouth College, class of 1913. At college he was member of the freshman track team in 1909, and of the football squad in 1911. He was high-point winner at the Dartmouth Winter Carnival in 1913, and second in one-mile New England swimming championship, 1914, 1915, and 1916.

On July 10, 1917, he enlisted in the U.S. Navy Aviation Corps, and trained at Akron, Ohio, from Oct. 10 to Jan. 21, 1918. He completed training at Rockaway Beach, N.Y., Jan. 30, and sailed overseas for Liverpool, Feb. 26, 1918. From March 9 to April 6 he was stationed at the U.S. Naval Air Station, Queenstown, Ire., when he was transferred to the Royal Navy Station at Castletown, Berehaven, Ire., as representative of U.S.N.A. forces. On April 29, 1918, this station was taken over by the U.S., and Lieut. Shumway was appointed Commanding Officer. From May 18 to July 3, 1918, he served as Executive Officer, and from then to Aug. 21 as Commanding Officer. The Castletown Station was the first of the five Irish stations under the U.S. to operate, as well as the first Kite Balloon Station in Europe to fly and operate patrols.

On Aug. 23, 1918, Lieut. Shumway was transferred to the U.S. Naval Base at Plymouth, Eng., where, until Nov. 29, he was Commanding Officer of the U.S. Naval Kite Balloon Detachment, attached to S.S.T.B.D. Parker, flying from R.A.F. Balloon Base No. 16.

He was commissioned Ensign, U.S.N.R.F., Jan. 24, 1918; and Lieut. (j.g.), May 1, 1918. He returned to the U.S. on Jan. 14, 1919.

EDWARD ANDRUS TERHUNE, Jr.

ENSIGN, U.S.N.R.F., SQUADRON B, NORTHERN BOMBING GROUP

SON of Edward Andrus and Emma G. Terhune; was born, June 3, 1895, at Dorchester, Mass. He was educated at the Dorchester High School and at Tufts College, graduating in the class of 1917, *cum laude* (B.S. in Structural Engineering). He played quarterback on the 1917 football team, and pitched on the 1917 baseball team.

He enlisted at Boston, Feb. 18, 1918, and was trained at the M.I.T. Ground School, and U.S. Naval Air Station, Key West, Fla., at which latter place he was Temporary Instructor. He studied flying-boats at the U.S.N.A.S., Miami, Fla.; and land-planes with the U.S. Marines, Curtiss Field, Miami, Fla. He was commissioned Ensign, July 10, 1918.

He was sent overseas, and trained in bombing and gunnery at Moutchic-Lacanau, France; he was then attached to the Northern Bombing Group at Calais, France (Champagne, Field B). Later he was stationed with the Italians at Malpensa, Italy, and received an Italian brevet, on Caproni bombing-machines. He returned to the U.S., and was stationed at Chatham, Mass., U.S.N.A.S. He was released from active duty, March 25, 1919.

After leaving the Service, Ensign Terhune inaugurated an Aerial Taxi and Transportation Company operating between Boston and the North Shore, using machines of the Canadian training-plane type, with wireless telephone connections.

Brother in Service —

Howard Haven Terhune, Ensign, U.S.N.R.F.

THOMAS T. HOOPES

Ensign, U.S.N.R.F.

Son of the Rev. and Mrs. Wilford L. Hoopes, of Newbury, Mass.; was born at Boston, Mass., March 31, 1898. He was educated at the Choate School, Wallingford, Conn., and at Harvard College, leaving at the end of his sophomore year to enlist. He was a member of the Harvard Flying Corps in 1915–16, and flew at Wright Field, Mineola, N.Y., in the summer of 1916, as a member of that corps.

He enlisted at Boston, on April 28, 1917, having in March enrolled for the Mass. School for Naval Air Service at Squantum, Mass. He remained at Squantum until Oct., 1917, when he was ordered to the U.S. Naval Air Station, Hampton Roads, Va., from Oct. 17, 1917, to Jan. 10, 1918. He was stationed at U.S.N. Air Station, Pensacola, Fla., from Jan. 10 to June, 1918, and was commissioned Ensign, U.S.N.R.F., June 13, 1918.

Ensign Hoopes was appointed Radio Officer at U.S.N. Air Station, Chatham, Mass., and has served there from June 17, 1918, to the present time. At last accounts he was still in Service.

RUSSELL NOYES HYDE

LIEUTENANT (*j.g.*), U.S.N.R.F.

SON of William Whitcomb and Flora M. (Valiquet) Hyde; was born at Lynn, Mass., Oct. 15, 1896. He was educated at the Classical High School, Lynn, and at the Northeastern College, Boston.

He enlisted in the U.S.N.A.S. at Boston, in April, 1917, and reported July, 1917, at the M.I.T. for ground training, being a member of Flight A. He had flight training at Pensacola, Fla., from Sept., 1917; and was commissioned Ensign in Dec., 1917. He was ordered overseas for active duty in Jan., 1918, and was in special service in England, Ireland, Scotland, and France, instructing and testing at various stations, and doing much patrol flying in search of enemy submarines and aircraft. In Oct., 1918, he was commissioned Lieut. (j.g.).

After the Armistice, Lieut. Hyde returned to the U.S. in Dec., 1918; but remained in the Service, reporting at the Naval Air Station, Key West, Fla., where he was stationed at last accounts.

Relatives in Service —

Great-great-grandfather: Jedediah Hyde, Capt., Revolutionary War.
Great-grandfather: Russell Brown Hyde, Major, Mexican War.
Grandfather: Breed Noyes Hyde, Col., Civil War.
Grandfather: Thomas Valiquet, Major, French Army.

ELMER LEIGHTON MITCHELL

LIEUTENANT (*j.g.*), U.S.N.R.F.

SON of Sidney A. and Maude A. (Canning) Mitchell; was born at Boston, Mass., Nov. 16, 1896. He was educated at the Stone School, Boston, and at Harvard College. He was coxswain of the Boston interscholastic crew, 1912–14; a member of the Stone crew, 1915; and of the Harvard freshman four-oared crew, 1916.

He enlisted at the Charlestown Navy Yard, as Machinist's Mate, 2d class, and was stationed at Pensacola, Fla., Sept. 6 to Nov. 26, 1917. He was later transferred to Student Officer, and completed work at the Ground School, M.I.T., Feb. 16, 1918.

He qualified as a Naval Aviator in May, 1918, and was ordered to Pensacola, Fla. He was commissioned Ensign, U.S.N.R.F., June 12, 1918. From May to Aug., 1918, he acted as Instructor to the 6th Squadron at Pensacola. On Aug. 3, 1918, he was made Division Commander, 6th Squadron, and on Dec. 23, 1918, he was commissioned Lieut. (j.g.).

Lieut. Mitchell, on Jan. 28, 1919, was made 6th Squadron Commander, and on Feb. 20, Commander of the Navigation School at Pensacola. He was ordered to inactive duty, March 12, 1919, at Pensacola, Fla.

JOHN MATTHEW MILLER

ENSIGN, U.S.N.R.F.

SON of John Matthew Miller and Fannie (Paddock) Miller, of Wellesley, Mass.; was born at Tacoma, Wash., June 3, 1896. He was educated at the Kent School, Kent, Conn.

He enlisted at Boston, Mass., July 23, 1917, and was assigned to the Naval Aviation School, M.I.T. He was subsequently trained at the Naval Air Stations at Hampton Roads, Va.; Pensacola, Fla.; and Rockaway Beach, N.Y.

He was commissioned Ensign, March 16, 1918. On the cessation of hostilities he was ordered to inactive service, and on Dec. 15, 1918, was appointed to the Post-Office Department, Aerial Mail Service, as manager of the Philadelphia Field, and later of the Mail Field, at Belmont Park, Queens, N.Y.

Ensign Miller comes from a family notable for its military record: one ancestor, Charles Fanning, was at Valley Forge; another, Nathaniel Fanning, was second in command to John Paul Jones, on the *Bonhomme Richard;* a third, William Bradford Whiting, was on the staff of Commodore Perry in the expedition to Japan, 1854. His family records show that thirty-five members served in the Revolutionary War, fifteen in the War of 1812, thirty-two in the Civil War, and nine in the Great War.

EDWARD SLOCUM BREWER

LIEUTENANT, U.S.N.R.F.

SON of Joseph and Helen (Slocum) Brewer; was born, April 10, 1896, at Milton, Mass. He was captain of the football team at Milton Academy in 1914, and graduated in 1915, entering Harvard College in the class of 1919.

He attended the Plattsburg Training Camp from July 5 to Aug. 8, 1916. In March, 1917, he enlisted in the Naval Reserve at the Charlestown Navy Yard, and was sent to Marblehead with the patrol fleet. On May 3, 1917, he was transferred to the Naval Aviation Service, and was trained at Pensacola, Fla. He was commissioned Ensign on Dec. 17, 1917. On Dec. 22 he was ordered to France, and arrived in Paris, Jan. 29, 1918; on Feb. 3, he was transferred to London.

He was attached to the R.N.A.S. from Feb. 8 to July 13, doing submarine patrol work at Westgate, Portland, and Felixstowe. He was ordered back to Paris on July 13, and joined the U.S.N.A.S. at St.-Trojan. From July 28 to Oct. 25 he served as submarine patrol and convoy. From Oct. 28 to Dec. 2 he was with the U.S.N.A.S. at Arcachon, in submarine patrol and convoy work as Chief Pilot. He was recommended Lieut. (j.g.) in July, 1918; Lieut., Oct., 1918. On Dec. 11, 1918, he was commissioned Lieut.; sailed from Bordeaux on Dec. 24, 1918, arriving in New York on Jan. 3, 1919. He was placed on inactive duty at Bay Shore, N.Y.

ALBION KEITH EATON

LIEUTENANT (*j.g.*), U.S.N.R.F.C., SQUADRONS 1, 3, 15, 16

SON of Albion Horace and Annie (Whidden) Eaton; was born at Calais, Me., June 14, 1891. He was educated at the Calais High School, Phillips Exeter Academy, 1911, and Bowdoin College, B.S. 1915. At Exeter, he played on the hockey and golf teams; at Bowdoin, on the hockey, tennis, and baseball teams; he was captain of the baseball team, and won the Maine intercollegiate championship in tennis.

He enlisted at Boston, Mass., on July 14, 1917, and trained at the M.I.T. Ground School; and at Pensacola, Fla., where he acted as Gunnery Pilot in advanced work. He spent six months as Instructor in Flying, and was Division Commander at Squantum. He was commissioned Ensign on March 8, 1918. At Pensacola he was Division Commander and Stunt Instructor; and Squadron Commander of Squadron 15, at San Diego, Cal. He was commissioned Lieut. (j.g.), dating from Dec., 1918, and on April 15, 1919, was honorably discharged at San Diego, Cal.

During his Service Lieut. Eaton made patrol flights along the Atlantic and Pacific coasts, totalling 400 hours solo work.

Married, Oct. 3, 1918, Mary E. Campbell.

Brothers in Service —

Carleton W. Eaton, Ensign, U.S.N.R.F.C.

Horace E. Eaton, Lieut., U.S.A., Field Artillery; Judge Advocate at Brest, France.

PAUL FROST IVES

Lieutenant, U.S.N.R.F., Casual Officer

Son of Archer Ward and Pauline (Frost) Ives; was born at Brookline, Mass., Aug. 12, 1893. He was educated at the R. G. Shaw School, West Roxbury High School, and Berkeley Preparatory School.

On May 5, 1917, he enlisted at Dedham, Mass., in U.S.N.R.F., Class 445. He attended Ground School, and Flying School, at Pensacola, Fla., from July 10 to Dec. 20, 1917. He sailed overseas on Jan. 13, 1918; was detailed to R.N.A. Station, Calshot, Eng., for advanced patrol training, Feb. 7, 1918. He was assigned to R.N.A. Station, Portland, for patrol duty, Feb. 13, 1918; and was transferred to Felixstowe, May 7, 1918, for reconnaissance work. On July 30, 1918, he was ordered to the U.S.N.A. Station at Killingholme, Eng., where he served as Pilot and Flight Commander until the Armistice. He sailed for America on Nov. 24, 1918. He was commissioned Ensign, U.S.N.R.F., Dec. 21, 1917; Lieut. (j.g.), April 24, 1918. He was detached from active duty, Jan. 17, 1919, having been previously commissioned Lieut.

The following is an extract from a report issued by the Navy Department at Washington, and signed by Franklin D. Roosevelt, relative to the services of Ensign Ives, U.S.N.R.F., attached to the Royal Navy Air Station, Calshot:

> . . . The Department quotes below for your information the report of Vice-Admiral Sims, relative to your operations while on scout duty against enemy submarines, under orders from the Commanding Officer of the Royal Navy Air Station, Portland, England: "The attached correspondence relative to the performance of duty of Ensign Paul F. Ives . . . U.S.N.R.F., reflects credit on both these officers. It is recommended that adequate recognition of their services be granted." The Department wishes to avail itself of this opportunity to express to you the very high appreciation felt upon receipt of reports similar to the above. It is strong evidence of the fact that earnest coöperation exists between the armed forces of our Allies and the United States Armed Forces. It is work of this character that will impress our enemies with the realization that the United States is a power very much to be considered. Accordingly, you are hereby highly commended for your valiant and earnest efforts on this particular occasion. It is to be hoped that a continuance of such work will be maintained in the future. . . .

Married, Dec. 16, 1918, Ruth Merrill.

HENRY SWIFT

LIEUTENANT, U.S.N.R.F.

SON of Dr. and Mrs. William N. Swift; was born at New Bedford, Mass., in 1893. He attended the Friends' Academy, New Bedford; Milton Academy; and St. George's School, Newport, R.I. He graduated from Harvard College in 1915.

In April, 1917, he volunteered for the Naval Aviation Service and was sent to Squantum, Mass., for training, then, in July, to the Ground School at Toronto University, Toronto, Can., and later to the flying school at Camp Rathbun; receiving final training at Camp Borden, Can. He was commissioned Ensign, in Dec., 1917, and sent to Hampton Roads, Va.; from there he was transferred to Pensacola, Fla., in Jan., 1918.

He was made Superintendent of Aviation Mechanics' Schools, and commissioned Lieut. (j.g.), U.S.N.R.F., Class 5, in Aug., 1918. In April, 1919, he was commissioned Lieut., and was at last accounts still in the Service, and stationed at Great Lakes, Ill., where he was Superintending Instructor of Miscellaneous Maintenance Force at the Navy Aviation Mechanics' School.

Married, in 1914, Josephine Ranlet, of Boston.

JOSEPH C. HALLETT

Ensign, U.S.N.R.F.

Son of Nelson A. and Mary E. Hallett, of Newtonville, Mass.; was born at Lynn, Mass., Aug. 5, 1894. He was educated at the Newton High School, the Stone School, and at Dartmouth College, A.B. 1917.

He attended the Plattsburg Training Camp in 1916, and enlisted at Boston, Mass., April 4, 1917. He was first stationed at Commonwealth Pier, Boston, then at Bumkin's Island. He was then trained as a night bomber at the M.I.T., N.A. School; and at the Naval Air Station, Pensacola, Fla. He sailed overseas, expecting to be transferred to the Marine Aviation Service, and used for bombing enemy cities and towns, but on account of lack of planes, he was sent to N.A.S., at Moutchic-Lacanau, France, for further training in coast patrol work. After a short period of instruction, he was detached for service at the Naval Station at St.-Trojan, on an island off the French coast, where he remained until the Armistice. He was commissioned Ensign, on July 8, 1918. He returned to the U.S. and was relieved from active duty Jan. 2, 1919, at New York.

Relatives in Service —

Grandfather: Nelson A. Hallett, Artificer, with the U.S. Engineers, Civil War.

Uncle: James H. Hallett, Sergeant, Heavy Artillery, Spanish-American War.

HOWARD JOHN ROWEN

LIEUTENANT (*j.g.*), U.S.N.R.F.

SON of Edward George and Annie Matina (McNeil) Rowen; was born at Jamaica Plain, Mass., July 22, 1895. He attended the public schools of Jamaica Plain, and graduated from Boston College in 1916. At college he was for two years captain of the track team, and one year manager of the football team.

He enlisted in the U.S.N.R.F., May 5, 1917, at the Boston Navy Yard, and trained at the M.I.T., from July 21 to Sept. 16. He was then sent to Pensacola, Fla., where he trained until Dec. 21, 1917, when he was commissioned Ensign. He sailed overseas Jan. 15, 1918, and after being stationed at London for a month, was transferred to the Bombing School at Moutchic-Lacanau, France, where he remained until April 15, when he was ordered to the Naval Air Station at Île Tudy. He was commissioned Lieut. (j.g.), and made Chief Pilot at this station about May 25, 1918. He was stationed there on duty until the end of the war.

On July 5, 1918, Lieut. Rowen received a submarine warning from some twenty-five miles distant, and he and his observer, in company with another plane, at once started out; finding traces of the enemy they let go their bombs and succeeded in destroying a submarine which was known to have been doing much damage in that vicinity. The destruction of this submarine was officially credited to Lieut. Rowen and his observer, and they also destroyed a number of mines in that vicinity. The station at Île Tudy was especially commended as a model for its excellent work and efficiency.

Lieut. Rowen returned to the U.S., Dec. 1, 1918, and was assigned to the N.A. Station at Key West, Fla., as Squadron Commander. In connection with recruiting, he did considerable "movie" work for the Government, and before his return from France was selected to be sent home as Instructor in Patrol Work, which plan was given up on account of the Armistice. He was placed on inactive duty at Key West, June 20, 1919.

Brother in Service —

Edward Joseph Rowen, U.S.N.R.F., Engineer Officer at Pauillac, France.

RICHARD A. MARSCHAT

Ensign, U.S.N.R.F.

Son of Albert and Karoline (Vicital) Marschat, of Ashley Falls, Mass.; was born at New York City, June 15, 1894. He was educated at the Morris High School, New York City, at Mercersburg Academy, and at Dartmouth College. In both preparatory school and college he was a member of the track and cross-country teams.

He enlisted as Seaman, 1st class, May 18, 1917, in the Naval Reserve Force at New York, and was in training at Pelham Bay, until Dec. 13, 1917. He entered the Naval Aviation Detachment at M.I.T., Feb. 18, 1918, and was transferred to Pensacola, Fla., as Student Naval Aviator, training from May 18 to Aug. 20, 1918. He was commissioned Ensign, Aug. 20, 1918.

Ensign Marschat was detailed to the U.S. Naval Station at Chatham, Mass., Sept. 6, 1918, for active duty as Coast Submarine Patrol.

Brothers in Service —

Albert J. Marschat, Private, Signal Corps, A.E.F.
Arthur G. Marschat, Private, Signal Corps, A.E.F.
Lawrence Marschat, Midshipman, Junior Naval Reserve.

*PHILLIPS WARD PAGE

ENSIGN, U.S.N.R.F.

Killed in airplane accident, Dec., 1917

SON of Cyrus Andrew and Anna M. (Phillips) Page; was born Nov. 28, 1885. He graduated from Harvard College in 1909. In April, 1917, he enlisted in the Aviation Service, and was stationed at Squantum, Mass., during the summer of 1917. In Nov. he was sent overseas to France. He was commissioned Ensign in 1917. During a trial flight off the English coast, he was killed in an airplane accident in Dec., 1917. (Portrait on opposite page.)

PHILIP THAYER STONEMETZ

ENSIGN, U.S.N.R.F.

SON of Harry M. and Flora Cooley Stonemetz; was born at Newton, Mass., April 8, 1899. He was educated at the Newton High School, and at Williams College, class of 1921. In the high school he was a member of the hockey team. In 1916 he attended the Officers' Training Camp at Plattsburg. He enlisted, May 26, 1918, and trained at the M.I.T. Naval Aviation School until Aug. 16, 1918. He was then assigned to the Naval Air Station, at Miami, Fla., where he remained until Oct. 20, 1918. He was then transferred to the Air Station at Pensacola, Fla.; there he was commissioned Ensign, Jan. 14, 1919, and placed on inactive duty, Feb. 11, 1919.

*MICHAEL JOSEPH DELEHANTY

Ensign, U.S.N.R.F.

Killed in airplane accident, March 25, 1918

Born at Boston, Mass., Jan. 17, 1896. He was educated at the English High School and at Bowdoin College. He entered the Naval Aviation Service, and attended the M.I.T. Naval Aviation Ground School. He continued his training at Norfolk, Va., and at Pensacola, Fla. On March 25, 1918, he was killed in an accident at Pensacola. (Portrait on opposite page.)

JOHN M. PETTINGELL

Second Lieutenant, A.S.A., U.S.A.

Son of Capt. John Mason and Caroline (Fowler) Pettingell, of Cambridge, Mass.; was born at Newburyport, Mass., May 26, 1890. He graduated from the Newburyport High School in 1908, and from the Mass. Institute of Technology in 1912. He enlisted at Chicago, Ill., Sept. 27, 1917. On Dec. 29, 1917, he graduated from Squadron 25, at the School of Military Aeronautics, Austin, Tex., and was assigned to the 3d Cadet Squadron at Ellington Field, Houston, Tex. He was subsequently Acrobatic and Cadet Flying Instructor at Payne Field, West Point, Miss. He was commissioned 2d Lieut., April 20, 1918, and completed final training at the 3d A.I.C., Issoudun, France, as Pursuit Pilot. He returned to the U.S., and was honorably discharged on Feb. 24, 1919, at Camp Dix, N.J.

Father in Service —

John Mason Pettingell, Capt., 8th Mass. Inf., Spanish-American War.

HAROLD COBB HARRIS

LIEUTENANT (*j.g.*), U.S.N.R.F.

SON of Samuel Tibbets and Caroline S. (Cobb) Harris, of Dedham, Mass.; was born at Somerville, Mass., Dec. 16, 1895. He was educated at the Powder Point School and at Dartmouth College.

He attended the Plattsburg Training Camp in June, 1916. He enlisted at Boston, Mass., on April 3, 1917, and was attached to the U.S. Naval Aeronautical Detachment, at Akron, Ohio, from Oct. 8, 1917, to Jan. 15, 1918. He was trained at the Naval Air Station, Rockaway, N.Y., from Jan. 16 to Jan. 30, 1918. He sailed overseas, and was attached to the U.S. Naval Air Station, Queenstown, Ireland, from March 9 to March 19, 1918. He was subsequently stationed at the R.N.A.S. School, Rockampton, Eng., from March 20 to April 20, 1918; U.S. Naval Air Station, Wexford, Ireland, April 25 to July 3, 1918; U.S. Naval Air Station, La Trinité, France, July 11 to Aug. 17, and Sept. 27 to Nov. 25, 1918; U.S. Naval Air Station, Brest, France, Aug. 18 to Sept. 26, 1918; U.S. Naval Air Station, Cape May, N.J., from Jan. 25, 1919, to date. He was commissioned Ensign, U.S.N.R.F., Jan. 24, 1918; and Lieut. (j.g.), U.S.N.R.F., Oct. 1, 1918. Lieut. Harris was a member of the first class of naval kite balloon pilots to be instructed and graduated, as a class, in this branch of Naval Aviation. At last accounts he had qualified as a dirigible pilot at Cape May, N.J.

HENRY COMYN CLAYTON

ENSIGN, U.S.N.R.F., NAVAL AIR STATION, CHATHAM, MASS.
NORTHERN BOMBING GROUP, SQUADRON 1

SON of Henry Helm and Fawn (Comyn) Clayton; was born at Milton, Mass., April 29, 1894. He was educated at the Canton High School, and at the Mass. Institute of Technology, where he took a three-year course in electro-chemistry before his entry into the Naval Service. He attended the Plattsburg Training Camp in 1915 and in 1916.

On May 10, 1917, he enlisted at Boston, in the U.S. Naval Reserve Flying Corps. From July 23 to Sept. 15, 1917, he trained at the M.I.T. Ground School. From Sept. 15 to Jan. 9, 1918, he was attached to the U.S. Naval Air Station, Hampton Roads, Va., and from Jan. 11 to Feb. 24, to the N.A. Station, Pensacola, Fla. He was commissioned Ensign, Feb. 18, 1918. Receiving overseas orders, he trained from April 3 to June 10, at the U.S.N. Air Station, Moutchic-Lacanau, France. He was then transferred to the Italian Army School of Aviation, at Malpensa, Italy, where he remained from June 19 to July 22, 1918. From the latter date until Oct. 26, he acted as Ferry Pilot from Milan, a fortnight of this time being spent at Gioia del Colle, Italy. From Oct. 30, 1918, to Jan. 15, 1919, he was a member of the Northern Bombing Group, Squadron 1. Early in 1919, Ensign Clayton returned to America and was stationed, from Feb. 28, 1919, at the U.S. Naval Air Station, Chatham, Mass.

Married, June 23, 1917, Augusta Frances Capen.

ALDRED K. WARREN, Jr.

Ensign, U.S.N.R.F.

Born July 2, 1897, at Staten Island, N.Y. He graduated from the Salem High School in 1916. He served for five months on the Mexican Border, at Fort Bliss, El Paso, Tex., with the 1st Mass. F.A., N.G., from June to Nov., 1916. He enrolled in the Naval Reserve Flying Corps, in April, 1917; was called to active service in July, and was assigned to the Naval Aviation Ground School at the M.I.T. In Sept., 1917, he was sent to Pensacola, Fla., for flight training, and in Nov. qualified as a Naval Aviator. He was commissioned Ensign, in Nov., 1917, and ordered to San Diego, Cal., as a Flight Instructor, in Dec., 1917. There he remained, fulfilling the duties of a Division Commander until ordered to Pensacola, Fla., for advanced training in Dec., 1918. (Portrait on opposite page.)

GEORGE LINWOOD HALL

Second Lieutenant, A.S.A., U.S.A.

Son of George W. and Effie B. Hall; was born at Mansfield, Mass., May 2, 1898. He was educated in the Mansfield public schools, and at the M.I.T. He enlisted at Boston, on Nov. 12, 1917. He trained successively at Princeton Ground School, Dec. 8, 1917, to Feb. 16, 1918; Camp Dick, Dallas, Tex., Feb. 21 to March 12; Taliaferro Field, Ft. Worth, Tex., March 13, to June 13. He was commissioned 2d Lieut., A.S., June 5, 1918. He was on duty at Camp Dick, Dallas, Tex., June 13 to July 28; Armorers' School, Wilbur Wright Field, Fairfield, O., Aug. 1 to Aug. 28, 1918. On Sept. 15 he sailed for France, and was stationed from Oct. 13, 1918, to Jan. 20, 1919, at 3d A.I.C., Issoudun, France. He completed his training as pursuit pilot late in Nov., 1918. He returned to the U.S. on Feb. 17, 1919, and was honorably discharged Feb. 20, 1919, at Garden City, N.Y.

GORDON C. PRINCE

Captain, A.S., U.S.A.

Son of Gordon and Lillian (Chickering) Prince; was born at Boston, Mass. He graduated from Harvard College in 1910. Before the declaration of war by the U.S. he volunteered for the Aviation Service, passed his examinations as an aviator, and began training at Newport News, Va. He attended the M.I.T. Ground School and sailed for Italy in Aug., 1917. He continued his training at Foggia, and was commissioned 1st Lieut. in Oct., 1917. In the spring of 1918 he was sent to France, where he was ill with malaria all summer; upon recovery, he was made Instructor at Issoudun, his health not permitting him to fly in high altitudes. Lieut. Prince returned to the U.S. and was honorably discharged in March, 1919. He subsequently received notice of his promotion to Captain. (Portrait on opposite page.)

CHESTER I. CHASE

Cadet, A.S.A., U.S.A.

Son of George Burton and Maud A. (Ingalls) Chase, of Melrose, Mass.; was born at Malden, Mass., Dec. 10, 1896. He was educated in the public schools of Melrose, and at the Mass. Agricultural College. At college he was a member of the Cadet Battalion. He enlisted in the Air Service at Boston, Mass., Dec. 31, 1917. From May 18, 1918, to Aug. 14, 1918, he received ground school training at M.I.T. He was then transferred to Camp Dick, Dallas, Tex., where he remained from Aug. 17 to Sept. 21, 1918. He was subsequently stationed at Barron Field, Everman, Tex., from Sept. 21 to Nov. 27, when he received his honorable discharge from the Air Service.

LISPENARD BATHE PHISTER

Second Lieutenant, A.S.A., U.S.A.

Son of Walter Bell and Elizabeth J. Phister, of Hartford, Conn.; was born at Chicago, Ill., Sept. 27, 1896. He was educated in the public schools of Chicago, at Williams College, and at Trinity College. He enlisted at Cambridge, Mass., July 26, 1917, and graduated from the M.I.T. Ground School, Nov. 10, 1917. On Nov. 23, 1917, he sailed overseas, and continued his training at St.-Maixent, France, until May 15, 1918. He was commissioned 2d Lieut., S.O.R.C., May 18, 1918; placed on active duty and commissioned 2d Lieut., A.S.A., dating from June 13, 1918. He received flying training at Voves, and at Avord, and served as staff-pilot at Observers' School at Tours, from Sept. 24, 1918, to Feb. 8, 1919. Received Brevet d'Aviateur Militaire, July 22, 1918, and civilian brevet from the Aero Club of France. He arrived in N.Y., May 6, 1919, and was honorably discharged at Camp Dodge, Ia., May 22, 1919. (Portrait on opposite page.)

LEO J. LEEBURN

Second Lieutenant, A.S.A., U.S.A.

Son of Samuel A. and Catherine E. Leeburn; was born at Pawtucket, R.I., Nov. 28, 1890. He was educated at the Pawtucket High School. He enlisted in the Air Service at Providence, R.I., Nov. 30, 1917, and was assigned to the M.I.T. Ground School, where he remained from Dec. 1 to Dec. 22, 1917. He was transferred to Cornell University, Ithaca, N.Y., where he finished the course, Feb. 9, 1918, and was then stationed at Camp Dick, Dallas, Tex., until April 11. He was subsequently ordered to Eberts Field, Lonoke, Ark., where he trained from April 12 to July 19, 1918. On July 20, 1918, he was commissioned 2d Lieut., and detailed to Eberts Field, as Flying Instructor, from July 20, 1918, to Feb. 8, 1919. He was then assigned to Love Field, Dallas, Tex., as Flying Instructor, and served from Feb. 12 to April 1, 1919, when he was honorably discharged.

Brother in Service —

William J. Leeburn, Ambulance Driver, 42d Sanitary Train.

JAMES ALLAN HODDER

Cadet, A.S., U.S.A.

Son of Alfred LeRoy and Jessie D. Hodder, of Framingham, Mass.; was born at Rosemont, Pa., May 29, 1897. His childhood was spent in Neuchâtel, Switzerland. He attended the Kent School in Conn., graduated from Newton High School in 1915, and entered the University of Neuchâtel, Switzerland, in 1915. He drove a hospital supply ambulance at Paris in the summer of 1916, then returned to the U.S. and entered Harvard College, class of 1920. He left Harvard after the declaration of war, enlisting in the U.S. Ambulance Service, and was assigned to the Harvard Unit. He reached France in Dec., 1917, and passed examination for transfer to the Aviation Division, which Service he entered in France on his twenty-first birthday, May 29, 1918. He trained in France at Tours and Châteauroux. (Portrait on opposite page.)

IRAD EDMUNDS WILLIS

Second Lieutenant, A.S., U.S.A.

Son of Newton Allen and Clara Isabel (Edmunds) Willis; was born at Concord, N.H., July 20, 1887. He was educated at the Concord High School, and at Harvard and Cornell Universities.

He enlisted in the Air Service at Boston, Mass., Jan. 29, 1918, and was assigned to Camp Dick, Dallas, Tex., where he remained from June 1 to June 25, 1918. He attended the M.I.T. Ground School from June 29 to Sept. 6, and the Ground School at Cornell University from Sept. 7 to Sept. 21, 1918. He then trained at Camp Dick, Dallas, Tex., where he remained from Oct. 4 to Oct. 16. He was subsequently ordered to the Coast Artillery School, Fort Monroe, Virginia, Oct. 20 to Dec. 6, 1918, and to the School of Aerial Observation, Post Field, Fort Sill, Okla., Dec. 10, 1918, to Feb. 14, 1919. He was commissioned 2d Lieut., Dec. 6, 1918, and applied for discharge at Post Field, Fort Sill, Okla., Feb. 14, 1919.

GEORGE H. MACKAY, Jr.

First Lieutenant, R.A.F.

Son of George H. and Maria Mitchell (Starbuck) Mackay; was born at Boston, Mass., Oct. 13, 1885. He attended the Noble and Greenough School, and graduated from Harvard College in 1908. He served for over nine years in the National Guard, being with the 1st Corps of Cadets; the Coast Artillery Corps; and the 1st Squadron of Cavalry, with which he served as Sergeant, on the Mexican Border.

On March 17, 1917, he enlisted in the Royal Flying Corps, and trained at Camp Borden, Toronto, Can. He was commissioned 2d Lieut., July 23, 1917, and 1st Lieut. April 1, 1918. While in Canada he was badly injured in a "crash." He sailed overseas and was stationed at Cranwell, Eng., where he served as a Flying Officer. He was discharged, owing to wounds, Dec. 21, 1918.

(Portrait on opposite page.)

MANSON McKOWN DILLAWAY

Second Lieutenant, A.S.A., U.S.A.

Son of George L. and Josephine Dillaway, of Wakefield, Mass.; was born at Bath, Me., Sept. 2, 1894. He graduated from Tufts College, and was studying at the Boston University Law School at the time of his enlistment. He had previously served in the 6th Mass. Infantry, N.G., from June, 1916, to Nov. 1, 1917. On the latter date he enlisted in the Aviation Service at Boston, and attended the M.I.T. Ground School from Nov. 3, 1917, to Jan. 4, 1918. From Jan. 5 to Jan. 12, he trained at the Cornell Ground School; then transferred to Gerstner Field, Lake Charles, La., where he trained from Jan. 19 to May 30. There he was commissioned 2d Lieut., May 8, 1918. In June he was stationed at Camp Dick, Dallas, Tex.; from June 17 to July 17, at Fort Sill, Okla.; from July 17 to Nov. 1, at Hicks Field, Fort Worth, Tex.; and later at Garden City, N. Y. Honorably discharged, Dec. 11, 1918.

Brother in Service —

George L. D. Dillaway, 6th Mass. Inf., N.G., entered West Point, U.S.M.A., June, 1917.

CHARLES R. MACAULAY

FIRST LIEUTENANT, A.S., U.S.A.

BORN at Beverly, Mass., Dec. 16, 1893. He graduated from the Beverly High School, and from Pratt Institute in 1915. On Feb. 11, 1916, he enlisted at Olean, N.Y., in the Infantry, N.Y. National Guard. He saw service at the Mexican Border, in 1916, and was promoted to Corporal. Following the declaration of war, he was chosen from the National Guard to attend the Officers' Training Camp, where he was commissioned 1st Lieut., U.S. Infantry, in Aug., 1917. He was a member of the "Iron Battalion" under Col. Azan at Cambridge, Mass. He was assigned to the 312th Infantry, at Camp Dix, where he remained until Jan., 1918; he then transferred to Aviation, and trained at Austin, Tex., from April 1 to June, 1918, and Kelly Field, San Antonio, and was commissioned 1st Lieut., A.S., U.S.A., Nov. 1, 1918. On Nov. 28 he was sent to San Diego as Instructor in Advanced Flying. Honorably discharged, Jan. 4, 1919.

Brother in Service —
A. Vernon Macaulay, 2d Lieut., A.S., U.S.A.

A. VERNON MACAULAY

SECOND LIEUTENANT, A.S., U.S.A.

BORN at Beverly, Mass., April 4, 1891. He graduated from the Beverly High School, and was engaged in business with the United Shoe Machinery Co., when the U.S. entered the war. He enlisted at Boston, Mass., July 15, 1917, in the Aviation Section, U.S.A. He attended the M.I.T. Ground School from Oct. 15 to Jan. 1, 1918, when he was transferred to the School of Military Aeronautics at Princeton, N.J. On Feb. 2, 1918, he was sent to Dallas, Tex., for some weeks, continuing his training at Chanute Field, Rantoul, Ill., where he qualified as a Pursuit Pilot, and was commissioned 2d Lieut. on June 8, 1918. Lieut. Macaulay was sent to Dallas, Tex., where he took a course in Aerial Navigation, and then to Dayton, Ohio. He received overseas orders, and arrived in France, Oct. 10, 1918. Had completed training at time of Armistice.

Brother in Service —
Charles R. Macaulay, 1st Lieut., A.S., U.S.A.

WILLIAM PLATT

ENSIGN, U.S.N.R.F.

SON of Mr. and Mrs. Charles A. Platt; was born at New York City, Feb. 6, 1897. He was educated at St. Mark's School, Southboro, Mass., and at Harvard College, class of 1919. At St. Mark's he was captain of the football and hockey teams. At Harvard he was a member of the freshman football and hockey teams.

He attended the Plattsburg Training Camps in 1915 and 1916. On March 16, 1917, he enlisted in the U.S.N.R.F. at the Charlestown Navy Yard, Charlestown, Mass. He was trained successively at the Naval Air Stations at Hampton Roads, Va., Pensacola, Fla., Marine Field, Miami, Fla.; and was stationed at the Naval Air Station, Anacostia, D.C., until he sailed overseas, on Aug. 24, 1918. In France he was stationed at the U.S. Naval Air Stations at Moutchic-Lacanau, and at Brest. He was commissioned Ensign, March 16, 1918.

STEPHEN PAINE

ENSIGN, U.S.N.R.F., SQUADRON 12

SON of William A. and Ruth (Felton) Paine; was born in Boston, Mass., July 30, 1897. He attended the Country Day School in Newton, Mass., from 1907 to 1916, and was manager of the school track team. He entered Harvard College with the class of 1920; trained with the Harvard R.O.T.C., and enlisted in the U.S.N.R.F. at Boston, in April, 1918, in his freshman year.

He began his training at the Naval Aviation Ground School, M.I.T., and was later assigned to Key West, Fla., for flight training. In Oct., 1918, he was commissioned Ensign at Key West, Fla., and made an Instructor. His designation as a Naval Aviator was received Oct. 28, 1918. He remained at Key West until returned to inactive duty on Feb. 5, 1919.

MORRIS HALL BAILEY

Lieutenant (*j.g.*), U.S.N.R.F.C.

Son of Albert E. and Marion Breed (Hall) Bailey; was born at North Scituate, Mass., Oct. 25, 1898. He attended the Newton High School and Worcester Academy, and entered Harvard College in 1915.

He enlisted in Naval Aviation as soon as that branch of the Service was created in June, 1917. He trained at the Naval Aviation Ground School, M.I.T., and later at Pensacola, Fla. He was commissioned Ensign, in Feb., 1918, and sailed for France, March 6, 1918, finishing his training at Moutchic-Lacanau, France. In May, 1918, he was transferred to Areachon, in the Gironde, and saw active service there, as well as at Île Tudy, Finistère.

He returned to the U.S. on Dec. 18, 1918, and was placed on active duty at Chatham, Mass., where he was made Flight Commander. He was later stationed at the Naval Air Base, at Norfolk, Va. He was commissioned Lieut. (j.g.) in March, 1919.

WILLIS DUER THOMPSON, Jr.

Ensign, U.S.N.R.F.

Son of Willis Duer and Abby E. (Whiton) Thompson; was born at Concord, N.H., May 26, 1895. He was educated at the Concord High School, and at Dartmouth College, class of 1917. Previous to enlistment he trained with the Dartmouth College Regiment, in 1917.

He enlisted at Boston, Mass., on May 4, 1917, and spent two months with the M.I.T. Naval Aviation Detachment; then four months at the Naval Air Station, Hampton Roads, Va. Following this he trained for two months at the Naval Air Station, Pensacola, Fla. He was commissioned Ensign, March 4, 1918, ordered overseas, and stationed at the Naval Air Station, Moutchic-Lacanau, France. His permanent assignment was at the U.S. Naval Air Station, L'Aber Vrach, Finistère, France.

Released from active service at Bay Shore, N.Y., on Dec. 20, 1918.

Brother in Service —

Raymond M. Thompson, Lieut., U.S.A., 2d Marine Corps; died of influenza, Sept. 13, 1918.

THEODORE PHINNEY GROSVENOR

LIEUTENANT (*j.g.*), U.S.N.R.F.

SON of William and Rose D. (Phinney) Grosvenor; was born at Providence, R.I., Jan. 3, 1897. He was educated at St. George's School, Newport, R.I., and at Harvard College, class of 1920.

He attended the Plattsburg Training Camp in 1916, and the Harvard R.O.T.C. for one year. He enlisted at Squantum, Mass., and was attached to the U.S.N.A. Station there from May 10 to Oct. 15, 1917. He trained at U.S.N.A.S., Hampton Roads, Va., from Oct. 15 to Feb. 5, 1918. He was commissioned Ensign, Jan. 2, 1918; attended Camp Hicks, Tex., School of Aerial Gunnery, R.F.C., from Feb. 5 to March 1, 1918; was attached to Headquarters, Washington, D.C., from March 1 to March 29, 1918. He sailed overseas, March 29, and was stationed at U.S.N.A.S., Killingholme, Eng., till Dec. 1, 1918. He was commissioned Lieut. (j.g.), Oct. 1, 1918. Placed on inactive duty, Jan. 15, 1919.

Brother in Service —

William Grosvenor, 2d Lieut., A.S.A., U.S.A.

WILLIAM FORBES MUDGE

LIEUTENANT (*j.g.*), U.S.N.R.F., NORTHERN BOMBING GROUP

SON of Arthur W. and Alice (Green) Mudge; was born at Jamaica Plain, Mass., Sept. 1, 1895. He was educated at Worcester Academy, Phillips Andover Academy, and at Princeton University.

He attended the Plattsburg Training Camp in 1916, and enlisted on June 4, 1917, at New York City. He trained with the Royal Flying Corps at the School of Military Aeronautics, Toronto, Can.; at Camp Rathbun; Deseronto; and Camp Borden; from July 10 to Nov. 9, 1917, when he was commissioned Ensign, U.S.N.R.F. He was stationed successively at Bay Shore, N.Y., and Pensacola, Fla., until June 25, 1918. He sailed overseas, and was attached to the Northern Bombing Group, U.S.N.A. Force from July 17 to Nov. 23, 1918. On Dec. 3, 1918, he was commissioned Lieut. (j.g.). Placed on inactive duty Jan. 1, 1919.

Brother in Service —

Arthur W. Mudge, Jr., Capt., U.S.A., 22d Regiment, Infantry.

JOSHUA CRANE, JR.

LIEUTENANT (*j.g.*), U.S.N.R.F.C.

SON of Joshua and Ethel (Hill) Crane, of Westwood, Mass.; was born at Brookline, Mass., Nov. 15, 1897. He was educated at Milton Academy and at Harvard College. He enlisted at Boston, Mass., in May, 1917. From May to Sept. he trained at Squantum, Mass.; from Sept. to Dec., 1917, at Norfolk, Va. In Jan. and Feb. he was stationed at Fort Worth, Tex., being commissioned Ensign, U.S.N.R.F.C., in Jan., 1918.

Receiving overseas orders, he sailed for England in March, 1918, and was stationed at Killingholme Air Station, near Hull, Eng., until Dec. 18, 1918. He was commissioned Lieut. (j.g.), in Nov., 1918. In Feb., 1919, Lieut. Crane was honorably discharged.

LAURENCE CURTIS

LIEUTENANT, U.S.N.R.C., NAVAL AIR STATION, PENSACOLA

SON of Mr. and Mrs. Louis Curtis; was born at Boston, Mass., Sept. 3, 1893. He was educated at Groton School, Groton, Mass., and at Harvard College, class of 1916. He won the John Harvard Scholarship at college; played on the hockey and tennis teams, and was substitute on the 'Varsity football team.

He enlisted at Washington, D.C., on April 26, 1917, in the U.S. Naval Reserve; and was assigned to Aviation duty. While flying with an instructor at Newport News he had a severe fall, in May, 1917, and received injuries which incapacitated him from further flying. On Nov. 15, 1917, he was commissioned Ensign, Aviation Ground Officer, and was attached to the Naval Air Station, Pensacola. He was promoted to Lieut. (j.g.), March 23, 1918; and was commissioned Lieut. Oct. 1, 1918. He was detached to inactive duty, Jan. 27, 1919.

Brother in Service —

Louis Curtis, Jr., Capt., U.S.A., F.A., 77th Div., A.E.F.

WALTER HARMON HELLIER

SECOND LIEUTENANT, R.A.F.

SON of Mr. and Mrs. Charles E. Hellier; was born at Boston, Mass., Aug. 5, 1893. He was educated at St. Mark's School, Southboro, Mass., Yale College, B.A. 1916, and at the Harvard Law School.

He enlisted in the Royal Air Force, at Toronto, Can., in Nov., 1917. From Nov. 17 to Feb. 18, 1918, he trained at the School of Military Aeronautics, at Toronto. He was attached to the 84th Canadian Training Squadron at Camp Bembrook, Tex., in Feb. and March, 1918, and was stationed at Armour Heights, Can., in April, May, and June, 1918. On July 8, he was commissioned 2d Lieut. R.A.F., and ordered overseas, to No. 6 T.D.S., Boscombe Down, Wilts, Eng., where he remained from Aug., 1918, to Feb., 1919.

Lieut. Hellier was demobilized at Boscombe Down, Eng., Feb. 5, 1919.

Brother in Service —
Edward Whittier Hellier, 1st Lieut., R.A.F.

EDWARD WHITTIER HELLIER

FIRST LIEUTENANT, R.A.F., CRANWELL AERODROME
LINCOLNSHIRE, ENGLAND

SON of Mr. and Mrs. Charles E. Hellier; was born at Boston, Mass., Dec. 11, 1895. He was educated at St. Mark's School, Southboro, the Florida-Adirondack School, and at M.I.T.

He enlisted in Aug., 1917, in the Royal Air Force, at Toronto, Can., and trained at the School of Military Aeronautics, Toronto, from Aug. to Nov., 1917. From Nov., 1917, to Jan., 1918, he was attached to the Northern Canadian Training Squadron. He was commissioned 2d Lieut., R.F.C., in Jan., 1918, and was appointed Instructor at the Aerial Fighting School, Camp Hicks, Tex., where he remained until April, 1918. He was then commissioned 1st Lieut., R.A.F., in April, 1918, and ordered overseas to the Cranwell Aerodrome, Lincolnshire, Eng., Aug., 1918, where he was stationed until the end of the war.

Brother in Service —
Walter H. Hellier, 2d Lieut., R.A.F.

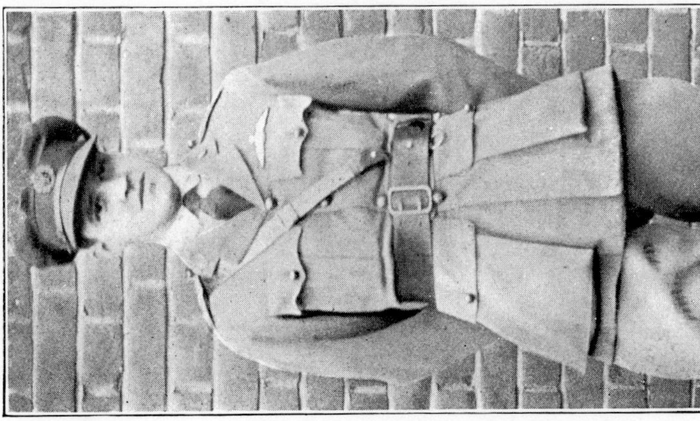

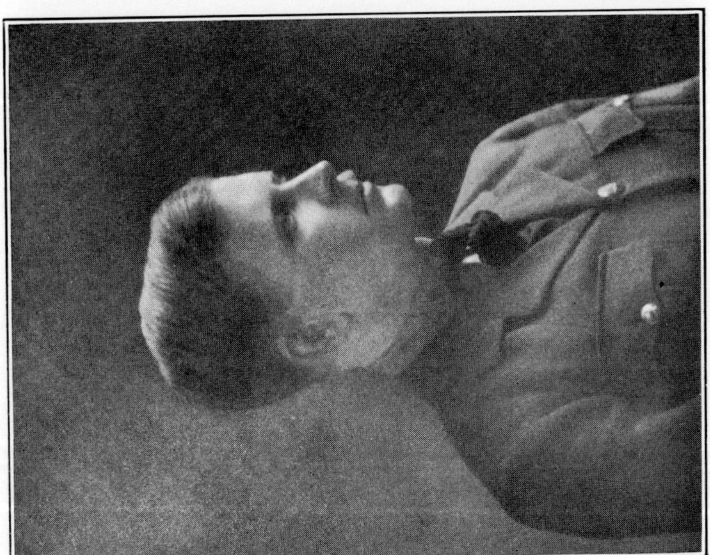

JAMES ARNOLD LOWELL

CADET, R.A.F., EIGHTY-FIFTH CANADIAN TRAINING SQUADRON

SON of James and Mary Wharton (Churchill) Lowell, of Chestnut Hill, Mass.; was born at Boston, Aug. 15, 1899. He was prepared for college at the Country Day School in Newton, Mass., and at the Evans School in Mesa, Arizona. He entered Harvard College in Sept., 1917, only to leave before the close of his freshman year to join the Air Service. Being too young to enter the U.S. Service, he enlisted, on May 15, 1918, with the Royal Air Force, in Canada. Cadet Lowell received his training at various Canadian camps: at the Recruits' Dépôt in Toronto; the Discipline Camp at Long Branch; the School of Aeronautics at Toronto; the School of Armament at Hamilton; and at the Flying Camp at Deseronto, where he was first attached to a Ground Instruction Section, and later to the 85th Canadian Training Squadron. He received his honorable discharge from the British Service upon the cessation of training for the Royal Air Force in Canada, Dec. 4, 1918.

ALBERT N. PARKER

SECOND LIEUTENANT, A.S.A., U.S.A., FIFTIETH AERO SQUADRON
FIRST OBSERVATION GROUP

SON of Eric W. and Lena N. (Goldsmith) Parker, of Malden, Mass.; was born at Cambridge, Mass., April 8, 1896. He was educated in the Malden public schools and at Huntington School, Boston.

He enlisted in the Air Service on Aug. 9, 1917, at Cambridge, and was trained at the Ground School, M.I.T.; Lower Field, Fort Sill; and at Taliaferro Field, in aerial gunnery. He was commissioned 2d Lieut. at Lower Field, Texas, on March 16, 1918. Lieut. Parker sailed overseas on July 1, 1918, and completed training at Issoudun, France; after which he was attached to the 50th Aero Squadron, 1st Observation Group, and saw active service at the front until the signing of the Armistice. He was cited in General Orders No. 33:

> Second Lieutenant A. N. PARKER, Pilot of the 50th Aero Squadron, has exhibited commendable courage and ability in his work over the line during the St.-Mihiel and Argonne-Meuse offensives.
>
> *By order of Colonel* MILLING

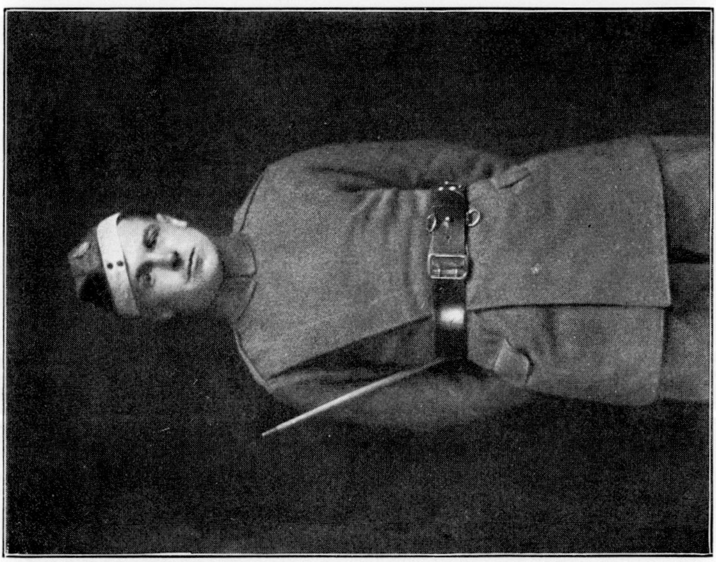

BENJAMIN M. GREELY, Jr.

Ensign, U.S.N.R.F., Northern Bombing Group

Son of Benjamin M. and Helen P. Greely; was born at Boston, Mass., Jan. 10, 1897. He was educated at the English High School, and at the Mass. Institute of Technology. In 1916 he went on a civilian naval cruise. On May 23, 1917, he enlisted at Boston, and trained at the M.I.T. Naval Aviation Ground School ("Flight A"). From Sept. 15, 1917, to Jan. 10, 1918, he was attached to the U.S. Naval Air Station, Hampton Roads, Va.; from Jan. 10 to Feb. 26, to the U.S. Naval Air Station, Pensacola, Fla. He was commissioned Ensign on Feb. 26, 1918. He was ordered overseas, and from April 1 to June 10, 1918, was stationed at Moutchic-Lacanau, France. Ensign Greely was then transferred to the U.S. Naval Air Forces in Italy, where he served from June 10 to Oct. 25, 1918, and qualified as Italian Military Aviator (Brevetto Superiore), July 4, 1918. From Oct. 25 until Nov. 18 he was attached to the Northern Bombing Group, in France. After the signing of the Armistice he returned to America, and was placed on inactive duty at Hampton Roads, Va., Jan. 17, 1919.

HENRY TURNER STANLEY

Lieutenant (*j.g.*), U.S.N.R.F.

Enlisted in March, 1917, and in July he attended the Ground School at the M.I.T. In Sept. he was sent to continue his training at the Flying School, Pensacola, Fla. He was commissioned Ensign, in Dec., 1917, and sailed for England on Jan. 13, 1918. He was assigned to the Royal Naval Air Service Station at Newlyn, Cornwall, Eng., remaining there for six months, when he was transferred to France, Aug., 1918, and stationed at the U.S. Naval Air Station at St.-Trojan, where he was at the time of the Armistice. He was commissioned Lieut. (j.g.), Oct. 1, 1918.

GEORGE KNOWLTON KEITH

Ensign, U.S.N.R.F.

Son of Mr. and Mrs. J. L. Keith, of Boston; was born at Grafton, Mass., April 29, 1896. He attended St. George's School, at Newport, R.I., and graduated from the Noble and Greenough School, Boston, in 1917. In May, 1917, he enlisted in the Naval Reserve, and entered the Naval Aviation School at the M.I.T., in April, 1918, graduating in June, 1918. He was later assigned to the Kite Balloon Division, at Akron, Ohio. In Oct., 1918, he was commissioned Ensign at Rockaway, N.Y. He was subsequently stationed at Norfolk, Va.

HOWARD CROSBY SARGENT

Ensign, U.S.N.R.F.

Born at Malden, Mass., April 11, 1896. He attended the public schools of Malden; and the Worcester Polytechnic, from Sept., 1914, to May, 1917. He enlisted in the U.S. Naval Aviation Service, June 28, 1917, and attended the Naval Aviation Ground School at the M.I.T. from Sept. 4 to Oct. 27, 1917. He trained at Pensacola, Fla., from Oct. 27, 1917, to March 3, 1918, and was commissioned Ensign in Feb., 1918. He sailed overseas for France, March 29, 1918, and was stationed at Moutchic-Lacanau, France, where he trained from April 17 to July 1, 1918. He was stationed, as pilot, at St.-Trojan, Isle d'Oleron, France, and engaged in patrol, convoy, and anti-submarine warfare, from July 1 until the end of the war.

FRANK HOPEWELL UNDERHILL

First Lieutenant, A.S., U.S.A., Twenty-Fourth Aero Squadron

Son of William P. and Margaret (Huber) Underhill, of Newton, Mass.; was born at Jersey City, N.J., Dec. 3, 1895. He graduated from the Newton High School in 1914, and attended Wesleyan University for three years, leaving to enter the Officers' Training Camp at Plattsburg in May, 1916. In Sept., 1916, he volunteered for the Aviation Service, and trained at Toronto, Can., being later sent to Fort Worth, Tex. He sailed overseas in Dec., 1917, and continued his training at Issoudun and at Tours, France. He was then attached to the 24th Aero Squadron and saw service with this Squadron until after the signing of the Armistice, doing observation and reconnaissance work. Lieut. Underhill took part in the St.-Mihiel and Argonne offensives. He returned to the U.S. early in Feb., 1919, and was honorably discharged during the first week in March, 1919.

Brother in Service —
Donald Prince Underhill, 1st Lieut., A.S., U.S.A.

DONALD PRINCE UNDERHILL

First Lieutenant, A.S., U.S.A.

Son of William P. and Margaret (Huber) Underhill, of Newton, Mass.; was born at Jersey City, N.J., March 10, 1897. He graduated from the Newton High School, in 1916, and attended Norwich University for one year before enlisting in the Aviation Service. He trained at Taliaferro Field, Fort Worth, Tex., and at Lonoke, Ark.; he continued his training at Langley Field, Old Point Comfort, Va., and was then transferred to Camp Dick, Dallas, Tex., where he was at the time of the signing of the Armistice. He was honorably discharged in Jan., 1919.

Brother in Service —
Frank Hopewell Underhill, 1st Lieut., A.S., U.S.A.

EDWIN BEAUMONT HUBBARD

Second Lieutenant, R.A.F., Twelfth T.D.S.
Southwestern Area

Son of William B. and Carrie N. (Haynes) Hubbard, of Roslindale, Mass.; was born in Dedham, Mass., on Nov. 16, 1896. He was educated in the Boston public schools; at the Mitchell Military School, Billerica, Mass.; the English High School, Boston; and at the Bryant and Stratton Commercial College. He saw service at the Mexican Border with Troop A, 1st Mass. Reg., F.A., N.G.

He enlisted in the Royal Air Force (British), in New York City, on Nov. 2, 1917. He was trained at the University of Toronto Ground School, and at various Canadian camps: 90 T.D.S., Camp Rathbun, Deseronto, Can.; 48 C.T.S., Camp Leaside, Toronto, Can.; and the School of Aerial Fighting, Beamsville, Can. After he had qualified as a flyer, he was commissioned 2d Lieut., R.A.F., on Aug. 8, 1918, and soon after sent overseas. Upon his arrival in England, Lieut. Hubbard was taken seriously ill with influenza and pneumonia. After a period of convalescence he continued his training at Netheravon, Wiltshire. He was discharged from the British Air Service at Netheravon, Eng., March 13, 1919.

APPLETON KING

Flight Cadet, Class A, Eighty-Fourth Aero Squadron, R.A.F.

Son of Mr. and Mrs. Tarrant Putnam King; was born at Milton, Mass., March 15, 1899. He was educated at St. Mark's School, Southboro, Mass., and at Harvard College, class of 1921.

He enlisted on April 29, 1918, in the Royal Air Force, at Toronto, Can. At the time of enlistment he was below the U.S. draft age, and so unable to enlist in the U.S.A. He passed through the Jesse Ketchum School (the Recruits Dépôt at Toronto), on May 4, the Camp of Discipline and Instruction at Long Branch, Ontario, on June 16. He trained at the School of Aeronautics, at the University of Toronto (Aerial Navigation); and at the School of Armament, at Hamilton, Ont.; concluding his training at the Flying Camp at Lake Mohawk, Deseronto, Ont., where he secured a pilot's certificate, and was assigned to the 84th Aero Squadron. He was honorably discharged with the rank of Flying Cadet, on Dec. 19, 1918.

CHARLES FRANCIS NASON

Second Lieutenant, A.S.A., U.S.A.

Son of Frederic A. and Susie M. (Tuttle) Nason; was born at Ipswich, Mass., Jan. 7, 1896. He was educated at the Ipswich High School and at the Boston University Law School.

He enlisted in the 8th Mass. Infantry Band, on May 18, 1917, and was transferred to the Air Service, Feb. 20, 1918. He took his ground-school training at Ohio State University, and work in primary and advanced flying, at Ellington Field, Houston, Tex. Subsequently he attended the San Leon Gunnery School, Dickinson, Tex. He was commissioned 2d Lieut., Oct. 23, 1918, and was awaiting assignment to overseas squadron, on Nov. 11, 1918.

He was honorably discharged at Ellington Field, Jan. 3, 1919.

Brother in Service —

Myron F. Nason, Musician, 102d F.A. Band, 26th Division.

THAYER FRANCIS

Second Lieutenant, A.S.A., U.S.A., Observer

Son of Dr. George H. and Elaina (Thayer) Francis; was born at Brookline, Mass., Aug. 10, 1894. He was educated at the Noble and Greenough School, Boston, and at Harvard College, class of 1915.

He served two years in the Home Guard of Lowell, Mass., and attended the Plattsburg Training Camp in 1916 and 1917. He enlisted at Plattsburg on May 12, 1917; trained at Fort Sill, Okla., Aug. to Sept., 1917; was stationed at Camp Devens, Co. A, 303d Infantry, from Oct., 1917, to April, 1918; he was Statistical Range Officer at Still River, Mass., from April to July, 1918. He went overseas with the 76th Division, but was transferred to the Aviation Service in France in Sept., 1918. He trained at St.-Maixent, Camp de Songe, Bordeaux, Tours, and at Châtillon-sur-Seine. He was Student Aerial Observer from Sept., 1918, to Jan., 1919; graduated from 2d Corps Aeronautical School, A.E.F., Jan. 25, 1919. He was commissioned 2d Lieut., Aug. 10, 1918; Military Observer, Feb. 1, 1919. He was assigned to the Army of Occupation. In April, 1919, he returned to the U.S., and was honorably discharged May 2, 1919.

Brother in Service: Augustine S. Francis, Ensign, U.S. Navy.

RAY BAXTER BROWN

SECOND LIEUTENANT, A.S.A., U.S.A.

SON of Richard Baxter and Ruth Abbie (Emerson) Brown; was born at Haverhill, Mass., Feb. 25, 1892. He was educated at the Haverhill High School; Phillips Exeter Academy; Brown University, 1913–14; Harvard College, 1914–17. He trained with the Harvard Regiment in 1916–17, and attended the First Officers' Training Camp at Plattsburg. He enlisted on May 8, 1917, and entered the Air Service in July, 1917. From Oct. to Dec. 8, 1917, he attended the Ground School, M.I.T., and was then sent to Park Field, Memphis, Tenn., from Dec. 15, 1917, to March 29, 1918. He was commissioned 2d Lieut., A.S.A., U.S.A., March 30, 1918.

From April 15 to May 1, Lieut. Brown was at Camp Dick, Dallas, Tex.; and on May 5 was ordered to Ellington Field, Houston, Tex. He attended the Aerial Gunnery School at Taliaferro Field, Fort Worth, Tex., from Oct. 11 to Oct. 26, 1918. He received overseas orders Nov. 11, 1918, which were at once recalled. He was honorably discharged at Taliaferro Field, Jan. 9, 1919.

CHARLES H. ROHRBACH

SECOND LIEUTENANT, A.S., U.S.A.

SON of Charles L. and Magdalena (Schmid) Rohrbach; was born at Bridgeport, Conn., July 15, 1890. He attended the Bridgeport High School, and entered Yale College with the class of 1912. He left Yale in 1910. He enlisted, Nov. 17, 1917, at Cambridge, Mass., and was assigned to the Ground Schools at the M.I.T. and at Cornell University. He was then ordered to Ellington Field, Houston, Tex., where he was commissioned 2d Lieut., May 9, 1918. He was subsequently sent to Payne Field, West Point, Miss.; and to Mitchel Field, Hempstead, N.Y., where he was attached to the 51st Pursuit Squadron, 1st Prov. Wing. Lieut. Rohrbach was honorably discharged at Hazelhurst Field, Mineola, N.Y., Jan. 16, 1919.

Married, Aug. 13, 1910, Nina Gilbert.

Grandfather in Service —

Charles H. Rohrbach, Corp., Conn. Volunteer Regiment, Civil War.

PHILIP BROOKS CRAIGHEAD

SECOND LIEUTENANT, A.S.A., U.S.A.

SON of John and Susie (Brooks) Craighead, of Malden, Mass.; was born, Jan. 5, 1895. He graduated from the M.I.T., B.S. 1918.

In Dec., 1917, he enlisted in the U.S. Air Service, but was allowed to finish his course at Tech., not being called to the colors until March 2, 1918. He attended the Ground School, Cornell University, graduating with honors, first in a class of 90 men. On May 2 he was ordered to Hazelhurst Field, No. 1, Mineola, N.Y., where he graduated as a Solo Pursuit Flyer, and on July 6, 1918, was ordered to Souther Field, Americus, Ga., for acrobatics. He made a record for the field in consecutive loops; also in cross-country flying. In Aug. he was commissioned 2d Lieut., and was also made a member of the Aero Club of America. On Sept. 3 he was ordered to Wilbur Wright Field, Fairfield, Ohio, and on Oct. 4 to Payne Field, West Point, Miss., where he received overseas orders on Nov. 10, which were cancelled after the Armistice. He was honorably discharged on Dec. 30, 1918. In Feb., 1919, he received a commission as 2d Lieut., in the Reserves.

ROLAND H. KINDER

SECOND LIEUTENANT, A.S.A., U.S.A.

SON of John T. and Minnie F. Kinder; was born at Marlboro, N.H., Nov. 14, 1893. He graduated from the New Hampshire State College, B.S. 1915.

He enlisted at Boston, Mass., Nov. 12, 1917, Aviation Section, Sig. E.R.C., and trained at Princeton, N.J., Dec. 10 to Feb. 27, 1918; and at Camp Dick, Dallas, Tex., March 2 to April 1. He had primary flying at Chanute Field, Rantoul, Ill., and was commissioned 2d Lieut., R.M.A., at Rantoul Field, on May 30, 1918. He was stationed for one month at Camp Dick, Dallas, Tex.; then ordered to Taliaferro Field, Hicks, Tex., July 9, 1918, where he qualified as Corps d'Armée Gunnery Pilot. Lieut. Kinder followed this training with a Pilot's course at the School of Aerial Observers, Langley Field, Hampton, Va., Aug. 14 to Sept. 28, 1918, from which he was transferred to the Air Service Dépôt, Garden City, N.Y., and was honorably discharged, Dec. 11, 1918.

RICHARD SKINNER WHITNEY, Jr.

Second Lieutenant, A.S.A., U.S.A.

Son of Richard Skinner and Mary (Lewis) Whitney, of Dedham, Mass.; was born at Brookline, Mass., July 25, 1898. He was educated at the Fessenden School, West Newton, Mass., and at the Noble and Greenough School, Boston.

He enlisted at Boston, Dec. 10, 1917; attended first the Princeton Ground School; was then stationed at Camp Dick, Dallas, Tex.; and later at Rockwell Field, San Diego, Cal., where he was attached to the 204th Aero Squadron; he continued his training at Armorers' School, Wilbur Wright Field, Fairfield, Ohio; and at Payne Field, West Point, Miss., where he acted as Instructor; he was transferred to the Port of Embarkation, Hoboken, N.J. He was commissioned 2d Lieut., A.S.A., U.S.A., July 27, 1918. On Dec. 4, 1918, he was transferred to the Reserves, at Hoboken, N.J.

Brother in Service: Holyoke Lewis Whitney, 2d Lieut., Co. H, 109th Infantry, 28th Division; died in service, Nov. 25, 1918.

CARL A. SARGENT

Second Lieutenant, A.S.A., U.S.A.

Son of George A. and Luella F. (Gates) Sargent; was born at Westminster, Mass., July 23, 1896. He attended the Fitchburg High School, Fitchburg, Mass., and entered the University of Maine, class of 1920.

In Sept., 1917, he enlisted at Cambridge, Mass., and entered the Ground School, M.I.T., Nov. 3, 1917. He was sent to Princeton University, Jan. 6, 1918, and upon graduation was ordered to Park Field, Memphis, Tenn. Here he passed R.M.A. tests and was commissioned 2d Lieut., March 20, 1918. He trained at Gerstner Field, Lake Charles, La., from June 28, 1918, to Aug. 10. He was then assigned to Rockwell Field, San Diego, Cal. He was ordered overseas on Nov. 1, 1918, but the order was recalled because of the Armistice. He was transferred to the Officers' Reserve Corps at Hoboken, N.J., Dec. 13, 1918.

Brother in Service: Chester E. Sargent, 1st Lieut., 21st F.A., A.E.F.

HORACE G. HAWKS

SECOND LIEUTENANT, A.S.A., U.S.A.

SON of Horatio C. and Annie G. Hawks; was born at Newton Centre, Mass., July 31, 1897. He was educated at the Newton High School and at Dartmouth College, class of 1919. He enlisted at Boston, April 6, 1917, in the Naval Reserve, and served in the Navy from April 6 to Sept. 25, 1917, when he transferred to Aviation. He attended the Ground School at Princeton University; and was stationed at Camp Dick, Dallas, Tex., from Feb. 14 to March 4, 1918. From March 5 to Dec. 28, 1918, he was at Kelly Field, San Antonio, Tex., where he was commissioned as 2d Lieut., May 27, 1918, and acted as Instructor. He was honorably discharged at Kelly Field, on Dec. 28, 1918, to return to Dartmouth College.

THOMAS C. QUINN

SECOND LIEUTENANT, A.S.A., U.S.A.,

SON of Joseph Francis and Elizabeth Ellsworth (Peart) Quinn; was born at Salem, Mass., March 30, 1889. He fitted for college at Dummer Academy, South Byfield, Mass., and graduated from Harvard College in 1910.

He enlisted at Plattsburg, May 12, 1917, and attended the Officers' Training Camp until he transferred to the Air Service, S.C., Aug. 14, 1917. He graduated from the School of Military Aeronautics, M.I.T., Dec. 15, 1917, and trained at Ellington Field, Houston, Tex. He was commissioned 2d Lieut. at Ellington Field, April 22, 1918, graduating from the Bombing Course on June 25. Subsequently he graduated from the Aerial Gunnery School, Taliaferro Field, Hicks, Tex., Aug. 24, 1918.

He sailed overseas, arriving at Liverpool, Oct. 17, 1918; and at Havre, Oct. 19. After five days at St.-Maixent, he was ordered to Clermont-Ferrand, 7th A.I.C., graduating there Dec. 6, 1918. He was then sent to Colombey-les-Belles, and assigned to the 20th Aero Squadron, on Dec. 9. On Dec. 24, 1918, he was ordered to the 2d A.I.C. at Tours. He returned to America and was honorably discharged at Garden City, N.Y., Feb. 11, 1919.

Married, Aug. 25, 1917, Elizabeth M. Conway.

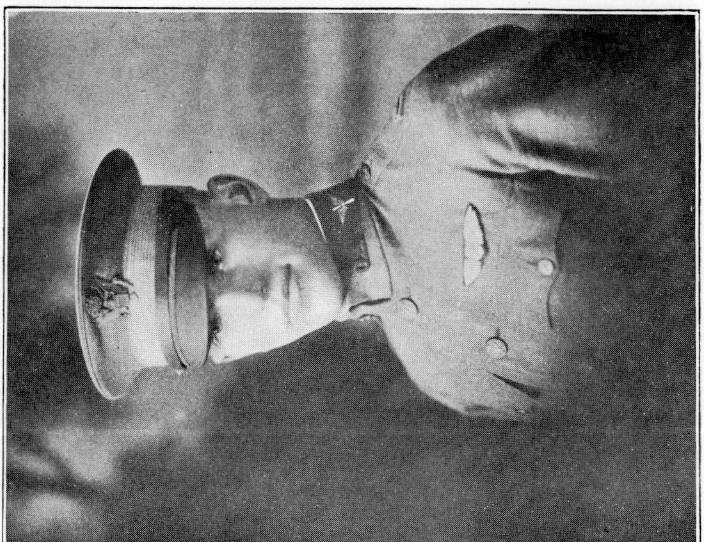

RAYMOND W. T. RICKER

SECOND LIEUTENANT, A.S.A., U.S.A.

SON of Leslie W. and Wendella (Tash) Ricker; was born at New Durham, N.H., Sept. 21, 1895. He attended the Rochester High School, Rochester, N.H.; the Farmington High School, Farmington, N.H.; and graduated from the Worcester Polytechnic Institute in 1916. At college he made records in the 220- and the 440-yard dash.

He enlisted at Essington, Pa., July 19, 1917, and sailed overseas, where he received his entire training for the Air Service. He attended flying schools at Foggia, Italy; at Tours, France; and at Galluate, Italy. Subsequently, he was attached to the U.S. Air Squadron 1111; and to the Italian Bombing Squadron 6, as Military Pilot in the Royal Italian Air Service, flying a Caproni bombing-biplane of 600 H.P. He was commissioned 2d Lieut., May 18, 1918. He was awarded the Italian War Service Ribbon by the Italian Director of Military Aeronautics, Nov. 18, 1918. He was honorably discharged at Garden City, N.Y., Jan. 6, 1919.

RALPH S. ROWE

FIRST LIEUTENANT, A.S.A., U.S.A., ATTACHED TO R.A.F.

SON of Jonathan N. and Margary M. (Kenty) Rowe; was born at New Haven, Conn., Sept. 27, 1894. He attended the public schools in New Haven, and graduated from the S.S.S. of Yale, with the degree Ph.B. in 1914; he received the degree of Met. E. from Yale in 1916.

He enlisted, May 1, 1917, at New Haven, and was sent to Newport News, Va., where he remained until May 25. He was trained at the M.I.T. Ground School, Cambridge, Mass.; at Chandler Field, Essington, Pa.; at Selfridge Field, Mount Clemens, Mich.; and at Gerstner Field, Lake Charles, La. He was commissioned 1st Lieut., March 1, 1918, and was transferred to Hicks Field, Fort Worth, Tex.; then to Hazelhurst Field, Mineola, N.Y.; and to Babylon, N.Y. He sailed overseas Aug. 17, 1918, and continued training in England. From Sept. 20 to Dec. 20, 1918, he was assigned to the Pursuit Group, C.F.S., at Upavon, Wiltshire, attached to the R.A.F. He was honorably discharged at Garden City, N.Y.

RICHARD H. GOULD

Second Lieutenant, A.S., U.S.A.

Son of John A. and Frances T. (Sabin) Gould; was born at Newton Upper Falls, Mass., June 14, 1889. He attended the public schools of Newton, and graduated from the Mass. Institute of Technology, B.S. 1911. He won 'Varsity letter in track and hockey, and was captain of the hockey team.

On Sept. 10, 1917, he enlisted, and entered the Ground School at Cornell University, graduating with the class of Dec. 1, 1917. From Dec. 6 to April 4, 1918, he trained at Love Field, Dallas, Tex. He was commissioned 2d Lieut., Sig. R.C.A.S., March 24, 1918, when he was transferred to Camp Dick for one month, and to Hoboken and Camp Merritt. He was then sent to Payne Field, West Point, Miss., where he completed the course, Sept. 10, 1918, and sailed for France. He finished his training at St.-Maixent and Issoudun, and was assigned to A.S. Casual Co. No. 1, Dec. 7, 1918, for transportation to the U.S. He sailed on April 18, for New York, and was honorably discharged, April 27, 1919.

Married Anna C. Spencer.

ALLAN NICHOLS DAVIS

Second Lieutenant, A.S.A., U.S.A.

Son of Arthur Eugene and Alice L. (Nichols) Davis, of Brookline, Mass.; was born at Worcester, Mass., Nov. 25, 1887. He attended the Classical High School, Worcester. At the time of enlistment he was manager of the Worcester branch of the Packard Motor Car Company of Boston.

He enlisted at Boston, Mass., Dec. 12, 1917; reported at Ithaca, N.Y., Feb. 16, 1918, and trained there at the U.S.S.M.A. until April 20, 1918. On May 1 he was ordered to Camp Dick, Dallas, Tex., remaining there until May 21. He was sent to Dorr Field, Arcadia, Fla., for primary flying, from May 24 to Aug. 24; then to Barron Field, Fort Worth, Tex., from Aug. 27 to Dec. 12, 1918. He passed all requirements for a commission on Nov. 13, 1918, and received his commission as 2d Lieut., A.S., O.R.C., Dec. 12, 1918, when he was honorably discharged.

THOMAS EMERSON PROCTOR RICE

FIRST LIEUTENANT, A.S., U.S.A.

SON of Charles G. and Anne (Proctor) Rice; was born in Boston, Mass., Dec. 10, 1894. He attended St. Paul's School, Concord, N.H. On Feb. 19, 1917, he enlisted, as Sergeant, A.S., S.E.R.C., and started flying at Curtiss Aviation School, Newport News, Va. He was injured in accident, April 26, and ordered home to recover. On May 28 he entered the M.I.T. Ground School, and, July 22, continued his training at Essington, Pa., where, Sept. 24, 1917, he was commissioned 1st Lieut. He sailed overseas, Oct. 27, 1917, in charge of 93 cadets, and trained at Issoudun from Nov. 28 to Jan., 1918, when he was made Instructor of Nieuports. On April 9 he was transferred to Clermont-Ferrand, where he trained for two months. From June until the middle of Oct. he was in active service at the front engaged in night bombing. After leaving the front he was prepared to return to the U.S. as a night bombardment instructor. He reported to Washington, D.C., Nov. 20, 1918, and was honorably discharged on Nov. 30.

Croix de Guerre

February 11, 1918

Le Lieutenant Bombardier RICE, THOMAS E. P.

Bombardier plein d'allant, a fait preuve dans l'attaque de nuit des arrières lignes ennemies de belles qualités d'audace et de sang-froid.

(*Signé*) T. VILLOME

WILLIAM BADGER LAWRENCE, JR.

ENSIGN, U.S.N.R.F., SQUADRON E (A)

SON of William Badger and Alice (May) Lawrence; was born at Medford, Mass., Oct. 3, 1896. He was educated at the Medford High School, the Volkmann School, Phillips Exeter Academy, and Harvard College. At the Volkmann School he was captain of the track team, and played on the football team. At Exeter he was captain of the baseball team, and was on the track team. At Harvard he played on the freshman football team. He enlisted at Savannah, Ga., on April 5, 1918, and trained at the M.I.T. Ground School; at Key West, Fla.; Miami (patrol); and Pensacola, acting as H 16, Chief Instructor. He was commissioned Ensign, R.F., on Nov. 2, 1918.

CHAUNCEY A. GALLOUPE

ENSIGN, U.S.N.R.F.

SON of Francis Ellis and Lilian Baker (Clark) Galloupe; was born at Lynn, Mass., Nov. 24, 1891. He attended Worcester Academy, and Exeter Academy; entered West Point with the class of 1916, attending for two terms. He enlisted in the U.S. Naval Aviation Service at Squantum, Mass., April 26, 1917. He trained at Squantum, from May 24 to the breaking-up of the camp there on Oct. 22, 1917. He was then stationed at Hampton Roads, Va., until April 10, 1918, and on Feb. 15, 1918, was commissioned Ensign. He was assigned to Pensacola, Fla., from April 22 to June 28, and sailed overseas, July 30, 1918. Ensign Galloupe was stationed at Killingholme, Eng., Aug. 15 to Dec. 11, on patrol duty over the North Sea. He was then ordered to the U.S., and detailed to Chatham, Mass., Jan. 23, 1919. He was placed on inactive duty at Chatham, Feb. 28, 1919.

Grandfather in Service —

Isaac Francis Galloupe, Bvt. Col., Surg., Army Medical Corps, during Civil War; prisoner of war at Libby Prison.

FRANK WEYMAN CROCKER

ENSIGN, U.S.N.R.F.

SON of George H. and Helen W. Crocker; was born at Fitchburg, Mass., Oct. 20, 1897. He was educated at the Groton School, and at Harvard College, class of 1922. He played for two years on the Groton football and baseball teams and was captain of baseball team in 1918. He was a member of the Harvard freshman baseball team. He enlisted at Washington, D.C., June 6, 1918, in Naval Aviation. He was called to M.I.T. Ground School, June 24, and on Sept. 28 was ordered to the Flying School at Bay Shore, N.Y. On Dec. 2, 1918, after completing the flying course, he was commissioned Ensign, with Naval Aviator's Designation, and was appointed Instructor in heavier-than-air seaplanes. On Dec. 2, 1918, he was ordered to the Naval Air Station, at Brunswick, Ga. There he received orders for inactive duty, Feb. 11, 1919.

Brother in Service —

George H. Crocker, Jr., 2d Lieut., U.S. Marine A.S.

JOHN LEWIS MURPHY

Ensign, U.S.N.R.F.C.

Son of Charles A. and Martha J. (Miller) Murphy; was born at Philadelphia, Pa., Jan. 4, 1896. He was educated at the John A. Andrew School in South Boston, the Mechanic Arts High School, Boston, and the Lowell Institute. He enlisted at Boston, Mass., May 9, 1917, and attended the Naval Aviation Ground School, M.I.T., July 23 to Sept. 17, 1917. He was assigned to the Air Station, Hampton Roads, Va., Sept. 19, 1917, to Jan. 9, 1918. He was transferred to Pensacola, Fla., where he remained from Jan. 11 to March 2, 1918. He was commissioned Ensign, Feb. 25, 1918. He received overseas orders, March 2, 1918, but while home on a furlough was sent to the U.S. Naval Hospital, Chelsea, Mass., March 13, ill with pneumonia. Upon his discharge from the hospital, July 30, 1918, his foreign orders were cancelled, and he was sent to Pensacola for advanced training. He subsequently became Instructor in H 16 Boat-Flying at Pensacola.

HERMAN J. JESSE

First Lieutenant, Squadron D, First Marine Aviation Force, Northern Bombing Group

Son of August E. and Annie M. (Beales) Jesse; was born at Rockland, Mass., June 27, 1894. He was educated in the public schools of Brockton and Weymouth, and graduated from the Lowell Institute, M.I.T., in 1916.

He enlisted in the U.S. Marine Corps at Philadelphia, Pa., June 7, 1917, and was sent to League Island, Philadelphia, for training, June 7 to Sept. 18, 1917; then assigned to the Army Aviation Station at Mineola, N.Y., where he remained until Jan. 1, 1918. There he qualified as R.M.A., and was commissioned 2d Lieut., U.S. Marine Flying Corps, Dec. 17, 1917. From Jan. 1 to April 1, 1918, he trained at Gerstner Field, Lake Charles, La., and was appointed Instructor at the Marine Flying Field, Miami, Fla., April 1 to July, 1918. He qualified as Naval Aviator, April 17, 1918, and was commissioned 1st Lieut., U.S. Marine Flying Corps, June 7, 1918. He sailed for France and was attached to the Northern Bombing Group. Placed on inactive duty, June 3, 1919.

RICHARD S. TOWNSEND

LIEUTENANT, U.S.N.R.F., NAVAL AVIATION CORPS

SON of Edward B. and Grace (Appleton) Townsend; was born at Roxbury, Mass., July 27, 1885. He was educated in the Brookline public schools, and at Harvard College, A.B. 1907. He was a member of the 'Varsity hockey team four years, and captain in his senior year. He enlisted at Washington, D.C., May 9, 1917, as Seaman, 2d class, U.S.N. He trained at the Naval Air Detachment, Curtiss Flying School, Newport News, Va., until Aug., 1917; finished training at the Naval Air Station, Hampton Roads, Va., Oct. 26, 1917, when he was commissioned Ensign. He was commissioned Lieut. (j.g.), March 21, 1918, and served at Hampton Roads until Sept. 15, 1918, as Construction Officer and Patrol Pilot. He was transferred to New London, Conn., and detailed as Officer in Charge of Flying and Experimental Work in connection with anti-submarine devices. Promoted to Lieut., Oct. 1, 1918. On Dec. 15 he received orders for inactive duty.

Married, Sept. 29, 1914, Edith Reed.

Brothers in Service —

Wendell Townsend, Ground Naval Aviation, U.S.N.R.F.
Prescott Townsend, Ensign, U.S.N.R.F.

LEWIS A. BURLEIGH, JR.

ENSIGN, U.S.N.R.F.

SON of Lewis A. and Caddie H. Burleigh; was born at Augusta, Me., July 20, 1897. He was educated in the public schools of Augusta, and at Bowdoin College, where he played on his class football team; was member of Bowdoin rifle and fencing teams, and Phi Beta Kappa. On April 6, 1917, he enlisted at Bath, Me., as Radio Operator, U.S.N.R.F. He was sent to the Harvard Radio School in May, 1917, and served on U.S.S. *Alacrity*, *Malay*, and *Machigonne* as wireless operator; entered M.I.T. Naval Aviation Ground School, March 25, 1918; had preliminary training in flying at Bay Shore, N.Y., where he received his "wings." He was commissioned Ensign, Sept. 21, 1918; took advanced training at Pensacola, Fla; sailed overseas Oct. 20, 1918; was stationed at Queenstown, Ire.; relieved from active duty, Jan. 15, 1919, at Bay Shore, N.Y.

ARTHUR R. HOLT

Ensign, U.S.N.R.F.

Son of Warren R. and Mary Elizabeth (Ratcliffe) Holt; was born at Newton Centre, Mass., Dec. 20, 1895. He was educated at the Newton High School, and at Amherst College. He enlisted on April 3, 1917, at Boston, Mass., and trained at Squantum, Mass., and at the M.I.T. Naval Aviation Ground School. He continued his training at Akron, Ohio, and at Hampton Roads, Va. He was then stationed at Akron, Ohio, until the end of the war, and was placed on inactive duty there, Feb. 12, 1919.

ADDISON C. BURNHAM, Jr.

Ensign, U.S.N.R.F.

Son of Addison C. and Emily Hudson (Bright) Burnham, of Newton Centre, Mass.; was born at Cambridge, Mass., Oct. 28, 1896. He was educated at the Newton High School; Phillips Andover Academy; and Harvard College, class of 1919.

He trained with the Harvard R.O.T.C., and enlisted at the Boston Navy Yard, June 27, 1917. He attended the Naval Aviation Ground School at the M.I.T. He was ordered overseas and continued his training at the Royal Air Stations at Roehampton, Cranwell, and at Polegate, Eng. He was commissioned Ensign, May 4, 1918, and was ordered to France and stationed at the U.S. Air Station at Paimbœuf. In regard to this station he wrote:

> This was the foremost dirigible station on the French coast. It was taken over from the French, early in 1918, and its patrol area extended from Brest to Rochefort. It was not until April, or May, that it became an efficient operating unit. Large incoming convoys, both troop-ships and cargo-ships, used Belle Île, some forty miles above our station, as a landfall. They would split there and proceed both up and down the coast to Brest, St.-Nazaire, and the southern bases. These large convoys, coming once or twice a week, were of course our first task, and subject to weather conditions, we met them from ten to ninety miles out.
>
> Next in importance were the daily convoys, eight to twenty or thirty ships, passing up and down the coast.

Ensign Burnham was released from active service, Feb. 3, 1919.

Brother in Service : John B. Burnham, Lieut. (j.g.), U.S.N.

GEORGE F. BAKER

ENSIGN, U.S.N.R.F.

SON of Dr. George T. and Marienne (Johnson) Baker, of Belmont, Mass.; was born at Boston Jan. 25, 1896. He graduated from the Winchester High School in 1912, from Phillips Andover Academy in 1913, and from Harvard College, A.B. 1917. Prior to enlistment he trained with the Harvard R.O.T.C. On June 25, 1917, he enlisted in the Naval Aviation Service at Boston, and trained at the M.I.T. Ground School, and U.S.N.A. Station, Pensacola, Fla. On Feb. 13, 1918, he was commissioned Ensign, U.S.N.R.F., Naval Aviation. The following month he sailed overseas, and was stationed at Moutchic-Lacanau, Gironde, France, where he was Instructor in Bombing. In Oct., 1918, he was transferred to the U.S. Naval Dirigible Station at Guipavas, Finistère, France. After the Armistice he returned to the U.S., and was placed on the inactive list at New York City Jan. 8, 1919.

WALDO HAYWARD BROWN

ENSIGN, U.S.N.R.F.

SON of Mr. and Mrs. Harry Hosmer Brown; was born at Salem, Mass., June 27, 1896. He was educated at Phillips Andover Academy, class of 1916, and at the M.I.T., class of 1920. At Andover he was a member of the 'Varsity track team. At M.I.T. he took a course in Military Science; left to enter Service at end of first year. He enlisted in U.S.N.R.F.C. at Washington, D.C., on Aug. 29, 1917; attended the Ground School at M.I.T., Nov. 12, 1917, to Feb. 2, 1918. He was stationed at the Naval Air Station, Key West, Fla., Feb. 7 to April 2, 1918. On March 19 he was commissioned Ensign, and on April 9 was ordered to the Naval Air Station at Chatham, Mass., where he was on patrol duty until Oct. 20, acting as Navigation Officer, and one of the Flying Staff. From Oct. 20, 1918, to Jan. 6, 1919, he was on sick-leave, as a result of influenza and pneumonia, contracted while flying. He was relieved from all active duty on Jan. 6, 1919.

Married, Jan. 15, 1919, Frances Martine Gray.

WALLACE J. FALVEY

LIEUTENANT (*j.g.*), U.S.N.R.F.

SON of Timothy James and Mary Elizabeth (Cosgrove) Falvey of Brookline, Mass.; was born at Norwich, Conn., on May 1, 1894. He attended the Brookline High and Boston Latin Schools; entered Harvard College with the class of 1918, completing his course in three and one half years. Member of the Institute of 1770, the D.K.E., and the Delta Upsilon fraternities. He enlisted in April, 1917, and was enrolled in the Flying School at Squantum, Mass., where illness disqualified him from continuing the course. Upon his recovery in July, 1917, he applied for admission to the Naval Reserve Flying Corps, and after twice being rejected, regained normal physical condition and was accepted at Washington, D.C., Oct. 28, 1917. He was called into Service in Feb., 1918, and was sent to M.I.T. for a ten weeks' Ground-School course, then assigned to Pensacola, Fla., for flight training. There he qualified as pilot, was commissioned Ensign on Aug. 13, 1918, and made Instructor. In Sept., 1918, he was transferred to the Experimental Station at Anacostia, D.C., where he served as Experimental Pilot, and was commissioned Lieut. (j.g.) on Jan. 1, 1919. He was honorably discharged at Anacostia in April, 1919.

ROBERT J. MUNKITTRICK

ENSIGN, U.S.N.R.F.

HE enlisted in the U.S.N.R.F. and was stationed at the U.S. Naval Aviation Operations Base, at Norfolk, Va. He was commissioned Ensign and was in Service for eighteen months. He had to his credit one hundred hours of active service, air patrol.

CLARENDON WAITE SMITH

ENSIGN, U.S.N.R.F.

SON of Mr. and Mrs. George Arthur Smith; was born at Worcester, Mass., May 16, 1893. He was educated in the public schools of Worcester and at the University of Michigan. He enlisted in the Naval Aviation Service April 10, 1918, and attended the M.I.T. Naval Aviation Ground School; he had preliminary flying training at Miami, Fla., and advanced flying at Pensacola. On Nov. 15, 1918, he was commissioned Ensign, and designated Naval Aviator, U.S.N.R.F.; he was ordered to Miami as an Instructor, and attached to the 17th Squadron. On Dec. 17, 1918, he was assigned to inactive duty.

Married, April 10, 1917, Margaret Deming.

Brothers in Service —

Paul S. Smith, 2d Lieut., A.S., U.S.A.
George Arthur Smith, Jr., Private, U.S. Coast Artillery.
David H. Smith, Private, S.A.T.C.

RALPH A. LEHAN

ENSIGN, U.S.N.R.F.

SON of Mr. and Mrs. D. F. Lehan, of Taunton, Mass.; was born in 1894. He enlisted in the U.S.N.R.F., June 12, 1917. On Dec. 23, 1917, he was commissioned Ensign. He sailed overseas, and was attached to the U.S. Naval Air Station, at Wexford, Ireland.

ROBERT WINTHROP KNOWLES

LIEUTENANT, U.S.N.R.F.

SON of Dr. Henry M. and Helen L. (Dykes) Knowles; was born at New Bedford, Mass., May 22, 1891. He was educated at Milton Academy, and Harvard College, class of 1912. He enlisted in N.R.F.C. at Washington, D.C., Dec. 19, 1917, and was commissioned Ensign. He trained at Naval Air Station, Pensacola, Fla., reporting there for duty Jan. 5, 1918. He was stationed successively at Pensacola; for temporary duty at Naval Air Station, Miami, and at Naval Air Station, Key West, Fla. He received Naval Aviator's designation, Aug. 7, 1918, and was commissioned Lieut. (j.g.) Oct. 1, 1918. On Oct. 7, 1918, he was detached from Key West and reported for duty at the Office of Naval Operations (Aviation) in Washington, D.C., where he remained until after the Armistice. He was commissioned Lieut., Jan. 1, 1919, and was placed on inactive duty April 1, 1919.

Married, Oct. 25, 1913, Amy Thorp.

WILLIAM GALLUP LASKEY

ENSIGN, U.S.N.R.F.

BORN Jan. 2, 1895, at Chicago, Ill. He graduated from the M.I.T. as an electrical engineer in June, 1917. He enlisted, Dec. 10, 1917, in the U.S.N.R.F., and was called to Service on Jan. 2, 1918. He trained at New London, Conn., and at Norfolk, Va. On Aug. 15, 1918, he was commissioned Ensign, and assigned to the Aviation Service as Instructor. He sailed from New York on Sept. 16, 1918, and was attached to the U.S. Naval Air Stations at Killingholme, England.

RALPH A. POWERS

LIEUTENANT (*j.g.*), U.S.N.R.F.

HE was educated at the Volkmann School, and at Harvard College, class of 1914. He enlisted in the U.S.N.R.F., and attended the M.I.T. Naval Aviation Ground School. He was stationed at Pensacola, Fla., where he was commissioned.

HAROLD SANFORD DOLE

FIRST LIEUTENANT, A.S., U.S.A.

SON of Nathan Haskell and Helen (Bennett) Dole; was born at Jamaica Plain, Mass., March 30, 1893. He was educated at the Roxbury Latin and the Stone Schools, and at Harvard College, class of 1917 (one year). He then took up the study of music, which he relinquished to enter the Service. He trained with the Harvard R.O.T.C. and graduated from the M.I.T. Ground School on Oct. 1, 1917. He sailed overseas in Nov., 1917, and after training at Tours and at Issoudun, was commissioned 1st Lieut., May 1, 1918. He had completed his training and was ready to go to the front when the Armistice was signed. He returned to the U.S. in Jan., 1919, and was honorably discharged.

Married, Oct., 1917, Thalia H. Smith, of New York.

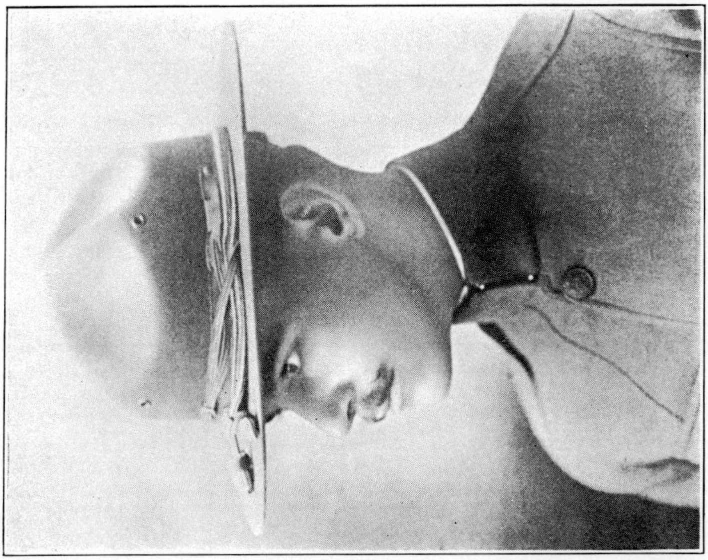

WILDER CRAWFORD CLARK

SECOND LIEUTENANT, A.S.A., U.S.A.

SON of Murdock Merrill and May (Crawford) Clark; was born at Winchendon, Mass., March 17, 1897. He was educated at the Cambridge Latin School, and at Harvard College. He attended the Plattsburg Camp in July and Aug., 1916, and trained with the Harvard R.O.T.C., Feb. to Aug., 1917. He enlisted Oct. 8, 1917, and attended the M.I.T. Ground School; Ground School at Princeton, N.J.; School at Dallas, Tex.; and received flying training at Scott Field, Belleville, Ill., April to June, 1918. On July 3, 1918, he was commissioned 2d Lieut., Air Service (Aeronautics). From July to Nov. he took the Gossport Instructor Course, and acted as Instructor. He was transferred to Langley Field, Hampton, Va., on Nov. 5; he completed his Army Corps Pilot's course on Dec. 1, and was honorably discharged on Dec. 7, 1918, at Langley Field.

LINCOLN ALVORD

SECOND LIEUTENANT, A.S.A., U.S.A.

SON of Ralph F. and Harriet Woodbury (Lincoln) Alvord; was born at Newton, Mass., Jan. 31, 1896. He was educated at the Newton High School, and at Harvard College, class of 1918. He trained with the Harvard R.O.T.C. He enlisted at Boston Nov. 3, 1917, in U.S. Army Aviation, and trained from Nov. 3 to Jan. 12, 1918, at M.I.T. Ground School. From Jan. 12 to April 8, 1918, he was at Kelly Field, San Antonio, Tex. He was commissioned 2d Lieut. April 8, 1918, and was stationed from April 8 to May 13, at Camp Dick, Dallas, Tex.; May 13 to Sept. 29, 1918, at Ellington Field, Houston, Tex.; and Sept. 29, 1918, to Jan. 7, 1919, at Taliaferro Field, Fort Worth, Tex. He graduated as a bombing-pilot. He was honorably discharged at Taliaferro Field, Tex., on Jan. 7, 1919.

Brother in Service —

Clark Alvord, Section 604, U.S. Army Ambulance Service, A.E.F.

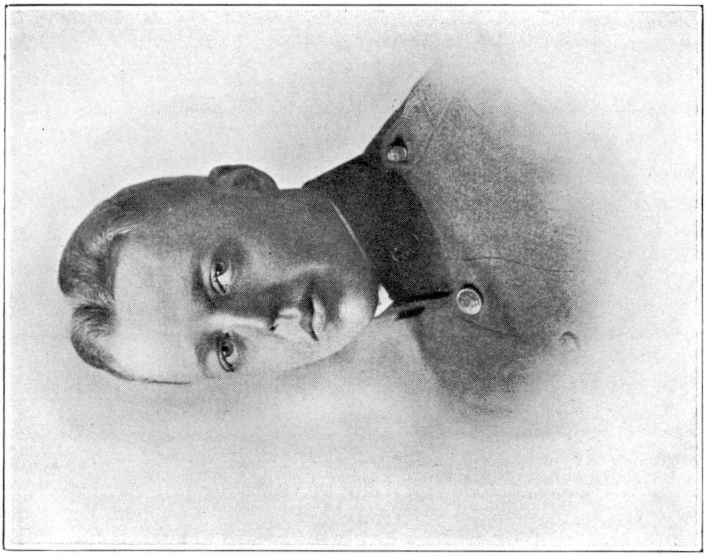

THOMAS CARSON CURTIS

Second Lieutenant, A.S.A., U.S.A.

Son of Harley B. and Susan D. (Carson) Curtis; was born at Newtonville, Mass., May 6, 1894. He was educated at St. George's School, Newport, R.I. He enlisted Dec. 1, 1917, at Cambridge, Mass., and began training at once at M.I.T., finishing Dec. 21. From Jan. 5 to Feb. 9, 1918, he trained at U.S.A.S.M.A., Ithaca, N.Y., and from Feb. 28 to April 12, at Camp Dick, Dallas, Tex. From April 13 to July 27, Flying Cadet at Eberts Field, Lonoke, Ark. He was commissioned 2d Lieut., R.M.A., A.S.A., July 27, 1918. He was Flying Instructor at Eberts Field, July 27 to Dec. 24, 1918. Honorably discharged at Eberts Field, Dec. 24, 1918. Dec. 6, 1918, Lieut. Curtis was put in charge of a flight of three ships, proceeding from Eberts Field, Lonoke, Ark., to Scott Field, Belleville, Ill.; returning Dec. 21. The object of the flight was to further public interest in flying and to look over the country as a possible air route between Little Rock, Ark., and St. Louis, Mo.

WILLIAM J. FITZ GERALD

Second Lieutenant. A.S.A., U.S.A.

Son of Michael J. and Annie M. (O'Neil) Fitz Gerald; was born at Boston, Mass., Oct. 28, 1894. He was educated at the High School of Commerce, at Chauncy Hall School, Boston; and at the M.I.T. He enlisted in the Air Service in Boston, Dec. 1, 1917, and was assigned to Cornell, for ground-school training. He was transferred to Dallas, Tex., and from there to Taylor Field, Montgomery, Ala., for flying instruction. He was subsequently ordered to Dayton, O., for a course in Aerial Gunnery, at the completion of which he was assigned to Payne Field, West Point, Miss. He was commissioned 2d Lieut., A.S.A., Sept. 12, 1918. On Jan. 7, 1919, he was honorably discharged at Payne Field, Miss., to resume his studies.

CHARLES F. WEEDEN, Jr.

Second Lieutenant, A.S., U.S.A.

Son of Charles F. and Mary Emma (Bassett) Weeden, of Newton Centre, Mass.; was born at Colchester, Conn., April 23, 1894. He was educated at Dorchester High School, and Amherst College, A.B. 1916. He enlisted in U.S. Army, May 15, 1917, at Plattsburg, N.Y., where he trained for Artillery Service. He was commissioned 2d Lieut. in Nov., 1917. He was transferred to Camp Dix, N.J.; and later to Princeton Ground School for Aviation work. In May, 1918, he won his "wings" at Mineola, N.Y. While at Mineola he made a flight to Camp Devens, 225 miles, in two hours and ten minutes. Later, he was stationed with the 280th Aero Squadron at Brindley Field, Cornmack, N.Y., under overseas orders which were recalled when the Armistice was signed. He was honorably discharged on Jan. 9, 1919. Lieut. Weeden was chosen as one of the assistants on the Near East Relief Commission, and sailed from New York on Jan. 25, 1919, for Constantinople.

Grandfather in Service: Chauncy J. Bassett, Col., U.S.A., Civil War, 1861–65. Killed in action leading colored troops.

JOHN A. LANGLEY

Second Lieutenant, A.S., U.S.A.

Son of John William and Annie Josephine (Dow) Langley; was born at Melrose, Mass., June 25, 1896. He graduated from the Melrose High School. After a year's work at the Junior Military Training Camp at Plattsburg, N.Y., he joined the 1st Prov. Officers' Training Regiment at Plattsburg. He enlisted at Boston, Mass., April, 1917; was ordered to Plattsburg in May, and later transferred to the Ground School at M.I.T., graduating Dec. 3, 1917; he was sent to the Primary Flying School at Waco, Tex., where he completed the course qualifying him for pursuit work, and was commissioned 2d Lieut., March 9, 1918. He was assigned to the Pursuit School, Gerstner Field, Lake Charles, La., and on completing the course was made Flying Instructor. He was transferred to Carlstrom Field, Fla., as Stage Commander and Instructor. Later was Instructor at Dorr Field, Arcadia, Fla., and was engaged in making special cross-country flights.

CHARLES CLARK MARSHALL

Second Lieutenant, A.S.A, U.S.A.

Son of John Knox and Sabina (Adamson) Marshall; was born at Brookline, Mass., Jan. 21, 1889. He attended the University Preparatory School, Ithaca, N.Y., and graduated from Cornell in 1911. Prior to the declaration of war, he served for five months in 1916 as a first-class private in Battery A, 1st Mass. Reg't F.A., N.G., and went to the Mexican Border. He enlisted at Boston, Mass., Nov. 1, 1917, in the Aviation Section, Signal Enlisted Reserve Corps. He attended the Army School of Military Aeronautics at Princeton, Dec. 8, 1917, to Feb. 16, 1918. March 13, 1918, he was assigned to Taliaferro Field, Fort Worth, Tex., for a course in primary flying, from which he graduated May 8, 1918, qualified to act as a gunnery pilot. He was classified Pursuit Pilot and commissioned 2d Lieut., R.M.A., May 23, 1918. He was ordered to Gerstner Field, Lake Charles, La., for an Advanced Pursuit course, July 20, 1918, and transferred to Rockwell Field, San Diego, Cal., for an Aerial Gunnery course which he completed Sept. 18, 1918. Lieut. Marshall was at Garden City, N.Y., awaiting assignment overseas when the Armistice was signed. He was honorably discharged at Garden City, Dec. 9, 1918.

THEODORE EDWARD BAKER

First Lieutenant, A.S.A., U.S.A.

Son of Irving H. and Jennie M. (Cleveland) Baker; was born at Somerville, Mass., Nov. 11, 1895. He was educated at the Somerville High School, and at Tufts College. He enlisted at Cambridge, Mass., Nov. 11, 1917, and trained at the M.I.T. Ground School; Cornell; and at the Flying School at Ellington Field, Tex., where he was commissioned 2d Lieut., Sig. R.C.A.S., May 3, 1918. He was Flying Instructor in Accuracy for six months; Assistant O.I.C., Accuracy Instructor in Formation; O.I.C. Formation, for three months; Assistant O.I.C., Primary Training, at Ellington Field, Tex. He was commissioned 1st Lieut., A.S., S.O.R.C., March 1, 1919. He was honorably discharged at Ellington Field, Tex., Jan. 9, 1919.

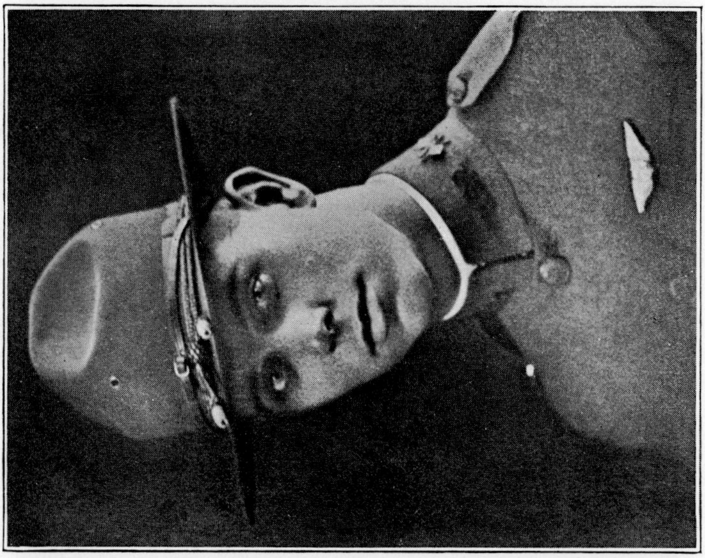

ALDEN S. FOSS

SECOND LIEUTENANT, A.S.A., U.S.A., SQUADRON 356

SON of Mr. and Mrs. Granville E. Foss; was born at Boston, May 21, 1896. Educated at the Noble and Greenough School, and at Harvard College, graduating in 1917. He attended the Plattsburg Training Camp in July, 1916, and the Harvard R.O.T.C. 1916–17. In the spring of 1917 he enlisted with the American Ambulance Field Service for six months. He sailed for France May 19, 1917, and during his stay served as a camion driver in the French Army. Returning to the U.S., he enlisted in the Air Service in Boston, Dec. 14, 1917. After a ground course at Cornell, he was ordered to Mineola, N.Y., where he passed the R.M.A. tests, and was commissioned 2d Lieut. July 18, 1918. He was attached to the 1st Provisional Wing, Hazelhurst Plateau, July 18 to Aug. 12, 1918. He was assigned to Camp Dick, Tex., for a short time, then transferred to the Bombing School at Ellington Field, Houston, Tex., for advanced training, Sept. 4 to Nov. 11, 1918. He was honorably discharged at Ellington Field, Houston, Tex., Jan. 6, 1919.

JOHN STETSON ALLARD, JR.

SECOND LIEUTENANT, A.S.A., U.S.A.

SON of John Stetson and Alice (Buckner) Allard; was born at Boston, Mass., Jan. 16, 1897. He attended the Medford High School, where he played left tackle on the football team. He enlisted at Boston in Nov., 1917, for the U.S. Air Service, and trained at the M.I.T. Ground School, and at Princeton. He was stationed at Dallas, Tex., and at Houston, Tex., where he was commissioned 2d Lieut. in June, 1918. He was transferred to Lake Charles, La., and later was made Instructor in Flying and Aerial Gunnery at Rockwell Field, San Diego, Cal. He was honorably discharged at San Diego, Cal., in Jan., 1919.

Brother in Service —
Norman B. Allard, U.S. Marine Corps.

CHARLES BURTON AMES

SECOND LIEUTENANT, U.S. MARINE FLYING CORPS

SON of Charles Henry and Henrietta Burton (Hunt) Ames; born at Newtonville, Mass., Sept. 11, 1892. He attended the Fessenden School, Thacher, Cal., and the Newton High School; he graduated from Amherst College, A.B. 1916. Member of swimming and track teams; captain track team. He trained at Plattsburg in 1915, and served from Sept. 2, 1916, to April, 1917, with the American Ambulance Field Service, Section 8, France; Lorraine, Somme, Argonne, and Verdun sectors. Returning to the U.S. he enlisted April 6, 1917, as Quartermaster, 1st class, in Naval Reserve Flying Corps. Trained at Pensacola, Fla., June to Dec., 1917. Commissioned Ensign, U.S.N.R.F., Dec. 7, 1917; stationed at San Diego, Cal., as Instructor in Flying, and Ground School Division Commander, Jan. to Aug., 1918. Stationed at Naval Aviation Headquarters, Washington, D.C., Aug. to Oct., 1918. Commissioned 2d Lieut., U.S.M.C.R., Nov. 1, 1918; transferred to Marine Corps, R.F.C., and sent to Marine Flying Field, Miami. He was Officer in Charge of Discharges, Flying Instructor, and Tester at Miami. Returned to inactive duty on request, at Miami, Fla., April 1, 1919.

LAWRENCE COFFIN AMES

SECOND LIEUTENANT, A.S.A., U.S.A.

SON of Charles Henry and Henrietta Burton Hunt Ames; born at West Newton, Mass., Feb. 9, 1897. He attended the Newton High School, and Berkshire School, Sheffield, Mass.; entered Amherst College, class of 1919. From June to Oct., 1917, he served in France with the American Ambulance Field Service; Oct., 1917, to April, 1918, he served with the Red Cross, operating just behind the lines in the Somme district. On April 29, 1918, he enlisted at Tours, France, in the Aviation Service. Trained in the 16th Foreign Detachment at St.-Maixent; breveted on Farman machine, at Voves, July 24, 1918. Continued training at Avord, France, and at the American School at Issoudun, on Nieuport machine, Sept., 1918. Commissioned 2d Lieut. Aug. 30, 1918. Stationed at 3d A.I.C. until the signing of the Armistice. Honorably discharged at Garden City, N.Y., Feb. 15, 1919.

CHANDLER BREWER GARDINER

Second Lieutenant, A.S.A., U.S.A.

Son of George C. and Mabel (Brewer) Gardiner; was born at Melrose, Mass., Feb. 22, 1894. He graduated from the Everett High School, receiving the Harvard Club Scholarship, and graduated from Harvard College in 1916. During his high school and part of his college course he played football; he was a charter member of the 1st Harvard Regiment. He was accepted by the American Aviation Service in Aug., 1917; taken by Draft to Camp Devens, in Oct., 1917. On Jan. 5, 1918, was transferred to Princeton, N.J., for training in Aviation; was later assigned to Dallas, Tex., Wichita Falls, Tex., and Wilbur Wright Field, Dayton, O. He was commissioned 2d Lieut., July 9, 1918, and sailed overseas, Oct. 16, 1918. He received further training as pilot in scout and pursuit work with French machines at the 3d A.I.C., Issoudun, France.

CHARLES MORRIS GARDINER

Ensign, U.S.N.R.S.

Son of George C. and Mabel (Brewer) Gardiner; was born at Everett, Mass., Sept. 16, 1897. He graduated from the public schools of Everett, and was awarded a scholarship for Amherst College; entered Amherst with the class of 1919. He left college in his sophomore year, and enlisted in the U.S. Naval Aviation Service in March, 1917, at Everett, Mass. He was assigned to Marblehead, and to Bumkin Island, Boston Harbor, for training. In Aug., 1917, he was made Quartermaster on U.S.S. *Whitecap*. He was transferred to M.I.T., Cambridge, for aviation training in Jan., 1918, and was sent to Pensacola, Fla., on March 30, 1918. Subsequently he was ordered to the Naval Air Station, Coco Solo, Canal Zone, Panama, where he served as Flight Officer. He was commissioned Ensign, N.A.S., June 17, 1918.

RIDGLEY GARRETSON SHEPHERD

Second Lieutenant, A.S., U.S.A.

Son of Joseph H. and Fanny G. (Van Reypen) Shepherd, of Holliston, Mass.; was born at Jersey City, N.J., Aug. 22, 1893. He was educated at the Ashland High School, the Franklin Union, and at the M.I.T. He enlisted at Boston, Mass., Dec. 14, 1917, and trained at the M.I.T. Ground School, and at Cornell University, where he graduated March 9, 1918. He trained for eight weeks at Camp Dick, Dallas, Tex., and was then sent to Kelly Field, San Antonio, Tex., where he was commissioned 2d Lieut., Aug. 28, 1918. On Sept. 10 he was transferred to Wilbur Wright Field, Dayton, Ohio, and on Oct. 22, to Payne Field, West Point, Miss. On Nov. 10, 1918, he was ordered to Carlstrom Field, Arcadia, Fla., where he was honorably discharged on Jan. 6, 1919.

Married, Oct. 15, 1918, Muriel V. Scott.

Brother in Service —

Joseph V. R. Shepherd, 2d Lieut., 101st Engineers, 26th Division, A.E.F.

RALPH E. FORSYTH

Second Lieutenant, A.S., U.S.A.

Born at Newton, Mass., Nov. 5, 1894. He was educated in the public schools of Newton, and at the M.I.T. (one year). He enlisted in the Aviation Service, and on Feb. 2, 1918, went to Cornell University, where he passed his examinations as Military Aviator. He was commissioned 2d Lieut. at Eberts Field, Ark., and from there was transferred to Wilbur Wright Field, Dayton, Ohio, where he completed a course in gunnery. He was then sent to an advanced flying school at Carlstrom Field, Arcadia, Fla.

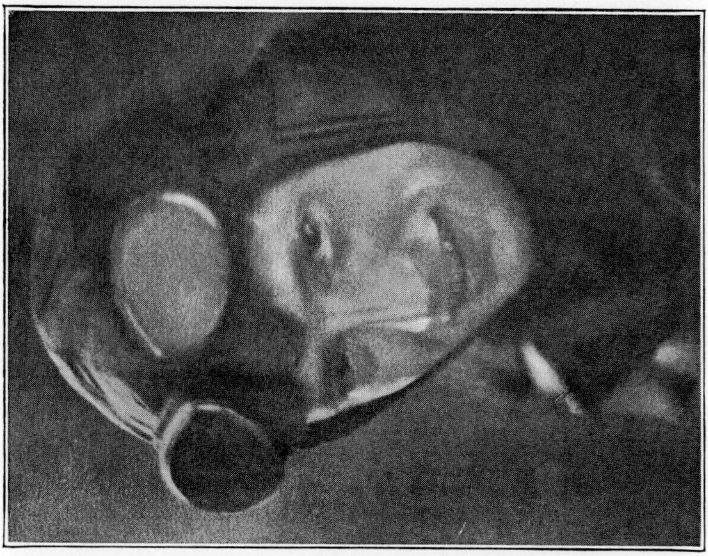

HORACE SCHERMERHORN

LIEUTENANT (*j.g.*), U.S.N.R.F., NORTHERN BOMBING GROUP
NA 208

SON of Edgar O. and Laura M. Schermerhorn, of Newton, Mass.; was born at Jersey City, N.J., Dec. 29, 1894. He was educated in the Newton public schools, and graduated from the Newton High School. He enlisted at the Charlestown Navy Yard, on April 23, 1917, and was sent to Squantum, Mass., for preliminary training. Later he was transferred to Hampton Roads, Va. He then proceeded overseas, and attended the French schools at Moutchic-Lacanau, Gironde, and Clermont-Ferrand. He was later stationed at Dunkirk, France. He was commissioned Ensign, Dec. 26, 1917, and Lieut. (j.g.), Oct 1, 1918. He was placed on inactive duty at Boston, Mass., Feb. 12, 1919.

CHARLES WHITE GREENOUGH

LIEUTENANT (*j.g.*), U.S.N.R.F.

SON of James M. and Katharine (Noble) Greenough; was born at Cambridge, Mass., Nov. 19, 1897. He was educated at the Noble and Greenough School, Boston, and at Harvard College, class of 1919.

He enlisted in the U.S.N.R.F. on May 21, 1917, at the Boston Navy Yard. He was trained at U.S.N.A. Station, Pensacola, Fla., where he was sent in June, 1917. He was commissioned Ensign, Dec. 21, 1917. With six others he was loaned to England and did patrol duty in various stations on the English coast. He sailed overseas in Jan., 1918, and was attached to the Royal Naval Air Service Seaplane Stations at Dover, and Newhaven, Eng., from Feb. 6 to June 1, 1918. He trained at R.A.F. Stations on Salisbury Plain, Eng., to Aug. 25, 1918, when he was attached to the U.S. Naval Northern Bombing Group, France, to Dec. 13, 1918. He was commissioned Lieut. (j.g.), Oct. 1, 1918. He was placed on inactive duty list, on Feb. 17, 1919, at Boston, Mass.

DONALD MacDONALD

First Lieutenant, A.S., U.S.A.

Son of Norman D. and Sophie (MacDonald) MacDonald, of Boston; was born June 30, 1894. He attended the public schools of Dorchester, and graduated from the English High School, Boston. In May, 1917, he enlisted in the Aviation Service and trained at the M.I.T. and at Mineola, N.Y. He was commissioned 1st Lieut., at Mineola, in Oct., 1917, and sailed immediately overseas to France. He served as Instructor at Issoudun, until the end of the war. In April, 1919, he returned to the U.S. and was honorably discharged at Garden City, N.Y.

Brothers in Service —

Neal C. MacDonald, 2d Lieut., A.S., U.S.A.
Murdock MacDonald, Bandmaster, U.S.N.
John Thompson MacDonald, 101st F.A., A.E.F.

NEAL C. MacDONALD

Second Lieutenant, A.S., U.S.A.

Son of Norman D. and Sophie (MacDonald) MacDonald; was born Jan. 18, 1890. He attended the public schools of Dorchester, and the English High School, Boston. In May, 1917, he enlisted in the Aviation Service, and entered the M.I.T. Ground School. There, after completing the course, he remained as Instructor until the fall of 1917, when he was ordered to Kelly Field, San Antonio, Tex. He was commissioned 2d Lieut., at Kelly Field, and was subsequently transferred to Washington, D.C., where he was made Inspector of Liberty Motors. He is still at Washington, and as Chief Engineer, is doing Inspection work.

Brothers in Service —

Donald MacDonald, 1st Lieut., A.S., U.S.A.
Murdock MacDonald, Bandmaster, U.S.N.
John Thompson MacDonald, 101st F.A., A.E.F.

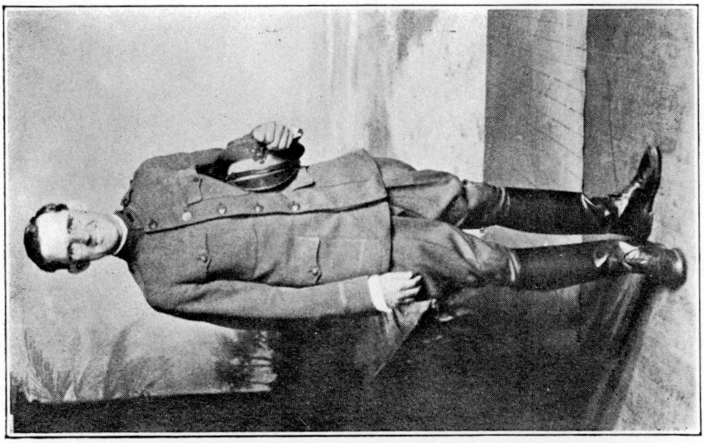

WILLIAM SCOTT KEITH

Second Lieutenant, A.S.A., U.S.A.

Son of Charles H. and Elizabeth C. (Allen) Keith; was born at Greenfield, Mass., Jan. 26, 1898. He was educated at the Salisbury School, Salisbury, Conn., 1911–15, and at Williams College, Williamstown, Mass., class of 1919. At Salisbury he was captain of the baseball team one year, and a member of the track, football, and baseball teams. At Williams he was a member of the track team. Prior to enlistment he attended Williams R.O.T.C. in the summer of 1917. He enlisted at Boston, Mass., Dec. 6, 1917, and attended the Military School of Aeronautics, at Cornell University, Ithaca, N.Y., from Feb. 2, 1918, to March 30, 1918. He was commissioned 2d Lieut., A.S.A., Pursuit Pilot, at Taliaferro Field, Hicks, Tex., July 18, 1918. Lieut. Keith was ordered to Garden City, N.Y., Oct. 1, 1918, and honorably discharged at Garden City, Dec. 7, 1918.

C. VINCENT DAIGER

Second Lieutenant, A.S., U.S.A.

Son of Mr. and Mrs. Charles V. Daiger, of Newton, Mass.; was born at Baltimore, Md., Aug. 11, 1892. He attended the Newton High School, graduating in 1911. On Oct. 26, 1917, he enlisted for the Air Service, at Boston, Mass. He reported for active duty at Kelly Field, San Antonio, Tex., Nov. 24, 1917, and was commissioned 2d Lieut., S.R.C.A.S., Jan. 20, 1918. In March, 1918, he was assigned as student to the Aerial Gunnery School, at Ellington Field, Houston, Tex., afterwards becoming a member of the staff of that school. Lieut. Daiger was ordered to Rockwell Field, San Diego, Cal., in May, 1918. Served as Instructor in Advanced Aerial Gunnery, and as Adjutant at Ream Field, Oneonta, Cal. In Oct., 1918, was awarded "wings," and rated as Reserve Military Aviator, being classed as "Pursuit Pilot." He was honorably discharged, Jan. 13, 1919. Afterwards he received commission as Flyer in Reserve Corps.

MAHLON COOK BUNDY

Second Lieutenant, Royal Air Force

Son of William H. and Marion C. Bundy, of Cambridge, Mass.; was born at Rice Lake, Wis., June 6, 1897. He was educated at the Newton High School, Phillips Exeter Academy, and at Wesleyan University, class of 1921; at college he was president of his freshman class, member of college Senate, and D.K.E. Fraternity. He attended the Officers' Training Camp at Plattsburg in 1916, and then served in France from Feb. 19 to Sept. 4, 1917, with the American Ambulance Field Service, Verdun sector. On April 12, 1918, he enlisted in the R.A.F. at Toronto, Can., and trained at the Toronto University, School of Armament, at Hamilton, Ont. (204 T.D.S.). He sailed for England, Aug. 31, 1918, and was stationed at East Church, Kent, from Sept., 1918, to April, 1919, when he was assigned to the Denham Repatriation Camp, and then to the Shorncliffe Repatriation Camp, where he was honorably discharged, for Repatriation, June 28, 1919. He was commissioned 2d Lieut., R.A.F., dating from Oct. 29, 1918.

JAMES E. KILEY

Second Lieutenant, A.S., U.S.A., One Hundred Sixty-Third Aero Squadron

Son of Mr. and Mrs. Kiley, of Concord, N.H. He attended the Officers' Training Camp at Plattsburg, completing his training there, Aug. 14, 1917. He was assigned to Princeton University, and graduated from the School of Military Aeronautics, Jan. 12, 1918. He was commissioned 2d Lieut., April 20, 1918, at Park Field, Memphis, Tenn., where he was stationed until he was ordered overseas. He sailed for France, and was attached to the 163d Aero Squadron.

JAMES WALLACE GIBSON

First Lieutenant, A.S., U.S.A.

Son of Charles Ellsworth and Helen (Knowlton) Gibson; was born at West Newton, Mass., Aug. 30, 1897. He attended the public schools of Newton, Chauncy Hall School, Boston, and the M.I.T., for two years, leaving to enter the Service. He attended the Officers' Training Camp at Plattsburg in 1917, and was there commissioned, on May 15, 1st Lieut., U.S. Infantry. He was on duty with the 310th Infantry at Camp Dix, N.J., until March, 1918, when he transferred to the Aviation Service. He trained at the Ground School, Austin, Tex.; and on Oct. 8, 1918, qualified as R.M.A., at Kelly Field, San Antonio, Tex. At Post Field, Fort Sill, Okla., he received training as Army Corps Pilot; and in aerial gunnery, at Taliaferro Field, Fort Worth, Tex., where he was honorably discharged, Jan. 6, 1919.

GEORGE B. CUTTS

Second Lieutenant, A.S., U.S.A.

He attended the First Officers' Training Camp at Plattsburg. He was commissioned 2d Lieut., Field Artillery; resigned his commission to enter the Aviation Service, and attended the M.I.T. Ground School for three months. He continued his training at Kelly Field, San Antonio, Tex., where he was commissioned 2d Lieut., A.S.M.A. He was transferred to Taylor Field, Montgomery, Ala., and served as Instructor for seven months. He was ordered to Gerstner Field, Lake Charles, La., where he spent a month training at the advanced bombing school. He was prepared to go overseas when the Armistice was signed.

WILLIAM FRANK BAKER, Jr.

First Lieutenant, A.S., U.S.A., Ninety-First Squadron

Son of William Frank and Mary T. Baker, of Dorchester, Mass.; was born March 7, 1889. He was educated in the public schools of Dorchester, and at the Missouri School of Mines; at college he played baseball and football. On May 28, 1917, he enlisted at Cambridge, Mass., and entered the M.I.T. Ground School, June 2, graduating July 29, when he was ordered to Mineola, N.Y. On completing his training there, he was commissioned 1st Lieut., Dec. 17, 1917. In Jan., 1918, he sailed overseas with the 153d Squadron, and trained in France at Issoudun and at Tours. On Aug. 15, 1918, he was attached to the 91st Squadron, and took an active part in the St.-Mihiel and Argonne offensives. Lieut. Baker's duties, as a long-distance reconnaissance pilot and observer, were to secure information of enemy fortifications, ammunition dumps, troop movements, airdromes, and artillery activity, and also to photograph the same; such missions often extended 100 miles over the enemy lines. Lieut. Baker sailed for the U.S. in Dec., 1918, and was honorably discharged at Garden City, N.Y., Jan. 10, 1918.

*JOSEPH GERARD MURPHY

Ensign, U.S.N.R.F.

Died, Oct. 18, 1918

Born Jan. 29, 1897. He was educated at the Somerville High School and at Boston College. He enlisted in the U.S.N.R.F.; was commissioned Ensign. Died in Service, Oct. 18, 1918.

GEORGE LOWELL ASPINWALL

SECOND LIEUTENANT, A.S., U.S.A.

SON of William Henry and Susan (Lowell) Aspinwall; was born at Chestnut Hill, Mass., Oct. 9, 1891. He attended the Volkmann School, and graduated from Harvard College in 1914. He then engaged in the banking business. He attended the Officers' Training Camp at Plattsburg in 1915 and 1916, and was there commissioned Capt., U.S. Infantry. Illness obliged him to retire from the Service, but upon recovery he enlisted in the Aviation Service, Feb. 15, 1918. On March 8 he began training at Princeton, N.J., where he graduated June 8, 1918. On June 10 he continued his training at Kelly Field, San Antonio, Tex., where he remained until after the signing of the Armistice. He was commissioned 2d Lieut., A.S., U.S.A., Nov. 12, 1918, and was honorably discharged in Jan., 1919.

Brother in Service —

Augustus Aspinwall, 2d Lieut., 110th Infantry, 28th Division; killed in action, Aug. 26, 1918.

HAROLD WAYNE PARKER

SECOND LIEUTENANT, A.S., U.S.A.

BORN in 1895. He received ground school training at M.I.T., and graduated from the U.S. School of Military Aeronautics, at Cornell University, Ithaca, N.Y., Jan. 19, 1918. He was commissioned 2d Lieut., A.S., U.S.A., at Gerstner Field, Lake Charles, La., May 18, 1918, and was appointed Instructor of Gunnery at that field. Lieut. Parker was transferred to Rockwell Field, San Diego, Cal., Aug. 22, 1918, where he completed his combat course. He reported for overseas service at Garden City, N.Y., on Nov. 1, 1918, but did not sail, owing to the Armistice.

FRANK H. MAHONEY

SECOND LIEUTENANT, A.S., U.S.A.

SON of Andrew J. and Josephine (Dowling) Mahoney; was born at Dorchester, Mass., Sept. 8, 1891. He attended the public schools of Dorchester, and graduated from the M.I.T. in 1913. He was a member of the 1st Corps of Cadets, M.V.M., and was with them mustered into the 101st Engineers. He transferred to the Aviation Service, and after training at the M.I.T., at Princeton, N.J., and at Dallas, Tex., he was stationed at Ellington Field, Houston, Tex., where he was commissioned 2d Lieut., A.S., U.S.A. He sailed overseas in Sept., 1918, and was in training in France at the time of the signing of the Armistice. He returned to the U.S. in the spring of 1919, and was honorably discharged from the Service.

*MARBEL LESTER DUNHAM

SECOND LIEUTENANT, A.S.A., U.S.A., NINETY-FIRST AERO SQUADRON

Killed in airplane accident, June 22, 1918

SON of Richard B. and Annie (Irving) Dunham, of Cambridge, Mass.; was born at Vernon Mines, King's County, N.S., Aug. 29, 1898. He was educated at the Cambridge High and Latin Schools. He left school to enlist in the Royal Air Force at Toronto, Can., June 23, 1917. He trained with the Royal Air Force in Toronto, for four months, and then at Fort Worth, Tex., for nine weeks. He sailed for France, Dec. 29, 1917, but to his disappointment was held in Chichester, Eng., for further training. There he was commissioned 2d Lieut., April 1, 1918. On June 22, 1918, while flying a scout machine, Lieut. Dunham met with a fatal accident. He was buried at Chichester, Eng., with full military honors.

Brothers in Service —

Clarence Dunham, Private, U.S.A.; killed in action at Battle of the Marne.

Gordon Dunham, Private, U.S.A.; wounded at Verdun.

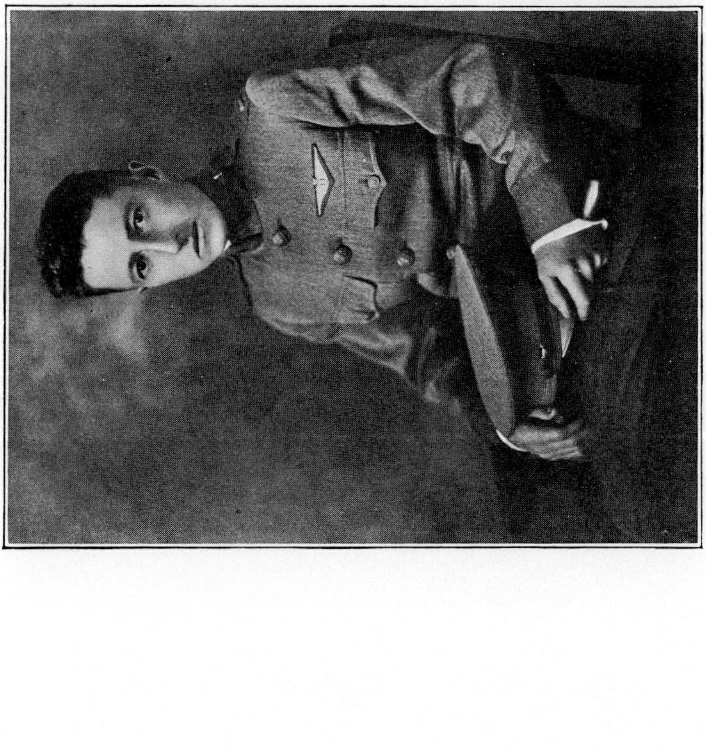

RICHARD de GOZZALDI

Second Lieutenant, A.S., U.S.A.

Son of Silvio M. and Mary I. (James) Gozzaldi, of Cambridge, Mass.; was born in Switzerland in 1889. He was educated in the public schools of Cambridge, and at Harvard College, graduating in 1913. He served with Battery A, 1st Mass. F.A., N.G., in 1916, at the Mexican Border. In the fall of 1917, he attended the 2d Officers' Training Camp, at Plattsburg, where he was recommended for the Aviation Service. He trained at the Ground School at Princeton, N.J., graduating March 16, 1918. He was then ordered to Camp Dick, Dallas, Tex., where he remained for five weeks; he was then transferred to Love Field. On May 1, 1918, he made his first flight, and continued to fly as Cadet, until Aug. 14, 1918, when he was commissioned 2d Lieut., A.S., U.S.A. He remained at Love Field, Dallas, Tex., until Nov., 1918, when he was sent to Garden City, N.Y., to await transport overseas, but did not sail, owing to the signing of the Armistice. He was honorably discharged at Garden City, N.Y., in Dec., 1918.

DANIEL W. POWDERLY

First Lieutenant, A.S., U.S.A.

He enlisted in the Aviation Service, in Dec., 1917, and trained at Cornell University, Ithaca, N.Y.; at Chanute Field, Rantoul, Ill.; and at Payne Field, West Point, Miss. He was then sent to a concentration camp at Long Island, preparatory to sailing for France. He sailed overseas on Oct. 26, 1918.

*WILLIAM G. SPRAGUE

Ensign, U.S.N.R.F.

Killed in seaplane accident, Oct. 26, 1918

Born at Chicago, Ill., July 13, 1893. He attended the University of Michigan for two years, and graduated from the M.I.T. in 1916. He joined the Naval Aviation Detachment at the M.I.T.; Motor Inspection Division, Jan. 11, 1917. He was transferred to the Naval Air Station at Pensacola, Fla., and trained there until May, 1917. He was commissioned Ensign, sent overseas, and stationed at Paris in Feb., 1918. He was ordered to the Moutchic-Lacanau Training School, and then to the U.S. Naval Air Station, Île Tudy, France, in Oct. On Oct. 26, 1918, he was killed in a seaplane accident at Île Tudy.

He was awarded the Croix de Guerre with Gold Star, which was presented at his funeral.

HENRY ALEXANDER MAGNUSON

Cadet, A.S., U.S.A.

Son of Axel Birger and Hanna Caroline (Johanson) Magnuson; was born at Cambridge, Mass., on Oct. 15, 1895. He was educated at the Harvard Grammar School, the Rindge Training School, Cambridge, and at the Mass. Normal Art School, Boston. He belonged to the Rindge crew in 1914, and won fourth place in the mile run at the Rindge track meet. During his freshman year at the Mass. Normal Art School, he received first honors, and in sophomore and junior years received the highest rank in the architectural course.

He enlisted in the Air Service at Boston, Mass., on April 23, 1918, and entered the School of Military Aeronautics at M.I.T., on June 29, leaving on Sept. 7 to complete his ground-school work at Cornell University, Ithaca, N.Y. He remained at Cornell with Squadron 59, until Sept. 21, 1918; then went to Camp Dick, Dallas, Tex., where he remained from Oct. 5 to Nov. 5. He was then transferred to Chanute Field, Rantoul, Ill., where he was trained from Nov. 7 to Dec. 4. Subsequently he was ordered to Camp Call Field, Wichita Falls, Tex., where he was stationed from Dec. 6, 1918, to Jan. 20, 1919; and to Love Field, Dallas, Tex., where he was held from Jan. 21 to March 17, 1919. On March 17, 1919, he was honorably discharged from the Service at Love Field, Dallas, Tex.

Brothers in Service —

Arthur Albert Magnuson, Q.M., Naval Aviation, Co. 4, Hampton Roads, Va.

Adolph Harold Magnuson, Corp., Co. C, 103d Infantry, 26th Division. On the evening of Nov. 12, 1918, as Co. C was celebrating the Armistice by firing off the rockets which had been used during the war as signals, a piece of one of the rockets, which had some metal in it, fell and struck Corp. Magnuson on the back of the head. He did not recover consciousness, and died Nov. 24, 1918.

DAVID PUTNAM

By Richard D. Ware

Up from the eyrie the young falcon leapt.
The fires of his fearless eyes
Outfacing the fierce flamings of the sun.
Then in wide circles swept
Against the skies,
More free than their own stars to run
His course in Liberty
Until, the Earth concealed
Beneath a cloud, he wheeled
          Free,
          Utterly.

Freed of all earthly things
Down through the void he pitched with folded wings,
Piercing the cloud like flashing sword
Full in the vulture horde.
Foul beaks and talons tore
The life from him, but on his spirit bore
The valiant heart, and back to Earth there sped
On stiffening pinions set, the falcon, dead,
To bear the message of his vision in the sky
          Of Liberty.

ABBREVIATIONS

A.A.A.P.	American Aviation Acceptance Park
A.A.P.	Aviation Acceptance Park
A.E.F.	American Expeditionary Forces
A.D.C.	Aide-de-Camp
A.I.C.	Aviation Instruction Centre
A.S.	Air Service; used in A.E.F.
A.S.A.	Air Service Aeronaut; used in U.S. to denote flyers only; ground officers in Air Service use A.S. only
A.S.M.A.	Air Service, Military Aeronautics
A.S.S.C.*	Aviation Section, Signal Corps
A.S.S.R.C.*	Aviation Section, Signal Reserve Corps
B.E.F.	British Expeditionary Forces.
C.A.C.	Coast Artillery Corps
C.E.F.	Canadian Expeditionary Forces
C.O.	Commanding Officer
C.T.S.	Canadian Training Squadron
D.A.C.	Division d'Application de Combat
D.F.C.	Distinguished Flying Cross (British decoration)
DeH. 4	De Haviland 4
D.S.C.	Distinguished Service Cross
D.S.M.	Distinguished Service Medal
D.S.O.	Distinguished Service Order (British decoration)
F.A.	Field Artillery
G.D.E.	Le Plessis-Belleville, where all French pilots were sent before being assigned to an escadrille
J.M.A.	Junior Military Aviator
M.I.T.	Massachusetts Institute of Technology
M.V.M.	Massachusetts Volunteer Militia
N.A.S.	Naval Air Station
N.C.T.S.	Northern Canadian Training Squadron
N.G.	National Guard
N.R.F.C.	Naval Reserve Flying Corps

* Obsolete as far as Aviation is concerned.

Q.M.C.	Quartermaster Corps
R.A.F.	Royal Air Force
R.F.C.	Royal Flying Corps
R.M.A.	Reserve Military Aviator
R.N.A.S.	Royal Naval Air Service
R.O.T.C.	Reserve Officers' Training Corps
S.E. 5	Type of British single-seater
S.A.T.C.	Students' Army Training Corps
S.M.A.	School of Military Aeronautics
S.O.S.	Service of Supply
S.E.R.C.*	Signal Enlisted Reserve Corps
S.O.R.C.*	Signal Officers' Reserve Corps
S.R.C.A.S.*	Signal Reserve Corps, Air Service
S.S.U.	Section Sanitaire États-Unis: official designation of an American Ambulance Section serving with the French Army
T.M.U.	*Transport de matériel:* the Camion Service which carried munitions and supplies for the Army
U.S.A.S.	United States Air Service
U.S.M.C.R.	United States Marine Corps Reserve
U.S.N.A.S.	United States Naval Air Service
U.S.N.R.	United States Naval Reserve
U.S.N.R.F.	United States Naval Reserve Force
U.S.N.R.F.C.	United States Naval Reserve Flying Corps
U.S.N.	United States Navy
U.S.S.	United States Steamship

* Obsolete as far as Aviation is concerned.